THE BEST
AUSTRALIAN
ESSAYS
2007

THE BEST AUSTRALIAN ESSAYS 2007

Edited by
DRUSILLA MODJESKA

Published by Black Inc.,
an imprint of Schwartz Publishing Pty Ltd

Level 5, 289 Flinders Lane
Melbourne Victoria 3000 Australia
email: enquiries@blackincbooks.com
http://www.blackincbooks.com

Introduction & this collection © Drusilla Modjeska
& Black Inc., 2007.
Individual essays © retained by the authors.

Every effort has been made to contact the copyright holders of material in this book. However, where an omission has occurred, the publisher will gladly include acknowledgement in any future edition.

ISBN 9781863954198

ALL RIGHTS RESERVED.
No part of this publication may be reproduced,
stored in a retrieval system, or transmitted in any
form by any means electronic, mechanical,
photocopying, recording or otherwise without
the prior consent of the publishers.

Contents

Drusilla Modjeska
  Introduction   xi

Gillian Mears
  Alive in Ant and Bee   1

Helen Garner
  From Frogmore, Victoria   16

Dan Chiasson
  Fire Down Below   26

Anne Sedgley
  In Fealty to a Professor   36

John Armstrong
  The Heart of Desire   43

Hazel Rowley
  The Ups, the Downs: My Life as a Biographer   49

Anna Goldsworthy
  Like Love in a Marriage   65

* * *

Don Walker
  In Shiraz   81

Kim Mahood
Blow-ins on the Cold Desert Wind   98

Tim Flannery
What Is a Tree?   112

Kate Rossmanith
Many Me   122

Guy Rundle
It's Too Easy To Say 'God Is Dead'   129

Kevin Rudd
Faith in Politics   139

* * *

J.M. Coetzee
Portrait of the Monster as a Young Artist   157

Inga Clendinnen
Lost in the Woods   172

Anna Funder
The Innocence Manoeuvre   182

Gert Reifarth
Born in the GDR   189

Mark McKenna
Being There   199

Clive James
Bons Mots No Match for Nazi Bullets   227

Nicolas Rothwell
Hard Cases and Hearts of Darkness   239

Anne Manne
Love Me Tender?   249

* * *

Noel Pearson
*White Guilt, Victimhood and the Quest for
a Radical Centre*   267

Robert Manne
Pearson's Gamble, Stanner's Dream   286

David Marr
Cowboys and Indians   304

Judith Brett
The Turning Tide   321

* * *

Luke Davies
Extravagant Stillness   331

Susan Hampton
Scale by Scale   336

Publication Details   347

Notes on Contributors   350

In memory of

ELIZABETH JOLLEY 1923–2007

GLENDA ADAMS 1939–2007

Introduction

Drusilla Modjeska

In Gillian Mears's 'Alive in *Ant and Bee*', one of this year's very best essays, the young – or no longer quite so young – writer recovers from an infection of the heart so severe it all but kills her, and sets out on the road to recovery in an old yellow ambulance. This essay, which was published in full in *Heat*, strikes me as an emblem of what's happening in our literary culture. After a rough decade in our political culture that has changed the terms of intellectual engagement, it's as if the trusted old form of the essay is setting out again, rekitted for recovery. This is not to say we haven't had good essays these last years, for we have, and I won't be the only reader who has turned to the likes of Robert Manne and Raimond Gaita, Judith Brett and David Marr for a steady hand on the wheel. Even so, as an advocate for the essay, *especially* in bleak times, it has been invigorating, in this my second year as editor of *Best Australian Essays*, to discover how much can change in a year. As I read from where I left off last year, which was a month or so before Kevin Rudd became the Leader of the Opposition, already there were signs of a change in mood. It's not that this year's crop of essays are more political in any obvious way, though there continues to be excellent comment on the dramatic events of a highly political year. Rather, it's as if we've come out from under the spell, or have woken from a torpor, and that we're talking again. More of us are talking, and talking more loudly. I've felt as if I'm reading through a clamour, that I've come in on a vigorous conversation. And then, in amongst the noise, I'd find that I'd stumbled on someone telling an intimate story from some kind of personal brink.

The personal essay, with its hallmark ingredients, is alive and well, in no need of an ambulance; it's a robust form and not one to be knocked out by a bit of chatter. You'll find some excellent examples here that work the familiar lode of individual experience and meaning, and the conundrum of artistic life; I'll leave it to you to assess the mood, for it's here that the change, if there's any, is most subtle. The more argumentative pieces, as you'd expect, are responding – as they did last year – to the play of political events and trajectories. These are the essays historians will look back to as they track the changes. But to my mind, the difference has shown itself most markedly in the review essays that have dominated the year. There were some good ones last year, but few as good as this year's best, and nothing like as many; I could have filled the volume with nothing else. It seems we've taken to arguing – in the most heartening of ways – about films and books, about God, and evil, about the echoes of history, about the lies we tell ourselves, about the slippery, and not so slippery, substance of truth.

It used to be said that we Australians weren't good at the review essay; it wasn't a form we had much scope to practise unless we went to the British or American press with their celebrated review pages. It may be that with the Friday Review of the *Australian Financial Review*, *The Monthly* and now *The Australian Literary Review* we have finally got on top of it. I think this shift in the way we give written expression to our thinking also has to do with the fall of Howard. By the time you read these essays, you will most likely know the result of the election, and just how far and literal the fall has been. But as I write this introduction, and prepare this collection for the printer, I don't even know its date. This has not made my task easier, and there have been times when I've fretted, as if forced to work blind. It's not just a matter of making a virtue of necessity that has brought me round to recognising this state of uncertainty, like Mears alive in her ant and bee, as a salutary practice for reading the moment. Is that not why we love the essay, those of us who do, because it is a kind of thinking aloud that loops back to the past and nudges us forward to the future, but depends for its life on its aliveness as a voice in the present?

Another image that has been with me as I've read my way through the year is of the two great landscapes by Anselm Kiefer that lodged at the Art Gallery of New South Wales during the first half of the year. Sydney readers will surely know them: those roads running straight up the centre of the picture, through landscapes of caked mud and clay that was left to dry and crack before being painted over. From where we stand, the road invites us forward into a landscape at once desolate and strewn with flowers of paint. The sky lowers and yet the sun is not absence. Is it Golgotha that we're headed towards? Or redemption? The answer to these questions is both and neither. Can we tell as we walk? For it is also just a road, the road we are on now, through a landscape that is as earth-bound as it is transcendent. It is the route we are walking, collectively and individually. The meaning I take from Kiefer is that, yes that road is made of history and will make the future, yes it is redolent of possibility and harsh disappointment, but at each step, at any moment, it is but the path we're on. Where it will lead is not determined – or not only – by whatever it is that lies out of sight beyond the horizon, but also by how we walk, right here, now. How we walk, how we write, how we read, how we think, how we argue.

It is in this spirit that I offer *Best Australian Essays 2007*.

Drusilla Modjeska

Alive in *Ant and Bee*

Gillian Mears

I am in the process of buying a thirty-year-old ambulance in 2004, sight unseen, and in the opinion of most people, I've gone crazy. Listening to Mr Bible from Homebush Motors in Sydney make his sales pitch on the phone, I think they might have a point.

'Just wait till you put your foot down out on the highway. It's like having a peach underneath. And the peach doesn't bruise. An icon, that's what you'll be buying.'

It was not so long ago that an invalid scooter had been my only transport. Even when I'd set it to 'rabbit', the fastest speed, the blind nun from down the road could overtake me on her cane. Before the scooter there was the wheelchair. In the winter sun of 2002, the spokes of its wheels cast shadows along the hospital patio in such a way that I couldn't stop crying. I'd had a seven-year-long struggle to walk, due to a form of multiple sclerosis that defied diagnosis, but that wasn't why I was being slid in and out of wheelchairs.

The open-heart surgery I underwent in 2002, following the emergency diagnosis of an infection in my heart, is like a penumbral eclipse of my life that can still seem incomprehensible. Why didn't I get myself to hospital sooner, before I was so nearly a corpse? How could it be possible that in so fervently following the advice of a macrobiotic practitioner whose treatment banned any recourse to Western medicine, I became part of a calamity so huge I almost died?

There were reasons. Imagine, after a lifelong passion for physical activity, suddenly finding movement itself becoming a mystery. Imagine, at the age of thirty-one, beginning to stagger like a Kurt Vonnegut syphilitic. Next, horrible feelings running along certain stretches of your skin, as if this were where Peter Piper's peck of pickled peppers had lodged.

As is common with multiple sclerosis, before diagnosis came many misdiagnoses. Everything from the trivial – my GP attributing my malaise to the effect of leaning on my elbow as I sat at my desk – to the extreme. The first MRI was to look for signs of multiple sclerosis but nothing was showing. Although no neurologist was convinced that my symptoms stemmed from an old horse-riding injury to my neck, pressure was intensifying that I must agree, the sooner the better, to major spinal surgery.

In my increasing alarm, I turned to the huge range of alternative health practitioners that anyone with an affliction in the twenty-first century might feel familiar with. I tried reiki, traditional Chinese medicine, holotropic breathing, reflexology and kinesiology. Under the directives of this or that healer, I drank disgusting molasses and soy-milk brews. I ate charcoal and seaweed. I fasted. I looked into colonic irrigations, iridology, numerology, Feldenkreis, Alexander technique, Bowen therapy, bone massage.

Again I consulted a range of GPs and specialists. Again I was scanned for multiple sclerosis. Again, no sign of any of the tell-tale scar lesions around nerves in the brain or spinal column. Vitamin B12 deficiency, syphilis, HIV, hepatitis C were also all ruled out. In the last MRI scan, the bit of osteoarthritis in my neck was neither better nor worse. A plump, small-fingered neurosurgeon diffidently suggested that a registrar could operate.

'We could book you in within the month. We'd come in through the front of your neck and put in a self-drilling cage. Take out the bony deposits around C5. It might help. But only in terms of you not deteriorating. I've seen necks on ninety-year-olds in far worse shape than your own. Yet with none of your symptoms.'

A fortnight later, by chance, I met a horse-rider who'd had just such an operation on her neck. One operation had led to three.

Her throat looked like the site of a chainsaw massacre. Some kind of permanent intravenous morphine drip only slightly numbed her pain.

I went home and, piling all my MRI scans and X-rays into a barrow, wheeled them out into a paddock to bury.

Apart from mental anguish, I was in no actual pain except from the financial. If I were to add up what I had spent on alternative health practices I could've had the deposit on two, maybe three houses.

Only Dr Seuss-style verse could properly convey some of the nonsense I again was forlorn enough to try. I was wrapping my middle in castor oil compresses. I was following the Fit for Life diet.

Eat thirty-two spirulina tablets three times a day. Cast out your demons. Talk to angels.

On the bicycle it was becoming increasingly impossible to pedal, I hurtled down hills with affirmations on my tongue. 'Every day and in every way, I'm getting better and better!' Except I was not. On certain days the creeping sensations began entering my eyes and I feared I was starting to go blind with something Western medicine had no name for.

Then I encountered the healing modality known as macrobiotics. At first it seemed a wise philosophy, shot through with a spare Taoist aesthetic. After so much gobbledygook, I found it irresistible. I soon became the charismatic macro man's lover and in my despair I helped to dig the doom that would overtake me two years on.

This had nothing to do with my walking mystery but was untreated endocarditis. My heart was infected. Five and a half months of physical agony and every new symptom gravely interpreted by my partner as my body being at last strong enough to detox.

*

After the ordeal my body has been through, how much easier seem the practicalities of buying the old F100 ambulance. As Mr Bible rants on, the afternoon breeze is causing the calico flour bag safety-pinned to the back of my old scooter to shift out and in.

'And the prior owner used the ambulance for camping?' I ask.

'More or less, mate. More or less. A bit eggs and ham in the back but nothing the feminine touch can't rectify.'

Much more than Mr Bible, it's a line out of Djuna Barnes's *Nightwood*, scrawled in texta onto the flour bag, which I so long to believe. That 'the unendurable is the beginning of the curve of joy'.

The ambulance is a gamble, I know, but not as big a gamble as staying motionless in Mary Street. Nothing chills me more than the thought of the institutionalisation that happened to my grandfather. Diagnosed at the age of twenty-two with the form of chronic progressive multiple sclerosis I'm living with, he eventually went blind. Just before he was put on the top floor of a hospice to die, they amputated both his legs.

This flat I've been renting on the Hoof Street–Mary Street corner, once such a sanctuary after open-heart surgery, has come to feel just like a smaller version of the Grafton prison diagonally opposite my bedroom window. The bricks of the flat resemble the worst Westons biscuits, adrift with flecks of inedible choc chips. On every side of me are frail neighbours in their eighties. When they kill ants in the patch of grass we share, fumes from the spray drift in to my flat's kitchen window.

As far as my eye can see, outside every neat house in every direction, stand red and yellow wheelie bins, ready for collection. It's as if I'm stranded in some giant version of a board game for fat children too unwell to play.

Something in me wants to scream. Needs to run.

*

In two-and-a-half months of searching, the ambulance is the only camper I find to fit the budget of a writer living below the poverty line on a disability pension of $228 a week. Once I sell the little white car to which I graduated from the scooter, there might even be enough for refurbishments.

'And it's yellow?' I check with Mr Bible.

'Harpers Gold, Gillian. Harpers Gold.'

So that in the two weeks it takes to organise transport of the ambulance to northern New South Wales, I keep wondering whether it's going to spangle in the way of that ex-girlfriend who danced topless up Oxford Street one Mardi Gras inside her replica of the Melbourne Arts Centre spire, or whether it will be more of a Christmas beetle gleam.

But the moment I see my ambulance coming through light autumn rain into a South Grafton service station, I realise the colour is that of *Calyptorhynchus funereus*, the yellow-tailed black cockatoos that always scream upriver when people I love die. From a distance, my camper, loaded on the back of a transporter, is a faded, ochre-yellow wonder around which Astroboy-bodied Hyundais are stacked like matchbox cars.

Because I'm so scared I know already that I'll call my camper *Ant and Bee*, after the Angela Banner books, which brought inestimable comfort through all the early years of my 1960s childhood.

'Be careful,' says the transport driver when the seatbelt anchor flies into my hand as I buckle up.

As I make my way into the heavy afternoon traffic burning south on the Pacific Highway, it's incredible no police siren stops me. With no speedometer, no rear-vision mirrors, and windscreen wipers that don't work, I take my maiden journey in *Ant and Bee*. I don't care that I'm about to find out there isn't a nut on the bolt holding the driver's seat onto a piece of ply. So what that the camper conversion described by Mr Bible appears to be an esky chucked in the back and a bit of old foam ockie-strapped to the roof? All will surely be fixable.

On this first drive, how marvellous seem the bends integral to the eccentricity of the Clarence River Bridge. From my lofty new driving height, the old trees of Grafton have never been so golden. How fantastic, how safe, this great bonnet of yellow iron stretching out in protection. Ah, the headiness of the promise of aloneness; of finally being, afflictions and all, the solo driver of my own life.

*

The last time I crossed the Clarence River in an ambulance, the siren was screaming and I was almost dead.

July 2002, the coldest winter on record for decades. Any recollection I allow of it always rolls out like the present.

The eve of my thirty-eighth birthday.

An old friend, working that night shift at Grafton hospital, hears that a woman's been brought in from Nymboida 'and they expect she'll die tonight'.

I have a fever of 41 degrees and veins so dehydrated that my arms turn black with bruises as the hospital staff search for a spot that will take a blood transfusion.

Acute endocarditis. An infection of the heart. Neither my macrobiotic partner nor I has ever heard of such a thing. As soon as the local heart specialist is convinced of his diagnosis, a succession of ambulances is taking me to Sydney for surgery. Although I'm in a state of physical anguish I feel absurdly safe, as if now my belly's full of hospital-issue, two-pack Arnott's Scotch Fingers, all shall be well, my agony soon over.

Even though I've never really watched television medical dramas, somehow I feel that they're part of my confidence; that surely this script of my own life is going to have a happy ending.

A streptococcal vegetation has been living off the mitral valve of my heart. In the absence of early detection by conventional medicine, it has become so vigorous, so mobile, that colonies are in my spleen and in both kidneys as well. The risk exists that at any moment a piece will ping off into my brain, causing a stroke big enough to end my life immediately.

If I survive the surgery essential to remove the main vegetation on my heart, grown as large as a four-centimetre-long caterpillar, another operation might be scheduled to remove my all-but-destroyed spleen.

In the air ambulance to Sydney, a guttural note enters my sobbing. It was only twenty-four hours before, at midnight, that my macrobiotic knight errant, apprehending at last the gravity of my condition, had eased my lightweight body into his truck to take me to hospital. Half a year since the excruciating onset of the heart infection. Half a year since I'd seen any of my family or my old hometown of Grafton. Macro-errantry. Macro-lunacy. It was as if by living in isolation along a stretch of the wild Nymboida River, surrounded predominantly by all the classic texts of the macrobiotic lineage, that I'd dried out my brains and lost my wits. A kind of warped, 21st-century healing version of Don Quixote. Almost a cult. Definitely a *folie à deux*.

The dual decline of my body – multiple sclerosis followed by endocarditis – is a mystery I've yet to decode fully. One day I'll recall all the bizarre facts. But not now. I don't want to spoil taking my new home-to-be on this first drive.

Driving back through Grafton to my flat, I push the past out of reach, focusing instead on the 4/3 rhythm that the abandoned intercom system makes as it hits the windscreen.

I'm alive aren't I? Alive in *Ant and Bee*, and the thin black steering wheel moves like a waltz in my hands.

*

My first task is to become an overnight petrol head. The intricacies of the internal-combustion engine are explained to me in that enthusiastic language of car-crazy boys. What better distraction from the past than craning over the bonnet or lying on my back under the chassis?

I discover who are the mechanics in my town with a relish for working on old Effies, as any F100 is affectionately called, and learn many things: when it might be necessary to put pepper into the radiator, how to clean spark plugs with a metal toothbrush, the miracle of WD-40 at work on ancient rust.

The mechanics are making the old ambulance sound. They're as cordial as Darjeeling monks: I could weep with gratitude when the auto-electrician throws a piece of canvas over a stash of MS-induced incontinence products he's had to uncover to get some wiring finished. The radiator man, without asking, rigs up the new airconditioner with a bit of PVC tubing from his backyard. Only then does the unit, which cost more than the ambulance itself, blast cold air in the right direction. This is essential because, as is the case for many people with MS, the moment my legs grow hot my ability to move them drastically declines.

Next I turn my attention to the interior. To cull forty years' worth of possessions so that they fit into a space no bigger than a bathroom is only a momentary challenge. 'Jettison' is becoming my favourite word. The more I give away, the more gleeful I feel. How fantastic to have a kitchen that fits into a red Coles shopping crate. How light my melamine bowl, cup and plate stacked like games in a toy box.

Alive in Ant and Bee

A narrow, sky-blue woollen carpet, afloat with white Tibetan cranes, doubles as my mattress and living-area rug. Sitting cross-legged here, I can wash dishes, brush my teeth, reach for CDs, check my hair in the small circle of mirror on the wall, and not have moved a step. Underneath the ply-sleeping platform I store an axe, spade, blockbuster, hatchet and campfire cooking tripod.

Painting the long cupboards that once held medical paraphernalia takes ten minutes and half a 250-ml tin of paint. They are the perfect height for holding kitchen canisters of pasta, rice, nuts and tea.

I've given notice at 'Brickland', and with only a fortnight left to go, each day is crammed with activity. I'm decorating now, removing my loveliest little watercolours from their frames. Sticking them onto the cleaned ambulance walls.

Cloth gathered long ago in different countries makes beautiful curtains. How fast my life has gone, I think, fingering a square of African cotton from the 16th arrondissement in Paris. How young and strong I once was, able to walk miles in a day. *My days are swifter than a runner.* How can it be that now I'm more than forty, with legs that haven't walked properly since the age of thirty? *They flee away. They go by like skiffs of reed. Like an eagle falling on the prey.* Maybe this'll be the decade to finish reading my tatty bible, which in *Ant and Bee* always seems to fall open in my hands at the Book of Psalms, as if this is where my reading of it stopped as a child.

No matter how sceptically people view my plan, everyone's rallying to help. If I sometimes have to pause, crouch down, it's due to the love washing over me from my family and friends, like the waves of some magical sea.

The increasing sense that my ambulance has become a cubbyhouse on wheels – new radial Firewalkers, their treads black and deep – brings delight. From the iron ceiling trusses I hang an assortment of charms, each object full of secret and lucky histories.

At certain angles *Ant and Bee* conveys the impression of a stationery shop. What a simple happiness to plump out a cane basket with new glue sticks, five different kinds of tape, rubber bands, pencil sharpeners, paintbrushes and stamps.

Favourite coloured nylon-tip pens hang by their lids along one side of a cardboard box rigged to hold cutlery. In no time at all pens will outnumber forks, as if words are to be my main nourishment.

Later still I'll come to appreciate that a roaming home means no cockroaches and no rodents of any kind. Soon, too, I'll be relishing bucket-and-jug washes, my body like a baby in my own hands.

A camping shop has an aluminium table that will serve as my writing desk, and a determined friend finally finds the perfect chair. Folded, they both tuck up neatly between a 12-volt fridge and three 20-litre plastic drums of grain. But would Rilke, I can't help but wonder, still advise his young poet to look into his heart and write? If the left cockle of the poet's heart were made of carbon?

As autumn arrives, I can feel the valve's artificial edge seated like a bit of meccano beneath my breast. It ticks as if made of tin, and sounds too small for my body. What if the neurocardiology researchers of the twenty-first century prove right and there is a brain in the heart? What might a new lover think? Will the valve handle the accelerated beat? Will there indeed ever be a new lover for one limping around in a body of such obvious wreckage?

Now I perch with unbearable anticipation on the two long shelves built to run either side of the van. Which books, which stories, which poems will I choose to travel with me? Four dictionaries, heavier than firewood, find the first space, and then my old paperback thesaurus. Not because it's ever been much use but because I like the smell of its thin yellowy pages, and the handwritten inscription of a sister whose gift it was when I turned sixteen. Tenderness is the sentiment that determines which old fictional favourites are chosen. Is there room for all my Randolph Stows? How about Virginia Woolf and Carson McCullers? I squeeze in a few equestrian classics and an assortment of poetry volumes I feel I can't live without. I also find the remains of my childhood edition of *1, 2, 3 With Ant and Bee* – a scruffy mascot for the glovebox.

The day arrives when, with no further funds left, I can hone my state of preparedness no more. As I cross the bridge one more time I say goodbye to the town of Grafton that I've loved so deeply, sometimes loathed, and written about for most of my life. The Clarence, my own river Alph, seems afloat with more memories than any story can accommodate. Farewell, old dear town that helped bring me back to life. Farewell, old, dangerously compliant self, who very nearly allowed her own death.

Travelling to no deadline, and with no fixed route, I'm on my way to live in Adelaide. As my first cautious weeks go by, I recognise the Way described with such a mixture of comedy and pathos in Farid Ud-din Attar's twelfth-century mystical classic, *Manteq ot-Teyr*, or *The Conference of the Birds*.

Even in the doggerel of the English translation I feel an enchantment, which is also connected to the beauty of my battered old Penguin paperback. The Persian miniature on the cover depicts a multitude of birds gathered by a decorative river. With as plucky a spirit as they can muster, they too are leaving the safety of their homes. Only with the assistance of each other, Attar's spiritual allegory emphasises, will the birds find their way. His riddling tales often mock the solitary attempts of desert Sufis, wrapped up in dangerous self-importance. Unless, warns Attar, you can see divinity everywhere and in everything, including every human being, then you're missing out on the mystery of the world.

For the first six months, though, once I've ascertained that even with MS the camping life is possible for me, I hide out alone in the state forests of north-eastern New South Wales.

In the bush I take respite from the inundation of people that occurs after you have almost died. Old trees and rain, starry skies and insects – these are the antidotes I crave. Frogs croaking, the songs of crickets, spider webs strung between fronds of lomandras. This is when my true recovery begins.

Moonlight can bring the impression that a galaxy of stars, a miniature Milky Way, is sliding into the tree closest to my camp. One morning, before light, my water bucket holds a reflection of the waning crescent moon at such a steep angle that the song of the first shrike thrush seems to touch its tip. To think that it was only due to catastrophe that I've chosen this way to live.

In order to avoid another medical emergency my van is rigged for safety not only with a two-way radio but also an EPIRB device that, if activated when I'm out of mobile phone range, instantly alerts an emergency centre and via satellite locates my exact position.

Life in these forest camps is calm and kind – my water dipper going in and out of a reed-rimmed wetland. Because I don't set up in well-known, overused beauty spots, all is fresh, the energy untrammelled and not a Vodka Cruiser can or chewing-gum wrapper in sight. The insects don't know how to bite and lizards are not afraid of me.

Every seven or eight days when I'm camping, I screw a small stone mill onto *Ant and Bee*'s back step. In less than an hour I have my flour for bread. A 25-kilogram sack of wheat berries costs less than five supermarket loaves. Dip a finger into fresh flour and it smells as alive as a little animal. Is there anything more peaceful or satisfying than turning flour into dough? This simple alchemy of sea salt, water and my own wild leaven; this dough forming like a head in my hands.

My balcony brush swish-swishing across the Tibetan rug is a rhythmic link to all the early morning sweepers of Asia and Africa, and even as far away as 12th-century Baghdad. In *The Conference of the Birds,* one of Farid Ud-din Attar's sweepers has just been given a bracelet sparkling with jewels from the king.

Who did *Ant and Bee* save? I'm always wondering. When it was used as an ambulance? Until 2002, my emergency year, ambulances had always been like fire-engines – an urgent wail for somebody else's disaster.

'Sorry,' a man who used to drive ambulances in the '70s tells me in a caravan park laundry, 'but your old ambo would've usually been heading for the morgue. Most people died.'

This, he claims, was mainly due to heart attacks, happening most frequently around eleven p.m., the body unable to cope with its last heavy meal. Ambulances back then carried little more than oxygen and a first-aid kit. Splints in the cupboard where I now keep my rolled oats and almonds.

'Probably shouldn't tell you this,' says the ex-driver, 'but one night we had a man who was smashed into smithereens. Come off from the thirty-third storey of a building in George Street. He was only young but we couldn't lift him. No bones big enough left.'

Alive in Ant and Bee

Back in *Ant and Bee* I turn on the radio. Just in time to hear that the day before, a young Sunni man strapped on his bomb belt, packed with nails, to blow himself and seventy others up, just before breakfast Baghdad time.

My glumness deepens. Ud-din Attar's anecdotes, often set in Baghdad, also tend towards bloody ends. Al-Hallaj, a Persian Sufi, was flogged, mutilated, hung on a gibbet and decapitated for his heretical pronouncement, 'I am God and I am the Truth.' Then Ud-din Attar himself was purportedly beheaded.

*

Which-a-where, which-a-where. In the camp I choose for my first solo bush birthday, almost a year after setting forth, the air's alive with small birds. *Which-you, why-you,* they sing. *Weech you. Wheeech you.*

Thinking back to turning thirty-eight three years ago, I try to cry but can't. The air of this clearing is too limpid, the noises from the small circle of a wetland too strong for tears.

Why you, which you, cry the black-faced fly-catchers, sallying in the air after insects.

So here at last, just before I turn forty-one, will be the place safe enough to fully remember. The urgent need for this makes me grind flour fast for my next loaf of bread. In less than half an hour I'm done. I check the leaven. Good. It's very active, its bubbles rising and popping. In haste I form the dough.

Flouring its bottom and setting it in the sun to rise, (it will take all of the bright day), at last I'm ready to allow the past to roll out like the present.

Like the Romans I believe memories are stored in your *cor,* in your heart of hearts. So in a sunny glade, lying on a blanket, I place my hands there over the vertical scar, to help let it be 2002 again.

In the few days' lead-up to surgery my sister nips open the restricted red patient file and at my behest reads 'Severely wasted, unwell lady, febrile, septic, with severe mitral regurgitation and acute heart failure. Limited movement due to extreme pain everywhere.'

From my hospital bed I weep at the sheer implausibility of how something as shining as macro-errantry has led me down a path this dark. When I dare a glimpse in the hospital bathroom mirror I think that if I were a wounded wallaby by the side of the road, I'd knock the life out of her with my car-jack. When I'm weighed in a basket I'm 39 kilograms. Naked I look like a concentration camp victim. My liver shutting down has lent my skin a dreadful, snakeskin-yellow hue. I feel stranded in a script penned by a horror writer devoid of skill.

That it's my drastic love affair that has brought me to this point is part of my pain. After trying so hard. So no, I decide in front of the hospital mirror, I won't look anymore into my own Knight of the Sad Countenance's face. I will avoid the appearance of my thighs, fallen like two twigs underneath the hospital gown. I won't dwell on the ash my lover used to treat the bedsore that smells of death, there at the base of my spine. Nor on his absence from this bedside of extremity he so helped to create.

Instead I tune in to the sheer pageantry of life. The whole hospital's a show on which I feast and feast, unable to take my fill.

Look! There go Dr Miriam Welgampola's shoes again, so small, so elegant that surely elvin cobblers create each new pair in the night. What is the exact tragedy of the chain-smoking Kurdish Iraqi doctor with the smouldering good looks? How come his eye got blackened at the Coogee Bay Hotel? And the friendly tableau of night nurses munching on the lollies that fuel them through their shift. Such scenes are a call to life more potent than any painkiller.

Here come processions of precious friends carrying baskets full of the most marvellous food and drink. After two years wherein the eating of sugar was equated with shooting up heroin, I tune in to home-baked puddings.

Human flirtation comes next to my bedside. Oh the lovely flitterings of it over me as I lie inert, surrounded by beloved members of my family. My dark-haired sister – the beauty of her, dressed like an eighteenth-century gypsy, as her deep brown eyes meet the nearly black ones of the bodybuilding male nurse from the Philippines. My father, too, laughing with happiness as he recognises he is indeed still attractive to the nurses.

Ah the light-hearted eddies across my shriven form, so that in the absence of fresh air, this is an almost greater tonic.

Finally there's Dr Grant, the cardiothoracic surgeon himself.

'Of all the doctors, he's my favourite,' declares my sister. 'Thank goodness he'll be performing the operation. Have you noticed his energy? He's like a bull.'

Matador, I secretly think, with his elegant moustache, especially when he goes by wearing a surgical gown as dramatic as any cape.

When one of the students confides that as a surgeon Dr Grant is renowned for his surgery on the hearts of children, I make a point of looking at his hands. His fingers are a poet's, long and pale. Due to my emaciated condition, the risks of open-heart surgery are high. Before I sign the permission form, I must be aware that I might die. But without this surgery my death is certain.

When the day of the operation arrives, my grief in saying goodbye to my colourful retinue is greater than all the towering floors of the ugly hospital. The ward's grey dullness runs in time in me with Psalm 55. *My heart is sore pained within me and the terrors of death are fallen upon me. Fearfulness and trembling are come upon me and Horror hath overwhelmed me.*

Regret flows in me. So this could be the last landscape of my life, this desolate place full of suffering people? According to the Socratic aphorism, I can't be judged to have excelled at philosophy because I haven't practised for my death, for my dying, not at all. I'd always taken it as given that, in the style of St Francis of Assisi, I would die outside, on solid ground, on grass. Far into the future, when I was old.

As orderlies slide me onto the surgical trolley, something unwanted begins to happen. Psalm 55, which even through pain I apprehend as being suitably charged for the situation, is being shoved aside. Instead, Edward Lear nonsense verse. *As soon as he saw our daughter Dell, in violent love that Crane King fell.* Taking over my mind.

Oh no, if I have to have Lear, rather than any plangent prayer or segment from some ancient saint, can't it at least be 'The Owl and the Pussycat'? Please, God or whoever, I want the owl and the cat. The dance by the light of the silvery moon. I hate 'The Pelican Chorus'. *Pelican Jee! Oh happy are we,* wading in on its great flippered feet. *Ploffskin, Pluffskin, Pelican Jill, we think so then and we thought so still.*

I never let anyone abbreviate my name to Jill. Now, due to a spelling error made on my admission, it's as 'Gorillian' that I'm being wheeled down the corridor to the theatre.

Somehow my sisters reappear for a last kiss goodbye. *She has gone to the great Gromboolian plain. And we probably never shall meet again.*

I have said goodbye to everyone except myself. 'Don't be crying now,' says the beautiful Irish anaesthetist, who also succumbed to my father's charisma.

For the king of the cranes had won her heart with a crocodile egg and an ice-cream tart.

What if the Buddhists are right, and from your last conscious thought comes your next reality?

In a moment the needle will go in. Why hasn't anyone mentioned God? Why did I stop praying when at the age of nine I lost my *Book of Poems and Prayers for the Very Young*, with the peaceful brown mare and foal on its cover?

My diseased heart will be exposed. The eyes of strangers will marvel at the extent of my gigantic mistake.

Was it an ice-cream tart or seaweed? Nori like mermaid's paper? Mists from the yellow Chankly Bore are rising up to greet me and someone is about to saw open my sternum.

Excerpted from 'Alive in Ant and Bee*', in Harpers Gold, HEAT 13*

From Frogmore, Victoria

Helen Garner

Last winter on a plane to the Mildura Writers' Festival I happened to sit next to Raimond Gaita. Like many people who have read his memoir *Romulus, My Father*, I felt I knew him better than I actually do. I asked him if it was true that Eric Bana was going to play Romulus in the movie adaptation that I'd heard Richard Roxburgh was directing. He opened his laptop and showed me some stills: the replica of Frogmore, the crumbling weatherboard shack of his childhood; Bana riding a motorbike with a plaster cast on his leg; a rangy boy running and laughing in a dusty yard. The movie-Raimond looked about nine. He had a face so open that it hurt to look at it.

'His name,' said Gaita, 'is Kodi Smit-McPhee.'

'Did you go to the shoot?'

'I kept away,' he said. 'I thought my presence might throw him off. He might think, Is *this* what's ahead for me?' He gave a small laugh. 'But near the end I went. Richard introduced us. We stood and looked at each other. We both cried. He said, "I've lived your life for the last three months." And then for an hour he wouldn't leave my side.'

There's a brief scene, quite early in the movie, in which Raimond is mooching along a street and sees a teenage girl dancing wildly to a record on her front porch. He calls out and asks her the name of the singer. She tells him it's Jerry Lee Lewis, from Ferriday, Louisiana. 'And who are you, when you're at home?' she asks coldly. The screen fills with the boy's eager, unbearably smiling and undefended face. 'I'm Raimond Gaita,' he says, 'from Frogmore, Victoria!'

At that moment a faint sound rustled through the first preview audience: half laughter, half sigh. Gaita was in the cinema that evening. I wondered how he would sit through this new telling of his childhood, a version over which he had little or no control.

It's a story of suffering: obsessive love, sexual betrayal and jealousy, abandonment of small children; violence, madness and despair; two suicides; repeated acts of forgiveness and loyalty that are nothing short of heroic; and threaded through all this, the miraculous blossoming of a child's intellect.

The book changed the quality of the literary air in this country. People often take an unusually emotional tone when they speak about it, as if it had performed for them the function that Franz Kafka demanded: 'A book must be the axe for the frozen sea within us.' Reading it, with its stiff, passionate dignity and its moral demands, can smash open a reader's own blocked-off sorrows. Out they rush to meet those that the book relates.

For a movie to be drawn from this memoir, the tale would have had to be taken apart, and the pieces picked up off the floor and compressed into a new configuration, without the one element that holds it all together on the page, makes sense of it, and redeems it: Gaita's unique narrating voice.

It's an intellectual's voice, a philosopher's, fastidious, restrained, wary. It's wonderfully serious, and terrified of being sentimental. At times it quivers with a suppressed, righteous anger. It can be disdainful, lofty to the point of chilliness, as when he refines and yet again refines his father's beliefs and motives, holding them away defensively from what he imagines the reader might lazily suppose them to have been: *no,* it wasn't *this,* he keeps insisting – it was *that.*

And then suddenly it will relax and open out into an image of sensuous joy: 'roads specially dusted to match the high summer-coloured grasses'; or a blunt domestic fact: 'the chickens came into the house and shat in it'; or a quiet statement of breathtaking simplicity and humility: 'I know what a good workman is; I know what an honest man is; I know what friendship is; I know because I remember these things in the person of my father, in the person of his friend Hora, and in the example of their friendship.'

How can film match this striding, all-creating, all-encompassing thing, the voice?

I saw Gaita emerge into the lobby after the preview. He looked vague, and numb. I would have liked to make a comradely gesture, but I didn't understand what the movie was doing to me, so I bolted for the train. I cried all the way home, and on and off for days afterwards.

*

'You can't imagine,' shouts Gaita over the rattling of his loose-jointed old ute, 'how much more beautiful it is round here when there's *grass*.'

But up here near Baringhup in Central Victoria, where Gaita is showing me the sites of his childhood story, the grass is gone. Drought has stripped the ground naked. Its surface is worn-out, grey-brown velvet. The paddocks are infested with a plague of wheel cactus, nasty, plate-shaped pads of pale green, fringed with sparse hairy spines.

'The stuff's out of control,' says Gaita. 'And it can grow straight out of a rock.'

We park and set out on foot towards the granite boulders among which Romulus Gaita's friend Vacek, a harmless hermit, made himself a fortress. I spot a baby cactus sprouting insolently from a dinted stone.

'Eww, gross,' I say. 'It *is* growing out of bare rock.'

'You thought it was mere hyperbole, didn't you,' says Gaita.

This is the first time I've ever heard anyone use the phrase 'mere hyperbole' in conversation. Before I can remark on this, which I'm not at all sure I'm going to, we fetch up against the first boulder.

Despite his grand philosopher's head with its white hair and glasses, Gaita is a small, agile fellow, a rock-climber from way back. Up he goes, smooth as a lizard. He leans down to me.

'Get your toe in *there*, see?'

I obey. He reaches down and grabs my hand.

'Now,' he says, 'you just *run* up it.'

Somehow my other foot gains a purchase on the granite. He lets go my hand and suddenly I'm running. I bound up the damn thing. In four light springs I'm standing on its flat top, not even out of breath. I glow with relief. Gaita is not the sort of person before whom one would like to appear foolish, or gutless; and I'm not yet sure why.

*

These austere volcanic plains, across which a vast, leisurely body of air is forever passing, have carried for Gaita since childhood an unabashedly transcendental meaning.

'I needed the film-makers,' he shouts as the ute rattles along, 'to understand how utterly fundamental to the story the landscape was. They saw it at all hours of the day and night – they fell in love with it. The first time Nick Drake [the British poet who wrote the screenplay] came to Baringhup, I drove him along this road. It was a bit later in the day. And when we came round this bend, the light over there was thick gold.'

Today the sky is partly clouded. The land is grey, grey, grey, racked and bare. But its bones are glorious – low contours under colossal, purifying skies.

'Now,' he yells, 'you're about to see what drought *really* is.'

We bounce over a rise and down the side of a large, lumpy, broad, grey valley, a couple of kilometres across. Right at the bottom lies a small, narrow body of water, sausage-shaped and murky. Its steely surface riffles in the wind. Gaita pulls off the track and stops. I look round vaguely. There's something odd about this place, something not quite natural.

'This is where Hora and I used to take the boat out,' he says.

What sort of boating could you do in these puddles?

'See that boat ramp?'

I glance at him. He's pointing up, not down. Way over there, quite high on the side of the valley with its craggy rim, I can see a length of cement footpath that ends a good hundred metres above the sausage-shaped ponds. My jaw drops. We are sitting in the ute at the very bottom of the Cairn Curran Reservoir. This whole valley was once full of water. This is the reservoir whose construction brought Romulus Gaita, his wife Christine, their small son Raimond, and their friends the brothers Hora and

Mitru all the way down here from Bonegilla migrant camp in 1950. And now it's empty. The water, like the grass, is gone.

I stare about wildly. 'What's that small building, right up at the top?'

'That,' says Gaita with a tiny, inscrutable smile, 'was the Yacht Club.'

*

Gaita and his wife Yael have recently built a house on a bare rise only eight kilometres from Frogmore. This autumn evening as the sun goes down, sending long fingers of light across the stripped grey ground where a dozen tiny wrens are hopping and peeping in a bush, Gaita and I sit on the veranda, drinking wine. He spreads out on the table a sheaf of old black-and-white photos.

'Here's my father's *real* ironwork,' says Gaita, 'rather than the garden settings he made for a living in Australia.' It's a beaten iron sign hanging on the façade of a building in Europe: so intricate and deft that it looks like something in nature, the flourishing tip of a branch.

Like Kodi Smit-McPhee's face, the family photos are hard to look at without emotion: unbearably poignant, some touched with a gentle playfulness, others shockingly dramatic.

'Here's my father when he was mad.' It's a tiny square headshot of a man from a Dostoevsky novel or a gulag: a dark face, thin, clenched, with blazing eyes and up-tilted chin.

The striking picture of Romulus Gaita that was reproduced on the book's cover shows, in its original, a much more complex expression: a wonderfully subtle play of humour and self-mockery round the mouth and eyes.

How handsome these people were! How *young*!

Christine Gaita is played in the movie by the German actress Franka Potente, who's blonde and strong-faced. The real Christine, the photos seem to show, was tiny, almost delicate, with curly dark hair that puffed lightly on a breeze. In the book Gaita describes her as 'highly intelligent, deeply sensuous, anarchic and unstable.' She plainly suffered from a mental illness: she heard voices, was self-destructively promiscuous, and aroused violent passions in men. In her son, whom she repeatedly left in the care of his father and Hora, she inspired an unassuageable longing: when she came back, and lay depressed in bed all day, unable to do the work of a wife and mother, he used to creep into the bed beside her, to bask in the warmth of her body.

'I was always afraid Richard Roxburgh would romanticise my mother,' says Gaita. 'He was very struck by these photos. But I don't think he does.'

In fact Potente in the part is restrained almost to the point of self-effacement, as if the film did not quite dare to understand or fully to inhabit Christine. The scenes in which we see her inability to mother, though, are terribly moving: the arms she dutifully holds out for her baby are as stiff as the prongs of a forklift truck.

Yet at its heart the movie is an unflinching study of the suffering, the desperation and the decency of men. Its failings, which are several and very thought-provoking, are swept aside, for me, by its four splendid male performances – Eric Bana as Romulus, Russell Dykstra as Mitru, the sublime Smit-McPhee as Raimond, and Marton Czokas as Hora, Romulus's lifelong friend whose loving faithfulness radiates from both book and film.

'The builder who made this house,' says Gaita on the veranda, 'had read the book, and so had the young fellow who was labouring for him. One day towards the end of Hora's life I brought him up here to have a look at the building. I told the builders he was coming. And when Hora got out of the car and walked towards the house, the builder downed tools and approached him like this' – Gaita bows his head and clasps his hands in front of him, like a man going up to take communion – 'and the young labourer took his peaked cap off. I'd never before seen him without his cap.' He laughs, almost tenderly.

'How did Hora take it?' I ask.

'Oh,' he says, filling my glass, 'I don't think he noticed.'

*

On Sunday morning the magpies are shouting when we set out in the car on what I am beginning to realise is a highly structured visit to a series of personal shrines.

Gaita shows me the site of the long-gone camp in which the Cairn Curran Reservoir labourers were accommodated, and the ramshackle hall opposite it, where dances were held and films shown. We visit his primary school, at which 'Professor Gaita' has recently instituted two awards: one for intellectual achievement, and the other the Romulus Gaita Prize for Kindness: 'though I did wonder,' he says, not quite joking, and I'm not quite sure if I should laugh, 'if it might be a *corrupting* prize – that kids might try to be kind for the wrong reasons.'

And then we head for Frogmore. He parks beside the bitumen road. We climb over a gate and walk a couple of hundred metres along a straight gravel track into the low, flat, empty landscape. My God, it's bleak out here. A steady, cool wind passes across the plain, coming from nowhere, going nowhere. Everything is brown or grey. Our boots crunch on the gravel. This is the road along which Christine Gaita trudged in her heels and waisted cotton dress, carrying her little suitcase, coming back to try again with her husband and son after each of her desperate flights to Melbourne.

'When I brought Nick Drake here,' says Gaita, 'it was a very hot day. The house had burned down years ago. Scotch thistles had grown all over it. It was … desolate. It shocked me to see how desolate it was. I insisted on bringing him back another day, in other softer lights.'

'What sort of life did your mother expect or hope to have?' I ask.

'She'd been training as a chemist, in Germany.' His tone is carefully neutral. 'She thought she would have a city life. When I brought my aunt Maria here from Germany a few years ago, she didn't say much. She just cried. To think her sister had had to live in such a place.'

We climb through a wire fence. There's a small dam.

'Is this where you chucked your dad's precious razor?'

'This is the real dam,' he says, 'in which my father's real razor still lies rusting. Not long before he died he asked me again what happened to the razor. I just shrugged.'

'You *never told him*? You held out for forty years? What a power struggle!'

He looks surprised. 'I suppose it was.' He puts his head on one side, and gives his rare, endearing smile.

The house was demolished in 1969. The place where it stood

is now just scraped-looking dirt strewn with old-fashioned brown beer bottles and studded with pieces of broken cement, rusty iron and smashed crockery. A crumbly patina of sheep shit coats everything. We mooch about with our eyes on the ground. I long to pick up a piece of the china and put it in my pocket, but one does not steal souvenirs from shrines. A large lump is starting to form in my throat.

In the dirt near the fence lies the metal head of a spade, rusted away into a graceful curve like a palm tree. I pick it up by the shaft and hold it out to him.

'Look. How beautiful.'

'That,' he says in a non-committal tone, 'is probably the one with which we buried Orloff.' In sentences of perfect syntax, as formally as if he were reciting a liturgy, he relates how the dog, which had taken a ground glass bait, managed to drag himself as far as the outside of the wire fence, and died there.

'My father lifted him over the fence, so that he could be buried on the right side. It was the first time I ever saw my father cry. The only time we ever cried together was beside the grave of Orloff.'

Looking down at the unmarked ground where the bones of Orloff lie, I feel my self-control begin to slip. There's a loud squawk above our heads in the pine tree. We look up with a start. Two brilliant white cockatoos glide down from a high branch in a big showy curve. I glance at Gaita. Down his cheek is pouring a sheet of tears.

'I know it's silly,' he mutters, wiping them away with the back of his hand, 'but for a second I thought it was my cocky Jack. They can live for eighty or ninety years, you know.'

We stand there in silence, in the steady wind, heads down, hands in our pockets.

He drifts over to a huge pine that has toppled beside the dam. Its bare upper branches, trained sideways by decades of wind, look like thick grey hair streaming. Its roots are in the air, but its lower branches are still putting out cones and fresh green needles. The symbolism of this is so obvious that we can't even look at each other.

*

From Frogmore, Victoria

Once we have inspected the collapsing shed on the nearby farm, where Romulus Gaita laboured over a forge at his ironwork, and once we have peered through the smashed windows of the derelict house where Raimond was often invited to afternoon tea by the old ladies of the Lilley family, the morning is gone.

As we drive into Maryborough, I spot a white tower on a bushy hilltop.

'What's that?' I say, making conversation.

'That's the Pioneer Tower.' He keeps his eyes on the road. 'From which Mitru jumped to his death.'

We drive to its base. The observation deck at the top has been enclosed with white cyclone wire: Maryborough is a town whose economic base has collapsed, and whose young people know despair and have acted on it. We climb the stairs, stand awkwardly at the railing for a few moments, and hurry down again. We drive in silence down the old town's handsome streets, and then he steers the car on to the overgrown land along the railway line, behind a deserted flour mill.

'This,' says Gaita in his quiet, neutral voice, 'must be where they shot the bit with the pram' – a scene in which the boy Raimond, trundling a pram that contains his baby half-sister, pursues his disturbed mother as she leads a stranger into a shed and has sex with him against a wall, while the frantic boy watches the encounter, with its violence and degradation, through a crack in the corrugated iron.

I don't know how much more of this I can take. I am struggling to hold on to some sort of self-command.

By the time we reach the cemetery and walk among the graves of these tragic people, Romulus, Hora, Mitru, and finally, near the fence, Christine, with its stone marked *She suffered deeply* (I read the dates, I do the sums; this woman killed herself a few weeks short of her thirtieth birthday), I am rigid with a distress so overwhelming that I know, with what's left of my mind, that it can't possibly be only mine. Some barrier between me and this man I hardly know has been breached by his story. I'm at the mercy of a tremendous force, a depth of sorrow that no book, no film can ever fully express or console.

Ritual behaviour is called for at shrines, but I can't think of a way to act. If we knew each other better, it would be natural for me to make some sort of human gesture of sympathy, or respect. But I'm paralysed by the fantasy of professional detachment, and by a strained sense of formality that I don't understand.

We stand side by side in front of Christine Gaita's grave.

Then Gaita moves slightly so that his shoulder lightly touches mine. I lean my shoulder against his. He puts his arm round my waist. I copy his movement, and we turn and walk back to the car like that, in silence, as if we were friends, though which of us is trying to comfort the other I have no idea.

The Monthly

Fire Down Below

Dan Chiasson

Poetry goes to the backwater to refresh itself as often as it goes to the mainstream, a fact that partly explains the appeal of Les Murray, the celebrated 'bush bard' of Bunyah, New South Wales, Australia. The son of a poor farmer, Murray, who was not schooled formally until he was nine, is now routinely mentioned among the three or four leading English-language poets. Because in Murray's poetry you learn, for example, that there exists such a thing as the 'creamy shitwood tree,' he has been mistaken for a neutral cartographer of far-flung places. But the key to Murray, what makes him so exasperating to read one minute and thrilling the next, is not landscape but rage. 'How naturally random recording edges into contempt,' Murray writes, identifying the poles of his own combustible poetic temperament.

Murray's poems, never exactly intimate and often patrolled by details and place-names nearly indecipherable to an outsider, reflect a life lived self-consciously and rather flamboyantly off the beaten track. Murray has always been associated with the land in and around Bunyah, where Aborigines harvested wild yams before Murray's own people, 'bounty migrants' from Scotland, displaced them in 1848. His childhood was marked by 'lank poverty, dank poverty,' a condition enforced by his grandfather, who kept Murray's parents in a brutal, resentful tenancy – sharecroppers, in essence, on their own ancestral lands. Murray's biographer, Peter Alexander, describes a slab house with a shingle roof and a floor of stamped earth covered by linoleum, sunlight streaking 'through the generous gaps in the walls.' Perhaps no major English poet since John Clare grew up in such destitution, and, like Clare, Murray enjoys the 'hard names' associated with being poor: 'rag and toejam, feed and paw.'

We associate the depiction of rural life with pastoral, a mode that was shaped by city sensibilities for city audiences. Pastoral is a sophisticated game pitting poets against earlier poets, like a chess match played across time. No poet writing about the natural world entirely opts out of the game, but Murray's poetry of elk and emus, bougainvillea and turmeric dust, comes close. For the sheer scarcity of its flora and fauna, this pastoral feels pretty far off the Virgilian grid. No poet who was 'kept poor,' as Murray believes he and his parents were, sees 'nature' – droughts and floods, the relentless summer heat on an uninsulated iron roof – in celebratory terms. Indeed, since the poverty that Murray suffered was an enforced poverty, it is hard even to see 'nature' in natural terms. Nature, for him, is the field where human motives, often sinister, play out.

If you've been as poor as Murray was, 'fate' can come to be synonymous with 'what people do to you.' The great struggle in his work is therefore between what Whitman calls the 'Me myself' and what Murray calls the 'Them and He.' Murray's poems tell an old story – the indignity that a small person and those he loved suffered at the hands of big, corrupt people, a long time ago – but they tell it with a ferocity that sharpens the farther away from the source the poet travels. You need to be a little bit of a lunatic to bear the specific, outsized grudges Murray has borne through his sixties, when all kinds of attention – including Alexander's fine biography (published in 2000), hundreds of articles and favourable reviews, and an invitation to write a new preamble to the Australian constitution – have come his way. And, indeed, there is always something demented about Murray's poems: even at their most painstakingly rational, it is as though, to quote Dickinson, 'a plank in Reason, broke.'

Rant-poems crop up everywhere in Murray: graffiti by other means, these blunt, scrawled mottoes are abandoned, like graffiti, the minute they get made. Murray has the habit of comparing people and things he dislikes to Nazis – including, most famously, in a poem called 'Rock Music,' sex:

> Sex is a Nazi. The students all knew
> this at your school. To it, everyone's subhuman
> for parts of their lives. Some are all their lives.
> You'll be one of those if these things worry you.

This poem is 'misunderstood,' Alexander claims, but then he quotes Murray's less than reassuring clarification: bullied by girls in high school, he came to view himself as the target of 'a kind of attempted psychic castration of people who are out of fashion in some way.' (The girls from Taree High School, Taree, NSW, might be forgiven for whatever ambivalence they now feel about being compared to castrating Nazis by their nation's pre-eminent poet.)

One way a child has of fortifying himself against the torments, real and imagined, of the outside world is to become an inveterate reader. Murray was aware of words at an early age, taking special delight, when he was three, in the phrase, from the Lord's Prayer, 'trespass against us.' (He is a faithful Catholic, dedicating his books 'to the glory of God.') He read Hopkins and Eliot early on and, the biography tells us, devoured the poetry of John Milton in a single weekend. Those three authors govern Murray's entire career. You hear Hopkins in the homemade compounds and heavy consonants ('Nests of golden porridge shattered in the silky-oak trees, / cobs and crusts of it, their glory box'); you sense Milton behind Murray's larger-scale works, notably his 1998 verse novel, *Fredy Neptune*; but most of all you detect the presence of Eliot, whose self-monitoring Christianity suggests an inner untidiness too vast to be tamed by ordinary secular means. Murray, who met his wife in a Passion play (they were both students at the University of Sydney; he played Satan, and she was in charge of his wardrobe), seems permanently shaped by a small archive of adolescent mortifications and slights. Flinch-prone and skittish, Murray (again, like Eliot) finds his defense in caricature, generalising about people from a few details or remarks. His temperament allows for only a beat or two between data and conclusion (synonymous too often for Murray with 'condemnation').

This bluntness can be off-putting; Murray often lacks a middle register of feeling. When he writes a poem about AIDS, for example, he seems almost sinister in his concision. Nobody who reads 'Aphrodite Street' (1987) feels exactly comfortable with the tone, and yet that discomfort makes the poem, alongside works by Thom Gunn and James Merrill, one of the best ever written about AIDS. These are the opening stanzas:

> So it's back to window shopping
> on Aphrodite Street
> for the apples are stacked and juicy
> but some are death to eat.
>
> For just one generation
> the plateglass turned to air –
> when you look for that generation
> half of it isn't there.

Surely there are more intimate and heartbroken stances toward one's subject matter (Gunn's great poems in 'The Man with Night Sweats' come to mind), and surely the very best poem imaginable would find a way to represent those stances, too. But never has the span between elation and tragedy – between plate glass 'turned to air' and the annihilation of half a generation – been depicted with such awful, chiming smoothness.

'Aphrodite Street' was roundly condemned. (In a letter to the *London Review of Books*, the Australian poet Alan Wearne called it kicking a group 'when they're down; or worse still, a poet attempting to play God, cheering on the kickers.') Indeed, Murray is often condemned, particularly inside Australia, where his anti-liberal views – anathema to a country trying rapidly to shake its old, bad mood – were nearly enshrined in law. In 1998, Murray was commissioned by Prime Minister John Howard to collaborate with him on a new preamble to the Australian constitution. (Howard, the son of a gas-station owner and, like Murray, the descendant of Scottish settlers, seems to have recognised himself in Murray's 'Subhuman Redneck' act.) The preamble (presented in a form much watered down from Murray's original draft) was put up for a vote and rejected when people detected, behind the official redaction, Murray's infamous grumpiness toward immigrants and indigenes. (Murray's positions are by no means simple: fascinated by the possibility that he has Aboriginal ancestry, he has asked about having his blood tested; he has advocated a 'Creole' Australia, free of identity politics.) Murray's homemade politics sometimes comes out leftist but, at its heart, carries the claims of the 'poor whites,' who 'must be suppressed, for modernity, / for youth, for speed, for sexual fun.'

Reckless, cantankerous, emboldened by a world view based on sexual resentment, Murray is (as he is the first to acknowledge) a cartoon hick in an overplayed idiom. Yet the perversities of his own position (both 'redneck' and elite, settler and indigene, 'English' poet and Bunyah farmer) make him seem to many of his countrymen all the more authentically 'Australian.' And Murray's real constitutional work has been to articulate a code true to the 'whipcrack country of white cedar / and ruined tennis courts,' home to 'passionflower and beige-bellied wonga vine.' This go-for-broke bush ethos, part Zen and part *sprezzatura*, is what Murray calls 'sprawl':

> Sprawl is doing your farming by aeroplane, roughly,
> or driving a hitchhiker that extra hundred miles home.
> It is the rococo of being your own still centre.
> It is never lighting cigars with ten-dollar notes:
> that's idiot ostentation and murder of starving people.
> Nor can it be bought with the ash of million-dollar deeds.

*

Murray nearly died in 1996 when some object, perhaps a chicken bone, punctured his gut and released deadly bacteria into his body. He spent twenty days in a coma. 'Conscious and verbal' once again (that phrase borrowed from a press release issued by the hospital, became the title of a 1999 poetry collection), Murray redoubled his efforts (as he puts it) to 'learn human,' banishing 'the black dog' of depression that, in his view, had sponsored much of his imaginative work. Murray's new book, *The Biplane Houses,* like everything he has done since the coma, seems to be the work of a person poured back into sentience the way molten copper is poured into a mould. Like the Mars spacecraft that came close enough to the planet to 'sniff and scan it / for life's irrefutable scent,' Murray's new poetry travels a long distance to get up close to life but spends much of its time airborne, en route.

All of Murray's recent work has been written under the protection of a fictional alter ego, the hero of his verse novel *Fredy Neptune*. (According to Alexander, 'Fred' was Murray's wife's code name for his depressive side; only when he reclaimed his genial spirits did she again call him Les.) *Fredy Neptune* has little competition aside from Anne Carson's *Autobiography of Red* for the claim to being the best verse novel of our time. It is the story of a German-Australian sailor in the First World War who, pressed into service by the German Navy, witnesses the death by burning of a group of Armenian women. Fredy then loses all feeling in his body; like Murray, he gets it back only when he realises that 'you have to pray with a whole heart.'

If *Fredy Neptune* is about what Murray earlier called 'my old theme of lack of communication,' *The Biplane Houses* is about trying to communicate across the chasm of moods, persons and cultures, or, at the very least, about the desire, often thwarted, to do so. This poet of elaborate language and affect-codes opens the new volume, tellingly, by decoding himself:

> The one whose eyes
> do not meet yours
> is alone at heart
> and looks where the dead look
> for an ally in his cause.

As talk of 'allies' and 'the dead' might suggest, Murray's new work encompasses the psychologically charged discourses of world politics. (Elsewhere in the book, Murray writes a poem in the voice of a suicide bomber: 'I implode. And laughter cascades in, / flooding those who suddenly abhor me.') But the first set of eyes we meet, or, in this case, do not meet, when we open the book are the author's. Murray won't look us in the eye, but he will, eyes averted, address us. 'Alone at heart,' this voice nevertheless seems newly interested in showing, for its readers and for itself, a modicum of empathy.

Always a riddle poet, Murray now likes to give the answers to his ingenious riddles; yet those answers inevitably pose their own riddles, like links in a chain. 'Twelve Poems' is such a chain-link riddle poem – among the best such poems to be written, it seems to me, since Stevens's 'Thirteen Ways of Looking at a Blackbird.' Following a poem in part about a horse and carriage, 'Twelve Poems' opens by correcting the reader's last sense impression:

> That wasn't horses: that was
> rain yawning to life in the night
> on metal roofs.

Even the corrected, 'accurate' perception – not horses but rain – carries within it a figural evasion of fact, 'yawning.' And so the riddle chain begins, linking an 'ampersand' ('smugly / phallic ... / in the deckchair of itself'), a bucket of fish (waving 'their helpless fan feet'), a spider (which, like Murray, walks 'in circles ... celebrating / the birthday of logic'). In the last link in the chain, a 'simple man' (who, like Murray in the act of writing this poem, is 'filling in a form') looks up at his mother and asks, heartbreakingly, '*Mum, what sex are we?*'

Murray has long been a master of depicting Murray-like creatures, greedily eager to introduce themselves as less-than-pleased-to-meet-you. The first-person bestiary of his 1992 sequence 'Presence: Translations from the Natural World' forces us to picture Murray now in terms of an ornery cat ('I permit myself to be / neither ignored nor understood'), now in terms of a pig, misty-eyed in recalling his wild days and speaking a pungent idiolect ('Us all fuckers then. And Big, huh? Tusked / the balls-biting dog and gutsed him wet'). The animals in *The Biplane Houses* share some Murray traits, to be sure (an octopus that lives, like a poet, in the 'pencilling of dark soil'), but by and large these animals represent impediments and counterclaims that Murray morally cannot but acknowledge. In 'The Mare Out on the Road,' a horse grows 'in moist astonishment' as a car hurtles toward it:

> Sliding fast, with the brakes shoaling gravel.
> Five metres down, and would the car capsize?

The moment was crammed with just two choices.
One of two accidents would have to happen.

Though the 'poor horse' is a 'beautiful innocent,' the real choice the driver must make is between dying in the ditch and living a life of local infamy ('No court case, just family slurs for life'). Village life – one might as well say 'poetry,' since this poem feels so adroit in reading its own symbols – involves learning one's right of way. The choice made in the moment – the car veers into the ditch, but nobody is hurt – depends on the speaker's determination to abide by codes other than his own.

Murray has raised a son, Alexander, who has autism, a simple fact that seems to me more central to his work than all the 'milk lorries' in Bunyah. Many of his new poems are haunted by the fear of social life, but Murray has learned to diagnose and correct that fear, perhaps for his son's sake. Or for his own. In 'The Tune on Your Mind,' Murray, mishearing the Latin of Psalm 51 (*'asperges me hyssopo,'* 'thou sprinklest me with hyssop'), sings, instead, *'Asperger, mais. Asperg is me.'* Characteristically for a poet so committed to self-portraiture, Murray has diagnosed Alexander's symptoms in himself. 'The coin took years to drop,' he writes:

> Lectures instead of chat. The want
> of people skills. The need for Rules.
> Never towing a line from the Ship of Fools.

The most impressive thing about the new poems is their capacity, writing 'with a whole heart,' to find the pathos in unlikely subjects. Keats once imagined that a billiard ball gets 'a sense of delight' from its own 'roundness, smoothness, volubility & the rapidity of its motion,' and there is something Keatsian about Murray's ability to locate the precise affect in image after image. 'Lateral Dimensions' might have been called 'Afterlives,' since the poem imagines a series of alternatives, most of them bad, for a poet's posthumous fate. Which of these two sorry creatures would you rather be?:

> rodeo bull
> he wins every time

> then back on the truck
> only one car
> of your amber necklace
> holds a once-living passenger.

The destiny of poets is to be, like the rodeo bull, triumphant over and over at the same rote act (Matthew Arnold is *always a winner* when we read 'Dover Beach'!) and, like the insect in amber, a primal speck, once alive, now merely a 'passenger' in the history of culture. The alternatives in Murray are not pleasing – but perhaps you would prefer to be like the 'newspapers soaked in rain / before they are read'?

Because, like all mature poets, Murray knows and represents his own imaginative limitations, his best poems show empathy lagging a little behind the imagination. The thrill of reading Murray is seeing how the heart that feels will catch up with the eye that sees. ('One might have thought of sight,' Stevens writes, 'but who could think / Of what it sees, for all the ill it sees?') 'Photographing Aspiration' is a boy's motorcycle accident in two takes. Take one:

> ... here's the youth swimming in space
> above his whiplash motorcycle:
> quadriplegia shows him its propped face –

and here, a moment later, is the same scene with empathy inserted:

> after, he begged video scenes
> not display his soaking jeans,
> urine that leathers would have hidden.

Stanza one is full of emotional redactions, seeing the spectacle entirely from the outside, even going so far as to attribute to it a ghoulish beauty (and projecting pain onto the 'whiplash motorcycle' and the 'propped face' of always looming 'quadriplegia'). That's how the boy of stanza two might like his accident to have been depicted; the old Les Murray, before he looked at his own 'propped face' face-to-face, might have been an ally in the boy's cause. A photograph shows a moment in time, the boy 'swimming above' his motorcycle; a 'video scene' can display the entire arc of the crash, including, to the boy's dismay, the soiling of his jeans; but only a poem (Murray's previous volume was called *Poems the Size of Photographs*) can show the begging boy's terror at seeing his fear represented. This new Les Murray, a poet equally of emotional obduracy and heartbreak, has learned what begging sounds like.

New Yorker

In Fealty to a Professor

Anne Sedgley

Professor Maxwell was so famous that we had heard of him when we were still at school. He was joint editor with A.A. Phillips of a very good anthology of poetry for use in schools: *In Fealty to Apollo*. When I first saw him at a first-year English lecture at the University of Melbourne he was exactly as I had pictured him: noble forehead, craggy face, deep voiced, with strong arms and a powerful upper body in a droopy tweed sports jacket. He had the head, arms and torso of a very powerful man joined to quite short legs; he was also slightly pigeon-toed, which gave his feet a tentative look, rather belying the majesty of his head and the authority of his voice. He brought books in to the lecture theatre, but never looked at them, lecturing in an intimate, spontaneous way, as if he and his listeners were good friends, joined in admiration of the works and the writers he spoke about. In his lecture on the Scottish Border Poets he would weep while reciting some of the ballads, which naturally became the stuff of awed legend.

Professor Maxwell loved all the masculine arts, boxing perhaps above all. The plaque that his friends and family have put on the site of the huts he built by the Howqua River in central Victoria carries one of his favourite quotations, from George Borrow's *Lavengro* (1851): 'We'll now put on the gloves; and I'll try to make you feel what a sweet thing it is to be alive, brother!' With his long arms and strong shoulders, Professor Maxwell was probably a good boxer himself. He was also said to be a tremendous axeman, who could split shingles with one blow.

At Melbourne University Professor Maxwell had one of the largest rooms in the Old Arts building: on the first floor, with several big diamond-paned windows looking onto the Law–Arts courtyard. His Icelandic classes were held in this room, where we read and translated Old Norse sagas. One thing that gave him particular pleasure in his later years was being made a Knight of an Icelandic Order for his services to Icelandic literature and culture. He showed us his chivalric medallion, and said with pride that there were very few knights of this order in Iceland, let alone in another country.

To illustrate the journeys in the sagas he had a map of Iceland, outlined in blue, hand-painted on the wall above the bookcase in his office. I spent many hours in this room, sipping sherry, smoking a preposterous number of cigarettes, and gazing out of the window at the twilight deepening in the old fig-tree that dominated the courtyard. Professor Maxwell valued strong drink – indeed he was the first tutor to provide us with sherry, in little glasses that were often topped up. I remember with my sherry glass carrying a little brass ashtray, tapping my ash into that, and trying to keep to only two cigarettes per hour, to reduce the smog.

I was normally late for classes, arriving breathless and apologetic, but I don't remember ever being reproved for this by Professor Maxwell. Shortly after I left the university, I asked him for a job reference. When I saw him next, he said, smiling: 'Well, Anne, I have written that reference you asked for, and now you will have to be diligent and punctual, or my name will be mud.' In anyone else, this would have been a reference to my lateness, but with him that was impossible. He was a gentleman in all things, above all, in his treatment of students. In return, we focused hard on the texts and grew to love what he loved.

Professor Maxwell sometimes stayed overnight at the university working, reading, drinking and thinking. The night watchman (no security men in those days) was accustomed to this. One night, so the legend got around, Professor Maxwell was alone in his room when he heard a sound outside in the broad corridor. Grasping his axe, he went outside and hewed at the man, cleaving him from top to bottom. Satisfied, he went back into his room. Next morning, the cleaners found a blackboard on wheels in the corridor, split right down the centre.

Professor Maxwell loved walking and horse-riding. He hated cars. I heard that for years he rode his horse in to the university from his home in Rosanna. Then, when this was no longer possible, he used to walk in, and only in later years consented to travel by train. I was luxuriating in ownership of my first car by then, and sometimes passed him on the streets of Carlton. I would pull up, open the car door and offer him a lift. The car was decrepit and sometimes had to be jiggled under the bonnet, but he would accept gravely, and we would have conversation while I struggled with driving and talking at once.

After I had left the university and was working in libraries, I heard that Professor Maxwell's Friday night Icelandic reading classes were still being held, and that he would be very pleased if I were to return. I went back, nervous about whether I would remember any of it, but it all came back of course. There we were, his colleagues Bob Priestley and John Martin, with three or four others, sipping sherry, smoking and struggling in the twilight with the hard bits. But Professor Maxwell had changed. He had had low blood pressure for years, and his legs had become very weak. He could walk, but only with calipers around both legs – iron rings joined to a vertical bar. I saw him quite often swinging his iron-bound legs slowly, painfully, one after the other, up Grattan Street, heading towards his room in the New Arts building. I caught up with him to talk and walk alongside a couple of times, but sometimes I avoided him, feeling guilty and ashamed. It seemed a dreadful downfall for so dignified a man: this barely managing to scrape one leg along in front of another. But he spoke quite openly about his incapacity.

Professor Maxwell loved the bush. He may have built the first of his famous huts by the Howqua in the 1940s, when he was a lawyer and before he turned to English language studies. When I was in my final undergraduate year in 1965, nothing would have given me more delight than to have been asked to go up there with him (I called him Ian by now), Bob Priestley and others. One dear friend of mine, Andrew Deacon, an outstanding lecturer in the English Department at that time, had been there with him several times and said: 'Ask him yourself. He'd love you to come.' But to me that seemed outside the furthest reaches of civilised behaviour: I felt I could not ask to be invited to something so personal. So Andrew said *he* would take me, together with my friend, Paul.

We went in two separate cars, and after Andrew managed to roll his on a straight road with no obstacles, we all piled into ours, Andrew nursing his dog Rani in the back. We left the car by the Howqua, hoisted our rucksacks on, walked downstream five hundred metres and waded through the river in our boots several times. Professor Maxwell's place was a cluster of little bush huts around a clearing, with a gigantic eucalyptus trunk in the middle. The huts were made of untrimmed tree trunks – 'bush poles' – nailed or lashed together, with beaten earth floors. Flattened kerosene tins nailed to bush-pole rafters with some sheets of corrugated iron served as roofing. The sleeping huts had two beds in each of them: fencing wire strung from a frame of rough bush poles. The intending sleeper, Andrew told us, had to collect masses of bracken and put it on the beds for a mattress. 'Quite comfortable,' he assured us.

The oldest hut was the kitchen hut, reserved for use by Professor Maxwell only, if he was there. The front of the hut was open, and the floor was built up at the front with river stones that formed the hearth of the cooking fire. The roof sloped sharply down at the back to his bush-pole bed, which was wedged in the angle between roof and floor. In later years, a rather splendid chair of bush poles and canvas was built in the north corner beside the fire. A few cooking pots hung from nails on the walls. Though I was never at the Howqua with him, I imagine him at night beside the fire, saying – or singing – his favourite Border Ballad, 'Sir Patrick Spens'.

Over the years he built more sleeping huts for other friends who stayed with him on the Howqua. The last one, the most northerly, he built for Professor Gabriel Turville-Petre, Professor of Old Icelandic studies at Oxford University. Professor Turville-Petre was invited to Melbourne University to read Old Norse with the fourth-year honours class for two terms in 1965. These two men were both knights of old-world courtesy, and both lived their passion for Old Icelandic. But in every other way they were as different as could be. Professor Turville-Petre was little, stooped, bald, with jug ears and a slow, beautiful smile. You had the feeling that asking him a question yanked him back from some other world – he would answer very precisely and literally, with respect for the person who asked the question even when it was foolish. He had worked at Oxford with J.R.R. Tolkien, and, having recently read *The Lord of the Rings* with great enthusiasm, I asked Professor Turville-Petre what he thought of it. It was all right, he said gently, but perhaps a misuse of his talents: 'In the time it took him to write *Lord of the Rings*, he could have brought out a truly definitive edition of *Beowulf*.' Turville-Petre's own special field was the Edda poetry of the Scandinavians of the ninth and tenth centuries. We translated it with him, line by line, conscious that we were working with the world expert in Edda poetry, and trying to rise to the occasion to make Professor Maxwell proud.

The last time I stayed at Professor Maxwell's was thirteen or fourteen years ago, when I went up for a weekend with my son Tom and a friend of his – both aged about fourteen – and a friend of mine, Sally. When we first arrived at the huts, they were already occupied. A great canvas marquee had been erected in the clearing in front of the kitchen hut, but there was no-one in sight. What a nerve! We had been going to stay there, and we *knew* Professor Maxwell. There was nothing I could do, however, so we continued on down-river, over the crag that juts out above the swimming hole, and pitched our tents and made our campfire a few hundred metres downstream.

I woke early next morning; the others were still asleep when I rolled out, put my clothes on and went back to the professor's encampment to see about these other people. A woman was sitting in the canvas chair in the kitchen hut, beside a smoking campfire, reading. She was tall and queenly, with a strong profile and impressive grey hair. It was very quiet. I went up and said, 'Lovely morning,' and conversation began. She offered me a cup of tea, my first for the morning. When I had drunk it gratefully, I asked casually (but preparing to pounce): 'Do you know anything about the history of this place?'

'Yes. My father built it,'

All my ideas flew round in circles. I said, 'You must be Camilla.'

'No, I'm Delia, the other one,' she said laughing.

I had been at the same school as Camilla. She was a couple of years older, and notorious as an eccentric who, against school rules, always wore a gabardine coat, whether inside, outside, hot, cold, raining or not. Her brother Danny came to our school once with his guitar, and for some reason played and sang lots of folk songs for us in a warm, gentle melodic voice. But I knew nothing of Delia. I told her how I loved Professor Maxwell – how we all did. I told her about the Norse reading classes, and how wonderful his lectures had been in the Epic and Romance course for Honours English II students – a course that had all his hallmarks, starting with W.S. Ker's study *Allegory and Romance* and our testing its theories against *Beowulf*, the Norse sagas, *Song of Roland*, Chrétien de Troyes, *Sir Gawain and the Green Knight*, *Piers Plowman* and so on. Professor Maxwell's idea was to introduce students to the best that's been thought and said, from Homer onwards as far as term time would allow: to Milton's *Paradise Lost*, at least. It was almost certainly his idea to introduce the honours students to 'Prose Dating'. This was a close study of the vocabulary, sentence structure, speech rhythms and so on of English in different periods, so that by the end of the course we could date any passage of prose correctly to within ten years. The important part of the exam was not the date we put forward but the reasons we gave to account for our decision.

Delia and I talked on beside the early-morning fire. She was obviously very pleased to meet someone who knew her father well and admired him. Suddenly she jumped up: 'Let's have a swim.' She went to the pool, unwound her dress or sari or whatever it was, and stepped in. I did the same, without quite the same insouciance, and we were soon sliding around the pool with long, slow strokes. This swim was a magical experience. We were talking about the prudery of the times when we were young. Delia began to sing. Pretty soon we were floating naked in the dark, still pool under the crag, singing song after song of the '50s as we tried to recall the more erotic ones. The most outstanding was Elvis Presley's with the deep reverberating line: 'I hunger for your touch.'

I responded to Delia's warmth and magnetism very strongly, although at another level I worked hard at resisting her overwhelming personality. I didn't get to say much, when I was with her! She could see that I loved her father – that was enough for her. She was like him, too. Like him in being striking, energetic in her talk and commanding loyalty and affection – but not, I think, loving back. Is this the description of the perfect teacher: someone you strive to please, who is always slightly aloof? Someone of whom it is natural to say, 'I admired and loved him, but I don't think he knew me very well'?

I see now that Delia and I, as we swam in that deep, dark river, were reaching for something that her father scarcely acknowledged: female eroticism. Active sexuality is almost invisible in much medieval literature, including the sagas. There are strong women in Icelandic literature, but they are not strongly feminine. It is a world of masculine virtues, where nobility lies in leading men, fighting without heed for their safety, hewing off a leg here or a head there within accepted codes of kinship, and knowing the ancient literature that embodies these virtues. I loved that world in Iceland through Professor Maxwell. It is there, too, in the all-male world of the bushman, the cattleman, the axeman. I was drawn to it in the Australian bush through Professor Maxwell and others, but what place ultimately was there in it for me or Delia? Now Professor Maxwell and Delia are both dead, and will never answer such questions.

No doubt Professor Maxwell knew how many students he brought to a love of Icelandic literature and culture. But I doubt if he knew what a powerful influence he was on me and many others, in interconnecting English, Scottish and Icelandic literature with the strength and beauty of the Australian bush.

Meanjin

The Heart of Desire

John Armstrong

For most people – I suppose – sexuality is something that lives, most of the time, underground. Swift famously remarked that if our inner mental workings were exposed we would appear mad. Goethe was devoted to this theme: the few who are clever, and stupid, enough to reveal their true feelings have been burned and crucified. 'There is not a crime of which I have heard that I could not have committed myself.' A few may be pure of heart; for them sex is light, benign. They are 'naive' – without fantasy. But for the majority sexual desire is formed by and contained within the private self.

Which may explain why convincing writing about sexuality is rare. We don't quite trust the writer until we sense the secret character of the mind, the unacceptable parts of the mind, at work. A thrilling passage in Richard Wollheim's memoir, *Germs* (2004), meets just this condition. Wollheim suddenly admits that he would like to break off writing and drive to a seedy part of town, wait for a thug to approach his car, and speed off. In general he is a prudent, cautious man; it is clear that such a confession is disturbing to himself; it is not there to shock – its purpose is security, for the reader. The impulse is sexualised only for Wollheim – to the outsider it is pointless. What we appreciate is the honesty of the remark: the familiar feeling of unhappiness, the sense that sexuality is – profoundly – a source of unhappiness. These admissions came only at the end of Wollheim's life

– only after he had had his career and gained his lion's share of academic honour and public money. This is not a reproach.

It is the privacy of sex – the privacy of its origins, I mean – that makes other, public elements of self-revelation irrelevant. And, in consequence, the dutiful avowal of public categories is merely irritating. C.D.C. Reeve's interesting recent take on the philosophy of sex, *Love's Confusions* (2005), opens with the weird admission that the writer is 'white, agnostic, deracinated, liberal, financially secure' – I don't presume to guess what percentage of philosophy professors published by Harvard University Press in recent years belong to this category. The point, however, is just how little that tells us about his experiences of sex. One longs for him to say: that's just the smug exterior; inside I'm a ravenous bitch. Compare with this:

> Cruelty is one of the chief ingredients of love, and divided about equally between the sexes: cruelty of lust, ingratitude, callousness, maltreatment, domination. The same is true of the passive qualities: patience under suffering, even pleasure in ill-usage.

This remarkable summation asserts something fearful: our most cherished, redemptive ideal – love – has allegiances and alliances with malign aspects, malignant parts, of the soul.

These sentences occur in one of the representative documents of Western cultural ambition: Goethe's early morning thoughts, imagined by Thomas Mann, which open the long penultimate chapter of *Lotte in Weimar*. It is the attempt of educated thoughtfulness to grasp, and somehow cope with, an unbearable tension in the human condition: 'cruelty is one of the chief ingredients of love.'

This idea is further explored in Mann's magnificent novella *Death in Venice*. The central character, von Aschenbach, is on holiday at the Lido. He has lived a life of exemplary devotion to noble values – he has worked extremely hard and achieved great success as a literary artist of the highest standing. But now, well into middle age, he is overwhelmed by the experience of love, and consciously he meditates on the most refined idea of erotic desire. He thinks of the Platonic ideal of the desire for beauty leading the lover towards a vision of the most perfect and comprehensive truth. But in his sleep von Aschenbach is assailed by the other side of love: lust. He dreams of the orgiastic, sadistic rites of Bacchus, in which every kind of sensual excess is desperately pursued, in which his personality seems to fall apart in a violent, ecstatic transgression of civilised values.

It is hardly surprising that there has been, at the core of Western civilisation, a powerful ascetic impulse. The longing to escape from one's own capacity for cruelty, to declare independence from one's Dionysian propensities: these are bids for freedom and decency. And this impulse shaped the ideals of Christianity.

By contrast, the classical notion of 'eros' has immense allure. And the early history of the idea helps to explain the appeal. In Greek, eros is at first the term for a primeval force: 'The force that through the green fuse drives the flower', as Dylan Thomas puts it, holding the hint of a broader, rising organic life: ire, orgasm, the budding leaf, the Leopard's returning appetite. Sexuality belongs here, in this glamorous category of animation; sexual desire is neither central nor strange.

Later, Eros is personified as the child of Aphrodite. This is a fateful lineage. Aphrodite is the goddess of love – and of beauty; it is to Aphrodite that Paris gives the apple. The personification, here, is a guide to conceptual liaisons. Eros – appetite – begins to have a purpose: beauty is the target and love is the name for desire when it is on target.

Our modern sense of eros as primarily linked to sexual desire – as in erotic literature or erotic art – is contrary to the original Greek meaning. What's so appealing – at least at first sight – is the way in which sexuality is regarded as continuous with, as part of, a larger 'erotic' project that aims at beauty and is experienced as love.

Plato's *Phaedrus* is a very serious attempt to discriminate between sexual desire that is genuinely erotic in this noble and ambitious sense – that is, sexual desire that really is the physical aspect of the love of beauty (the longing for what is good for beauty, the longing to enhance and increase beauty) – and sexual desire that is base, that has no higher ambition. The latter desire is not the dark truth about sex; it is rather how eros manifests itself in base people. What we call erotics – the 'science' of sexual arousal – turns out to be the residue, what's left over when things go wrong, rather than the heart of desire.

*

When I was seventeen I spent the early summer in the south of France with my father. Driving back to Glasgow we stopped for a couple of days in Paris. My father was keen to visit the Delacroix museum and suggested I come along. In principle I rather wanted to; but I'd been nurturing another plan. I told him – and it wasn't entirely untrue – that I preferred Claude and Poussin to Delacroix. I would go to the Louvre and meet up with him for lunch. As soon as I was on my own I headed for the red light district and squandered my holiday money in a hot little attic room, pursuing an erotic scenario that had long gripped my imagination.

Afterwards, descending the exceedingly shabby staircase, I felt a terrifying inundation of self-disgust. I was wicked, stupid, naive, vile, corrupt, irresponsible, thick, wasteful, out of control, nasty, brutish. As I wandered miserably towards the square where I was to meet my father I passed a bookshop. The peaceful, old volumes that I would love to have owned were now reproaches: my holiday money had all been squandered. I could have had one of these books; it would have been a joy forever, a memento of a lovely morning in Paris. I would have taken possession of its wisdom; in some imagined future I would take it down carefully from the shelf, turn its pages with a happy sense of the continuity of life.

But I'd destroyed all that. I'd had half an hour of what now seemed like pointless squalor. The evident boredom of the woman I had been with was ghastly to recall; her French had been even more limited than mine – a miserable token of our lack of intimacy. My pathetic attempts to make her grasp some particular action I wanted her to perform, some specific detail of my desires I wanted her to satisfy, were now my primary memories. This was what I'd locked inside myself.

A little further on I passed the front of a small church. A choir was rehearsing: their voices could just be heard in the street. I looked in; it was a scene of remarkable serenity and patient effort; the conductor was taking them through a limpid, simple – and astonishingly beautiful – piece by Fauré. The mild and tender line of the music felt like an invitation: you must be like me, then you will be happy. It seemed completely real and agonisingly far away. The music expressed what I wanted now; only it was too late; I had cut myself off. Standing in the porch of the church, listening as the conductor rapped his baton cleanly on the back of a chair and they sang again, I started to cry.

At lunch my father told me all about Delacroix; I lied a little about the Louvre, enough to signal that it would be embarrassing to ask me how I had actually spent the morning. As I ate my omelette and sipped my glass of beer I wondered idly if there was a new story I could spin to get my father to give me some cash and leave me free for the afternoon and whether I would be able to find again the door that led up to the tiny, sordid chamber.

This episode was, for me, unusual only in its dramatic neatness: the deception, the spending of money, the scene at the church door. Thematically it was all too familiar. It all seemed like an endless struggle between sex and civilisation. My troubles, I felt, originated in the fact that I was not civilised enough. If only I loved, or understood, Fauré or Delacroix or the pictures in the Louvre more and better, then I would no longer experience the urges that took me away from them.

The guiding image was to be found in an opera by the eighteenth-century German composer Gluck. In his *Orpheo* the hero has to rescue his wife, Eurydice, from Hades. But to reach her he has to get past Cerberus – the triple-headed dog–monster that guards the entrance to the underworld. Orpheus is, however, the first great musician and as he plays a noble, delicate theme on his lyre, the insistent growling of the beast is lulled; Cerberus is pacified, Orpheus can pass on and the redemptive work of love can proceed.

Cerberus was the sexual part of me and Orpheus was the civilised part. If the latter could get strong enough then it would quieten the beast. If only I could be civilised enough I could become a good and wholesome person – and maybe find a girlfriend. Or perhaps not. A few weeks later we were at the beach; lying on the sand in my bathing trunks I was (I thought) freakishly thin, a static exhibit of adolescent gawkiness. Everywhere there were graceful, curvy girls, doing things with suntan lotion. My mother kindly suggested that I should 'get to know some nice ones'.

*

A first reaction to von Aschenbach might be to think that his ideal vision, his cultivated idealism, is now revealed as a sham. It was just a screen for – a deceptive denial of – his real and very dirty nature. But something much more interesting is going on. For, within the narrative there is no shying away from this part of von Aschenbach's personality. Within this immensely civilised short story the inflamed, destructive imagination is allowed its place; it does not have to be shut up in a cage. At the same time it is seen as no more real than anything else about him.

We should be more pessimistic about sex: sexual unhappiness seems unavoidable in civilised societies; for the sexual drives – at least of many men – are only loosely tethered to the other concerns of life. Montaigne put it best: sexual desire holds us intently; while it lasts it grips fervently; but it 'holds us only by one corner'; pull that corner and the whole fabric of our nature has to follow.

The binding of sexuality and imagination is at the core of the problem. 'I call someone rich', says Ralph Touchett in Henry James's *Portrait of a Lady*, 'when they can satisfy the demands of their imagination.' So, the greater the range of demands in the realm of imagination, the more likely one is to feel – and indeed to be – poor. Sexual poverty might be said to be the natural result of sophistication.

Meanjin

The Ups, the Downs:
My Life as a Biographer

Hazel Rowley

My brother, an intensive care specialist, has been known to end phone conversations by saying: 'Gotta go, got lives to save.' He really does. I've never seen him at work, but I imagine he is mostly re-arranging tubes on whimpering bodies; I know that he once clambered into a helicopter to fetch a shark-savaged fellow with shredded limbs. The sight of blood makes me queasy, and I'm terrified of hospitals. But I once sat my brother down and tried to explain (between urgent calls on his mobile phone) that biographers also have someone's life in their hands. 'If you read a dull biography, you come away thinking that person's life was dull,' I told him, 'whereas in reality, it's almost never the *life* that's the problem; it's the *narration*.' My brother coughed. 'No wonder people are wary of biographers,' he said. 'It's bad enough to die; we don't want some dullard turning our lives into insipid gruel.'

My brother, sister and I have made such different choices in life: what is it, I wonder, that led me to biography? Looking back, I am struck by how fortunate I have been, both in terms of historical timing and my personal circumstances. I have also made some quite dramatic choices. They are complex things, choices. Existentialists would say they come from deep within us, reflecting some sort of 'original choice' we made in our childhood. Certain moments stand out when people said something to me that caused a click in my mind, but why these moments and not others? You have to *want* to hear those words; they have to strike a chord in you. Ultimately, other people influence you only in ways you choose to be influenced.

Since my early twenties, I have been deeply influenced by existentialism, a philosophy which is fundamentally a sophisticated reflection on the extent to which the individual is free or not free. The question that most interested the existentialists was: in what ways do we make ourselves out of what we have been made? In her memoirs, Simone de Beauvoir muses: 'How is a life formed? How much of it is made up by circumstances ... how much by chance, and how much by the subject's own options and his personal initiatives?'

In their own biographical and autobiographical writings, Sartre and Beauvoir examined their subject's *situation* (the historical period, social class, family dynamics, the person's physical constitution, and so on), while scrutinising, as if under a microscope, any actions that were signs of rebellion or compliance. They saw these as defining moments, which reflected a deep-seated choice of being. In other words, these were moments of existential choice.

I had no say in this whatsoever, but I often think how lucky I was to have been born in the early 1950s. I am grateful to have been brought up before the internet, mobile phones, BlackBerries and iPods made kids into jittery, easily bored, semi-autistic creatures who, by being so fanatically plugged into the virtual world, have no time left for the world of the imagination. When I was growing up in the 1950s and 1960s, our family did not have television, as a matter of principle, though we usually rented a set during the summer holidays. I was an avid reader, and it seemed to me there was nothing more noble and exciting than being a writer, having the power to transport people into another world.

From the age of nine or so, I wanted to be a writer. One summer in Adelaide, I wrote a novel with a girlfriend. We sat at a folding table beside her family's swimming pool. One wrote while the other read or swam; then the roles were reversed and the other one took up the story. Her father handed the manuscript to Nancy Cato, the South Australian writer, who was encouraging and told us to persevere. Every summer during high school, I wrote short stories in notebooks, then typed them up on my Remington manual and sent them to magazines. They were all rejected, but even the rejection slips made me feel proud. Real writers get rejection slips.

During my student years, I wrote less for the sheer pleasure of writing. I had less time, and more distractions – such as falling in love. This was the late 1960s and 1970s, when societies all over the Western world were undergoing fundamental changes. I had been politically active from the moment I started university (the anti-apartheid campaign, anti-Vietnam War demonstrations, women's liberation), and we students were convinced we were going to change the world *forever*. It was a heady period in which to come of age, especially for women. I remember feeling sorry for Simone de Beauvoir, who had done so much to inspire the women's movement and would not be alive to see what I took for granted my generation would see: a complete transformation of society, with all of us working half-time (due to technological advances), and true equality between the sexes.

I took a combined honours degree in French and German. I loved languages, and the worlds they opened up. A German fellowship allowed me to spend two years at the University of Freiburg, attending lectures, and making a start on my PhD. Then I went just across the border to Strasbourg, supported by an Australian Commonwealth Scholarship. In both Germany and France, I was active in the women's movement. In Paris, I interviewed the woman who by this time exerted more influence on my life than anyone else: Simone de Beauvoir. Altogether I spent three years away from Australia, and this was before email, before long-distance phone calls were cheap. There was no hand-holding from home. I was completely immersed in two very different cultures. A marvellous experience for a future writer.

I wrote my PhD dissertation on Simone de Beauvoir and Existentialist Biography. One of the many things I liked about Sartre and Beauvoir was their lifelong interest in biography. Another was their commitment to being public intellectuals, who considered it their responsibility to speak out about oppression, injustice and the forces that militated against individual freedom. They were also interested in our own complicity in our non-freedom, a state of mind they called 'bad faith'. (In *The Second Sex* (1949), Beauvoir shows how tempting it is for women to slip into certain roles, rather than taking the harder road, which is to assume the burden of their freedom.) After World War II – and the deaths of close friends at the front, in the Holocaust and the Resistance – Sartre and Beauvoir were highly conscious of the limitations of individual freedom. Nevertheless, they argued that individuals have a degree of choice, whatever our circumstances. This, to me, is the burning question at the core of biography. What makes it possible for a handsome, athletic man, who is struck by polio at the age of thirty-nine and never again able to take a single step on his own (and this at a time when the words 'infantile paralysis' and 'cripple' carried a severe social stigma) to become president of the United States? How does a shy, awkward woman with buck teeth and a wavering falsetto voice become one of the most effective speakers of her time, and the most outspoken, independent, courageous, admired, controversial and savagely mocked First Lady the US has ever known? (As you may have guessed, I am currently writing a book about the Roosevelt marriage.)

A humanities PhD is, of course, great training in research and mounting a sustained argument, but whereas in the United States, a humanities PhD involves three years of coursework, followed by a dissertation, supervised by a committee of three, a humanities PhD in the British-Australian system generally involves no coursework whatsoever. At least in my time, you would sit at home or in a library or postgraduate room for four or five years incubating a thick dissertation, with occasional meetings with your supervisor. It tested your powers to withstand isolation. I suppose that is quite useful for a future writer. You came out of the experience as chastened as a monk, quivering with self-doubts. I suppose that, too, is useful for a future writer. But one thing was not at all useful for a future writer, and it still isn't, and that is the language of the academy. English departments should impart the pleasure and power of playing one of the world's richest languages like a musical instrument, but sadly enough, they are among the worst strongholds of academic jargon. By the early 1980s, when I was finishing my PhD, postmodernism was in vogue, and postgraduate theses clanked with words like 'discourse', 'marginality', 'signifier', 'masculinist', and 'to problematise'. For the last thirty years, the reigning ethos in humanities subjects has been that in order to appear intelligent your sentences must be unintelligible. Fortunately for me, I was extremely resistant to this pressure. I regarded it as a nasty virus.

My PhD was in French Studies, but I wrote it in English, and it was about history and philosophy as much as about literature. I did not want to teach in a French Department, I was not qualified to teach in an English Department, I was thirty-one, and it was not at all clear what I was going to do with my life. I did various part-time jobs, some writing, and quite a bit of worrying. And then a piece of extraordinary luck came my way. Despite the fact that we had, for years, been talking about 'interdisciplinarity', universities were still rigidly divided into 'departments'. The very word, when you think about it, sounds like something out of Kafka. What good fortune I had, in 1984, to crack a job in 'Literary Studies' at Deakin University, at that time probably the most interdisciplinary university in the country. The Literary Studies area was keen to employ someone who did not have a standard English Department background, and I was thrilled to have the freedom to range across disciplines pretty much as I pleased.

Deakin was regarded as the equivalent of Britain's Open University, a progressive sort of place that offered education to working people who would not otherwise have the opportunity to study. In order to write course material for our long-distance students, we formed teams and planned the course content together. These meetings sometimes involved hefty arguments, but this was part of the stimulation. Even with our on-campus teaching, we 'team-taught', and I personally learned a great deal from my colleagues.

It was challenging to have two sets of students: the younger on-campus students, who mostly came from the Geelong area, and the highly motivated mature-age students, who came from all over Victoria and sometimes from interstate, whom we met at occasional weekend schools. Deakin academics were not segregated into departments; the 'Literary Studies' area was part of the School of Humanities, and our offices were scattered throughout the building. I shared my corridor with philosophers, sociologists and political scientists. The humanities staff was expected to attend each other's seminars. For me, this set-up could not have been more ideal. And dare I remind you, we had six months' study leave every three years on full pay, and provided we were presenting a paper, the university funded an international conference every year. Luckily, I was aware at the time how good these conditions were. It would have been sad to realise it only afterwards. Because we were going to look back on this as the tail-end of a golden period in the academy.

Academics are expected to write books, and there was nothing I wanted to do more. I had no trouble deciding to write a biography; that had been the thrust of my PhD thesis. Biography was 'interdisciplinary', and I would be writing for the general reader rather than the academy. But deciding on the subject proved a torturous process. I wanted to write about a woman writer – no doubt because I was looking for some sort of model. Since coming to Deakin, I'd been reading my way through Australian literature – for the first time in my life, I might add (my generation hardly touched upon Australian literature at high school) – and I wanted an excuse to dive in deeper. I was fascinated by Henry Handel Richardson, Katharine Susannah Prichard, Dymphna Cusack and Christina Stead. For various reasons, I whittled the choice down to Cusack and Stead. I lacked confidence, and it seemed far too daunting to take on Stead, a towering international figure. 'She's too big,' I told my boyfriend. 'Why start small?' he said.

I have found in life that the anticipation is nearly always worse than the challenge itself. Once I got started, I was in my element. I made an appointment with Brenda Niall, a biographer I knew and admired, and she gave me some excellent tips. She showed me how she organised her files, one manila folder for every year of her subject's life, and how she cross-referenced details on index cards. 'When you interview people,' she told me, 'don't just ask them about Christina Stead; ask them about themselves. After all, they are characters in your book.' We discussed taping versus note-taking, and agreed that it depended on the situation, but it was safest to take notes anyway. The most important thing was to sit down somewhere, straight after an interview, and go through your notes while the conversation was still fresh in your mind.

I set up a reading group in Australian literature, and four of us met each month for several years – a precious memory for us all. I gave my chapters to a friend who saw it as her mission to make me throw away what she called my 'academic boots', and who would write 'boring!' and 'cut!' in the margin whenever she felt the narrative pace was lagging. My working conditions were perfect: a six-month study leave spent in London and New York where I conducted dozens of interviews, and long summer breaks with no teaching. In the final year of writing, I took unpaid leave. The book came out in 1993, published by Heinemann, and won the Banjo Prize for Non-fiction.

In 1994 I had another six-month study leave. Of all places to go to, I freely went, of my own volition, to Austin, Texas. I owe this experience to my friend, Frank Campbell. We were sitting in the Deakin staff club, and I told him that much as I liked both places, I was tired of feeling lonely in New York and London. 'Go to Austin,' he said. 'Why on earth would I go there?' I said. 'The university has a fantastic library,' he said. 'Oil money. I have friends there, an interracial couple, who have a kind of open-house on Sunday afternoons. Through them you'll meet everyone interesting in town.'

Until I went to Texas I had to some extent swallowed the myth that America is a gigantic melting pot. It looks that way on the surface, especially on the streets and in the subways of New York. In Texas, I discovered American apartheid. I saw that poverty and police abuse had a great deal to do with skin colour. I saw that even in educated circles – perhaps *especially* in educated circles – black people and white people rarely had dinner at each other's houses. A notable exception was the verandah of the sprawling southern gothic house where I spent my Sunday afternoons, and where a handsome young African-American told me that Richard Wright had changed his life. Little did I realise, that steamy October afternoon, that he would change mine too.

While I was in Texas my Stead book was published in the United States, by Henry Holt, and received glowing reviews. Over lunch in New York, on my way back to Australia, my publisher asked me what I wanted to write next. I said I would like to write about Richard Wright. She put her head in her hands and looked at me through her fingers. She asked me why. I told her that I thought race the most fraught and complex subject in America, and I wanted to try to understand it, from the inside-out. Richard Wright was such a viscerally powerful writer that he made me feel what it was like to be a black boy growing up poor in segregated Mississippi in the 1910s and 1920s, with grandparents who had all been slaves, and an uncle lynched for running a business that was too successful. Wright had felt in exile in his own country, first in the Deep South, and then in the North. In 1946, he and his wife left the United States in disgust. As they sailed out of New York Harbor, Wright wrote in his journal, 'I felt relieved when my ship sailed past the Statue of Liberty.' They moved to Paris, and at first Wright could scarcely believe his new freedom. But it was the beginning of the Cold War, and as a black American writer who spoke out about American race relations, Wright could not escape the tentacles of the State Department. Paris was bristling with spies and informers, and Wright knew he was being closely watched. We will probably never know for certain whether his premature death in 1960, at the age of fifty-two, was natural or helped along by the CIA.

By this time, my publisher had taken her head out of her hands. 'I like your outsider perspective,' she said. 'It's fresh. And I like your passion. If you write a good proposal, we'll publish you.'

Back in Melbourne, I was intensely aware of my hubris. Would I ever be able to understand, let alone convey, the experience of a black man in America? I was not American, I was not black, I was not a man. I struggled with the question of legitimacy, the feeling that I didn't belong at the other side of that high invisible fence that separates black and white America. Henry Holt was courageous enough to offer me a substantial advance, but before I had signed anything, I backed out, scared. One day, the phone rang. It was Jock McCulloch, a friend of mine, then a colleague at Deakin, who had written a great deal about race. He said: 'I'm going to say something and then hang up. Listen, Hazel. A publisher has offered you a good advance. You want to be a writer. You want to broaden your horizons. You want to know more about race. You've got a fascinating subject. Do you want to spend the rest of your days knowing you did not have the courage? That's all I want to say. Think about it.' A click, and the line went quiet.

In the next few weeks, the figure of Richard Wright loomed before me. His whole life was about courage, daring and determination. He *always* grappled with the sense that he was an interloper in territory meant only for whites. He hadn't given in, had he? Needless to say, the people at Henry Holt were not impressed by my vacillations, and I had to write a very convincing proposal to persuade them to take me back on board.

At first I thought I would take unpaid leave to research the book in the United States. But by now it was the mid-1990s, and the Australian academic world had changed. Almost overnight, universities became businesses. We were seeing the rise of the bureaucrat and the demise of the intellectual. The government decreed that universities had to prove their worth in order to gain funding, but the criteria for measuring intellectual endeavour were so ludicrous that I came to the conclusion I could not be the kind of writer I wanted to be under these conditions. At the age of forty-five, I 'took a package'. Tied in with this decision was another, to leave Australia. I was eight when my family came to Adelaide from England; I had studied French and German; my soul has always belonged to Europe. North America was a new episode, and I would see whether I wanted to stay there or not, but at least it was closer to Europe. I sold my St Kilda flat; I sold my car. I had written an article for the *Australian* explaining why I felt obliged to leave the university system, and it came out on the very day I was leaving to spend Christmas with my family before departing for the US. That morning, before my phone was cut off at midday, I received fifty-eight phone calls from academics around the country thanking me for saying what I'd said.

I was stepping into the unknown, and taking a huge risk – financial, professional and personal. But sometimes in life you know what you *don't* want more clearly than what you want. It's funny, too, how your head rattles with clichés when you make an existential choice. 'Life is short,' I told myself. 'It's now or never. Take the plunge.' I even remembered something a Marxist boyfriend used to say, twenty years earlier in Germany: *'Wer, wenn nicht wir? Wann, wenn nicht jetzt?'* (Who, if not us? When, if not now?)

I went to the US on a three-year visa and had no idea what I would do when that expired. To my astonishment, I obtained a green card with remarkable ease, in a category the name of which I relish: 'Alien of exceptional ability'. But meanwhile, I *was* an alien, and I had a book to write on the most fraught and emotional subject in America: race. It wasn't just that I knew next to nothing about the subject matter; I did not know much about my readers, either. The least of my problems was to change over to American spelling. I had to find out fast what American readers knew about their history, about race issues, and how they talked about these things.

I am exceedingly grateful that the Du Bois Institute in African-American Studies at Harvard made me a visiting fellow, a privilege they extended year after year. Professor Henry Louis Gates welcomed scholars from Africa, Europe and elsewhere; he did not want African-American Studies to be a ghetto. We came together as a group every Wednesday for a two-hour lunchtime seminar. In that Harvard common room, among the Persian rugs, deer antlers and portraits of white men, we heard speakers from all over the world, and engaged in animated discussion about race issues.

Richard Wright took me to the black ghettoes of Mississippi, the South Side of Chicago, to Harlem. There were days when the only white person I would see was myself, in the mirror. As it turned out, it was a real advantage to be an outsider. My accent gave me licence to ask questions I could not have asked if I had been a white American. At first, my black interviewees would look at me with bemusement, but when they saw that I had done my research thoroughly and was open-minded, they talked to me more frankly than I had dared to hope. When I finished the manuscript, I gave it to American friends to vet – black friends and white friends. Nevertheless, I was scared of the reviews. Would they call me a naive white woman from Australia?

The publisher's blurb on the back of the book made me sound like an American. I also noticed that they had left off the author's photograph. When I asked about it, they pretended it was a question of space. In fact, the marketing people did not want to reveal my colour.

The book came out in August 2001, and had cover reviews in the *New York Times*, the *Washington Post*, and the *Chicago Tribune*. I was proud that the highest praise came from well-known black male intellectuals. The *Washington Post* reviewer, an African-American writer who lives in Paris, told me afterwards that he could tell from certain sentences that I was not American, but he had not been able to work out whether I was black or white, and the enigma had intrigued him throughout the book. (In the United States, the name 'Hazel' is possibly more commonly a black name than a white name.)

Two weeks after publication, a disaster occurred that took all discussion of books off the airwaves, devastated the New York theatre season, and made numerous businesses go bankrupt. September 11 reminded me what it was like for Christina Stead to publish *The Man Who Loved Children* in 1940.

I have sometimes compared writing biography to being in love. This sounds melodramatic, and nor is it quite accurate, since it is essential for a biographer to keep her lucidity and to remain in control of her subject matter, and that is not quite akin to my experience of being in love. But there are striking parallels. My books are voyages, risky voyages, involving a great deal of passion on my part. I choose subjects that will open up new worlds for me. It has always been a harrowing decision for me to commit myself to a subject; I know I will be living with that person day and night for two to four years. Much energy and empathy goes into putting yourself in someone else's shoes; you inevitably become obsessed. And you have to follow that person wherever he or she takes you. I write about people I deeply admire, but when you study them closely, they are always flawed, and you end up grappling with these flaws as if they were your partner's. Rather than judging them, my energy goes into understanding them, which is something I am prepared to do only with people I love. Finally, I finish the book. Do I feel relieved? No, I feel lost. It's the end of an affair.

To write about Sartre and Beauvoir, I moved to Paris, rented a fifth-floor walk-up looking out onto slate rooftops and terracotta chimney pots, filled it with my books and went out to talk to those who remained from Beauvoir and Sartre's intimate circle. I found this a much easier book to write than the previous two. This time, I was writing a book where I already knew a lot about the subject matter. By now I was far more confident as a storyteller. I had fun with *Tête-à-Tête: The Lives and Loves of Simone de Beauvoir and Jean-Paul Sartre,* from beginning to end.

Once again, it was an advantage to be an outsider. The Parisian intellectual world, I would discover, consists of cliques, which in their loyalties and hatreds are not unlike the gangs in *West Side Story.* I came with credentials, which was important, but the French could not quite place me. As a foreigner, I felt less bound by what I could and could not say about this iconic French couple. It was just as well that I was a more experienced biographer, because this time I was negotiating a path between two camps, the Beauvoir camp and the Sartre camp, which on the whole detest each other. I had to be constantly aware of the viewpoint of the person I was speaking to, and judiciously sift everything he or she told me. When I was younger, I would have been terribly intimidated by these French intellectuals. I had been duly warned that Claude Lanzmann, the film-maker and former boyfriend of Beauvoir, would probably not consent to see me and that if he did he would be abominably rude. Well, he put me through every possible hoop before agreeing to, but he saw me several times. On the first occasion, he had me come to his vacation home on the west coast of France. He set up his tape recorder – in case he needed to sue me, he said. We would talk for two hours at most, he said, and then we would go out in his boat. Ten minutes in, I asked him something and he exploded: *'Mais c'est une question idiote!'* I said: 'Maybe it is, but I'd like you to answer it anyway.' He looked at me with fury. I gazed at the sky. Two minutes passed. Finally he spoke. It was his most interesting reply.

What were the main difficulties I had writing *Tête-à-Tête*? Nearly all the books by Beauvoir and Sartre are fat door-stoppers. So are the biographies about them. I was determined to keep my story concise and rapid-moving. I wanted to write a medium-sized book that readers could hold comfortably in bed. But how to do that? I was dealing with not one central character but two, and then there was what they called *'la petite famille'* – the friends and lovers. I was drowning in material. The answer, I realised, was selectivity. Sublime detail, but no superfluous detail. I wanted the book to leave readers hungry for more.

My other worry was more of a moral one. I was writing a book about people I admired, and I was acutely conscious of the danger of trivialising them. I wanted to tell the truth about this relationship, and I didn't want to whitewash their behavior in any way, but the fact is that Sartre and Beauvoir's love lives do not always show them in their best light. I took pains to sketch in the broader picture – their philosophy, their incredible capacity for hard work, their courage as public intellectuals. (Both were, at times, the target of extraordinary hostility.)

Sartre and Beauvoir have always aroused passion – admiration and hatred – and the reaction to my book shows that they still do. Some reviewers praised me for not being at all judgmental and then proceeded to dance a furious little jig themselves, denouncing Sartre and Beauvoir as monstrous, immoral and sexually depraved. A reviewer in *Le Monde* surmised that we were once again experiencing American puritanism. Rosemary Sorensen wrote in the Brisbane *Courier Mail:* 'I do wonder if some of the animosity is envy hiding behind prissy puritanism.' For me, the surprise was when the book appeared in the United Kingdom, and a couple of reviewers in that country reacted like maddened seventeenth-century Salem witch-hunters – this time raging against me, as well as Sartre and Beauvoir. (The nastiest came from our own Peter Conrad, who seemed to think my problem was that I hailed from 'prissy Adelaide'.) One of the problems with biography is that it attracts reviewers who already have strong views about your subject, and sometimes, as their pontifications make clear, they scarcely even read your book.

This brings me to the question of judgment. In my last two books, I have left all judgment out of the narrative. I have done so deliberately. I see it as my task to present the facts, to tell a good story and leave it up to readers to decide what they think. You could argue that my choice of what to put in and leave out is already a kind of judgment; I am steering the reader's opinions. I would normally agree, but the fact is my steering lands readers all over the landscape. Those who were already attracted to Sartre and Beauvoir tell me they found my book deeply moving and they cried at the end. Those who already disliked them tell me it made them seem thoroughly dislikeable. With *Tête-à-Tête* I have finally learned that my readers and I do not necessarily think the same way, and it is probably not a good idea to write a book that provides a kind of blank slate on which readers project their own feelings. For my Roosevelt book, I've decided to include more authorial comment – as I did in my Stead book.

One of the rewards of writing biography is that it gives you a perspective on our own times; it gives you a 'long view' of history. My three biographies have been about people born in the first decade of the twentieth century, and I am more and more struck by the parallels between that generation and my own. Stead was born in 1902; Sartre in 1905; Beauvoir and Wright in 1908. They came of age in the late 1920s and 1930s, when the Left was strong, revolutionary Russia seemed to be a beacon of hope, and women enjoyed a new freedom. By the late 1940s, everything had changed. World War II was followed by the Cold War, and the United States was in a position of global eminence.

Joe McCarthy and J. Edgar Hoover created an atmosphere of fear, conservatism and guilt by association. The Left was brutally suppressed. As writers, Richard Wright and Christina Stead more or less disappeared from view. Stead's work was too angry, too critical of society for the conservative 1950s. Richard Wright was writing non-fiction: his book *Black Power* (1954), about the Gold Coast (soon to become Ghana) and *Pagan Spain* (1957), about Spain under Franco, contained some of his best writing ever, but the Western world was deeply threatened by the independence of Ghana, and the United States had just signed an important economic and military treaty with Franco. Wright told a friend: 'So far as the Americans are concerned, I'm worse than a Communist, for my work falls like a shadow across their policy in Asia and Africa ... Truth-telling today is both unpopular and suspect.'

As public intellectuals, Sartre and Beauvoir were famous in the 1950s, but they were widely hated, and Beauvoir writes that they felt in exile in their own country. France was fighting a vicious colonial war in Algeria, and the French press was in cahoots with the government. There was silence about the unbelievable torture methods the French army was using. The press did not even call it 'the Algerian War'; it was 'the Algerian question' or 'the troubles in Algeria'. Sartre and Beauvoir believed in Algerian independence, and their journal, *Les Temps modernes,* spoke out about the torture. In the early 1960s, their lives were in such danger that they had to go into hiding. Sartre's apartment was twice ripped apart by dynamite bombs.

My generation came of age in the late 1960s and 1970s, a time of revolutionary change and hope. Then – it happened some time in the 1990s – everything changed. These days, I think that most of my friends in the Anglo-Saxon world – whether we live in Australia, the United States or the United Kingdom – would say we feel in exile in our own country. With that mindless slogan 'war against terror', our governments have brought war *and* terror to Iraq, and have taken our own countries into an endless war. While our leaders jabber on about freedom and democracy, we are seeing our freedoms savagely curtailed. Kurt Vonnegut, a writer who could not contain his disgust with the Bush government and who never lost the courage to speak out, wrote in his memoirs: 'Our daily news sources, newspapers and TV, are now so craven, so unvigilant on behalf of the American people, so uninformative, that only in books do we learn what's really going on … I am a man without a country, except for the librarians.'

I would say the same. I do not have a country. In any event, I have always been wary of nationalism. I gain strength and nourishment from the people I write about, people who lived in difficult times and who never gave up the fight and hard work. And I am inspired by public intellectuals who speak out; by independent, un-embedded journalists; by publishers and newspaper and magazine editors who publish books and articles that are important rather than safe or commercially viable; and by the owners of independent bookstores who are fighting a heroic and losing battle against the chain bookshops that now determine which books 'make it' and which books don't.

When I toss and turn at 3 a.m., I sometimes ask myself whether the anguish of being a biographer is worth it. Writing is harrowing. Out of a spider web, a vague notion in your head, you have to create a book. You are expected to produce it on time, and it had better be a page-turner or the publishers will want their advance back. For every photograph, for every significant quotation, you need copyright permission, and this can take months and cost you several thousand dollars. There are always at least a couple of killer reviews, and you are supposed to take them with a shrug. If the book doesn't sell, somehow it's you, the author, who is to blame.

And yet, and yet … There are ups and there are downs, but as I see it, being a writer is an enormous privilege. Your life and work blur into one. Whatever you do, you can tell yourself it's *experience,* and that's what a writer needs most. While the world is full of people carrying out various forms of alienated labour, I look at my watch not because the days drag, but because they are far too short. I love visiting archives, gathering material and interviewing people. And I love sitting in a room by myself, with the phone turned down, lost in my own world, writing. You cannot believe how satisfying it is when the manuscript is finished and a whole team of people – your editor, copy-editor, indexer, cover designer and publicist – busy themselves turning it into a beautiful object that bears your name. Then your book is out there in the bookshops. You get letters from strangers thanking you for transporting them to another world. In one way, I have not changed at all since I was nine. I still think there is nothing more exciting than being a writer.

Australian Book Review

Like Love in a Marriage

Anna Goldsworthy

The first time I entered an international music competition I was seventeen. My entire future as a pianist seemed to hinge upon its outcome – and by extension, according to the equation I then lived by, so did my right to exist.

The competition was held in an ancient hall in the Italian seaside town of Senigallia; competitors practised in a nearby music school. As I wandered the school's corridors in search of a piano, the practice of the other contestants snowballed into the most terrifying white noise I had ever heard: part *Mephisto Waltz*, part *Paganini Variations*. It was a fearful avalanche of sound, and it threatened to consume me.

On the plane on the way home a woman casually asked my mother where we had been. 'My daughter took part in an international piano competition in Italy,' she said, 'but she was eliminated after the first round.'

I sank down in my seat. 'You don't need to tell her that,' I hissed.

'What do you want me to say, then?'

'Just say I didn't win.' I thought I might never recover from the shame.

I recovered sufficiently to enter further competitions, first as a soloist and then with my trio, and after a time it became clear that they were a numbers game. Sometimes they went well; more frequently they did not. Most musicians have a public CV of successes. We also have an alternative CV of failures that we keep tucked away in our back pockets, not to be shared with strangers on aeroplanes.

'Competitions are terrible,' says Stefan Heinemeyer, the diminutive, twinkling cellist of the Atos Trio, from Germany. 'You go in with certain expectations. It's a lottery. That's why you have to go in a lot.'

'Competitions are a necessary evil,' adds the group's pianist, Thomas Hoppe.

Formed in 2003, the Atos Trio has an impressive CV of competition triumphs, such as first prize at the Schubert Competition in Graz and at the Deutscher Musikwettbewerb. Its CV doesn't mention the trio's most recent competition appearance – at the Premio Trio di Trieste, in May – where it was eliminated before the finals.

In the second week of July the trio comes to Australia for the Fifth Melbourne International Chamber Music Competition. The night before its first competition appearance it performs at Labassa House, in suburban Caulfield, for the German consulate.

Unlike the perfect medium of a string quartet, the piano trio is a flawed instrumental combination in which a true homogeneity of sound is impossible. It is this flaw that lends the genre its friction, its drama. Because there can never be a perfect melding of sound, the piano trio operates as a conversation between three individuals.

In Labassa's ornate drawing room, as the Atos Trio plays, this friction could not be clearer. Even physically the group's members are entirely different. Pianist Thomas Hoppe is tall and broad, and looks even taller when sitting at the piano. 'I am what we call in Germany a *sit-giant*,' he explains. Heinemeyer is scarcely larger than his cello, and seems as he plays to be drawing its sounds out of his own body. Violinist Annette von Hehn is of aristocratic descent, and has the austere beauty of a Princess Leia. Her violin sound is unassailable, noble, and yet merges perfectly with Heinemeyer's exuberant cello. It is a combustible combination, and in the Brahms C Major Trio it takes the roof off the drawing room.

The German consul quickly stands up and normalises things:

'What an exquisite music. Now, ladies and gentlemen, this is the end of it.'

At the reception, a waitress brings the trio some champagne. 'Hot dang!' Hoppe exclaims.

'You are very kind, thank you,' says von Hehn.

'We are very different,' Heinemeyer explains. 'There is a German saying, *nie intim im Team*, or "don't be intimate with the team". We each have our own lives.'

Hoppe reaches for another glass of champagne. 'We will not rehearse tomorrow,' he says. 'If we are not already prepared, we have a problem.'

*

Music and competition is an odd coupling, though not a recent one. History abounds in legendary musical duels – Handel and Scarlatti, Mozart and Clementi, Liszt and Thalberg – that were frequently declared draws. Modern competitions tend to be less diplomatic, and their failings are well documented. There is the curse of the first-prize-winner, who rarely goes on to the expected great career; the compromising nature of juries, which can reward everyone's second favourite over the artist who thrills someone and offends another; the veneration of accuracy over artistry; the inevitable political corruptions.

But perhaps competitions also acknowledge a Darwinian reality about artistic careers. They encourage young musicians to work, and expose them to new audiences. And they can have a trickle-down effect into a larger culture, at least according to the founder of the Melbourne International Chamber Music Competition, the Dutch-born violist Marco van Pagee. Van Pagee is an unlikely visionary, cherub-faced and overheated. 'I wanted to raise the profile of chamber music in Australia,' he explains, blushing with enthusiasm. 'And I thought Australians like major events.'

Founded in 1989, the competition is now one of the richest of its kind, with almost $90,000 in prize money. Late last year van Pagee travelled the world for the entrance auditions, selecting eight piano trios and eight string quartets. Most of his choices are European, apart from two Canadian quartets, a Russian trio that calls itself American and Melbourne's TinAlley String Quartet.

The competition's first two rounds are held at the Australian National Academy of Music's headquarters, in the South Melbourne Town Hall. Van Pagee sits alongside the judges in the balcony, surveying the audience like a master puppeteer. Frequently he leans over the railing and addresses a comment to the back row of the stalls or photographs an oblivious head. After every performance he runs backstage and delivers a puffing verdict on ABC Classic FM.

It is clear from the first day that the piano trios are of a higher calibre than the string quartets. Trio Chausson, from France, presents a stylish, enlivening Haydn; the Russian-born Manhattan Piano Trio delivers authoritative interpretations of Rachmaninov and Shostakovich.

'I think the Rachmaninov is an absolute waste of time, to be very rude,' van Pagee declares on the radio. 'It is a fifteen-minute indulgence in romantic nonsense.'

The ABC receives a spate of complaints about his commentary. Announcer Emma Ayres jokes that he is earning a reputation as 'the Rex Hunt of chamber music'.

Van Pagee pops his head over the balcony. 'I don't understand at all,' he says, perplexed. 'Rex Hunt kisses fishes.'

*

Perhaps the most seductive thing about a competition is that it makes experts out of us all. The audience at the South Melbourne Town Hall is a warm one, but not short of opinion.

'Did you like that?' a woman demands of her companion in the toilets, after the Trio Fridegk, from Germany.

'Oh yes, I did,' says her friend, 'the violinist was lovely.'

'No,' the woman corrects her. 'No, no, *no*! The violinist was quite plain.'

'Oh yes, you're right,' her friend concedes. 'She was very plain.'

The plush red seats at the front of the auditorium are given over to Platinum Pass Holders, who have purchased tickets to the whole competition. Society hairdressers sit alongside distinguished conductors. Midway through a performance by Trio Novalis, a woman catwalks to her Platinum Pass seat, extravagantly re-arranges her pashmina and turns around to wave at a friend. A group of Melbourne's young chamber musicians sits in the back row of the hall, concentrating sternly.

It is a diverse audience, but it occasionally thinks as one. Late on Sunday afternoon the Morgenstern Trio, from Germany, walks slowly onto the stage. The three look unprepossessing, but launch into a gripping performance of Beethoven's 'Ghost' trio. At the reprise in the slow movement, the little boy in front of me turns despairingly to his mother. 'I'm bored,' he says. But no-one else is. There is an extra hush in the audience, as if an idea has arisen suddenly in the room. Afterwards the trio stands to bow and reels backwards from the applause, that great wind of gratitude. The three of them seem as surprised as we are, as if they have accidentally given the performance of their lives.

*

Years ago, at the Premio Trio di Trieste competition in Italy, my own trio approached the Russian judge for feedback on our semi-final performance. 'Your Beethoven was – how can I say – not bad, not good,' he said, and fixed his canny eye on us. 'It was … *normale.*'

Hearing these consistently impressive ensembles, it is easy to become careless about excellence. When you have heard so much polished music in one day, its currency becomes devalued. On Monday the Tecchler Trio, from Germany, plays first. It is a technically excellent performance. There is nothing wrong with it at all. It is *normale.*

Then the Atos Trio takes the stage. After a day of chamber music, you have to wait for the goose-bumps, for your body to decide for you. The Atos Trio begins with Beethoven's Op. 1 No. 2, and creates a room full of puckered skin. From the first note there is a sense of the music's drama, its gestural significance. In the Brahms C Major that follows, the trio feeds off the large audience and generates an even greater thrill than the night before. The audience stands as one, in the competition's first standing ovation; the trio's CDs are immediately sold out.

'We thought we were a little perverted, bringing ten CDs to Australia,' Hoppe says.

A young girl approaches. 'You have such delicate fingers,' she breathes at him.

Like Love in a Marriage

On the radio, Marco van Pagee does not mince his words. 'Suddenly we have this one ensemble that rises above everything else,' he declares.

*

That evening the trio is lured into a Lygon Street restaurant by the promise of free undrinkable wine. Heinemeyer has changed out of his suit into a smart white leather jacket. 'I bought this jacket from an Italian tailor in Berlin,' he announces, proudly.

'I never make fun of your clothes,' Hoppe says, 'but I do make fun of your face creams.'

Heinemeyer ignores this and turns to me. 'At five, my cello teacher put me on the stage,' he says. 'Afterwards a woman came up to me and asked, "Do you want to be a cellist?" And I said to her, "I *already am!*"'

I can see the five-year-old in his grin, pleased as punch.

'My story is different,' says Hoppe, thirty-five, the old man of the competition. 'Let me just say that adolescence hit me very hard. I was running around in a leather jacket, with a little plait down to my waist, a blonde streak here and a feather earring. At twenty I had never heard an orchestra live, had never been to an opera. But I always knew I loved music like nuts.'

They toast each other.

'It was always my dream to play in a trio,' says von Hehn softly.

'We work well together because we still can laugh at my jokes,' Heinemeyer suggests.

'We work well because we have the same goal,' says Hoppe, suddenly serious. 'To perform any piece as well as possible.'

They are in a triumphant mood and even bad food can't dent their cheer, nor undrinkable wine. When the waiter brings the bill, Heinemeyer glances over it and then sends it back. The waiter returns with a different bill, which Heinemeyer studies for a moment. He tears it up into confetti and sprinkles it on the table.

'Mate, what is your fuckin' *problem*?' the waiter asks.

'It is simple,' says Heinemeyer, with a beatific smile. 'You continue to overcharge us.'

The spruiker, who looks like he might sideline as a hit-man, steps up to our table.

'What the fuck is going on here?'

I imagine the Atos Trio in a Lygon Street brawl under my watch. I don't like its chances.

Hoppe stands up. 'Come on, Stefan, it's not worth it.'

But Heinemeyer remains where he is, arms folded, until the waiter reissues the bill.

'Sometimes Stefan has to fight for something to feel it's worth it,' Hoppe says later. 'I am not in a mood mostly to fight. My role is mediator.'

*

On Tuesday the second round begins. This year, for the first time, every group must program a work composed after 1985. Some selections are hideous. During one quartet, the four-year-old in front of me turns to his mother and strikes his head with his palm, astonished that such sounds could exist or that people could choose to listen to them. Other groups make better choices. Australia's TinAlley Quartet gives a compelling performance of Kurtag's *Six Moments Musicaux*, which displays its command over a range of techniques.

On Wednesday evening Heinemeyer accompanies me to hear the piano trios. He wears his white leather jacket and a pair of aviator sunglasses that push his hair out of his eyes. 'Normally I would never come along to listen to the others,' he says, 'but this competition is different. I feel so comfortable here.'

'You're in one of the trios, aren't you?' asks a man. 'I have a theory about the trios. They're going to take you all outside and stone you, and the three who are left standing will be the winners!'

Heinemeyer smiles and nods with the graceful forbearance of a celebrity. The highlight of the evening is the Manhattan Piano Trio's 'Arensky', in which the strings give dazzling, solo-like performances. At its conclusion, the pianist jumps from her stool and charges towards the audience, hoping to provoke a standing ovation.

'I loved this performance,' says Heinemeyer.

'Certainly I can't say that the "Arensky" is a piece that I would play every day,' Marco van Pagee tells the radio audience.

*

Like Love in a Marriage

On Friday morning the Atos Trio has a 'turbo-rehearsal' of the Schubert B Flat Major Trio, in preparation for its second-round performance that evening. Heinemeyer looks a little puffy. He was out until late the previous night. 'We are here too long not to enjoy ourselves,' he explains. Von Hehn requests more flow in the second movement; Heinemeyer asks for more *shwing* in the third.

At lunch, in Carlton's Rathdowne Street Food Store, the trio gradually becomes quieter. I show them a review in the *Age*, which identifies them as the competition's favourites. 'Cool!' say Heinemeyer and Hoppe in unison. Then they look nervous. 'After the standing ovation in the first round we thought, *Yikes*,' says Heinemeyer, 'we have to practise now.'

'It is a very nice competition,' von Hehn offers after a while. 'I like very much how someone brings you water as soon as you step off stage.'

'What I would like is a whisky or an ice-cold beer,' says Hoppe. 'Leonard Bernstein used to get this. Four measures before the end of his performance, someone backstage would light his cigarette. So that after the first applause he could walk off-stage, have a sip of whisky and take a drag at the fag.'

The three of them look thoughtful. Hoppe offers a lame pun on crab and mash; Heinemeyer ripostes half-heartedly on pea soup. No-one laughs, and they finish their lunch in silence.

*

There is a feeling of gravitas at the South Melbourne Town Hall on Friday night. It has been a long week of music, in which the audience has gradually lost tolerance for itself. In the fourth movement of the Tecchler Trio's prosaic Ravel, a flurry of unchecked coughs spreads through the crowd. Heads swivel; exasperated looks are exchanged.

The Atos Trio begins with a colourful folkloric trio by the Chinese composer Bright Sheng. In the Schubert trio that follows, Hoppe takes a more flowing tempo in the second movement, as promised, and Heinemeyer's cello entry is so fragile, so inward, that the entire audience seems to huddle into the stage. It shows a sweeter, less muscular side of their playing, which in the last movement expands to joy.

Backstage, the crew has ice-cold beers waiting. Clearly, Hoppe has been doing the rounds with his Bernstein anecdote. The three of them take their beers back into the hall for an ABC interview as the jury makes its decision. 'It doesn't matter how the result will come,' Heinemeyer declares. 'We love it here.'

The competition's jury comprises eight international musicians, with Melbourne QC Julian Burnside as the non-voting head. In a system that van Pagee describes as 'suspiciously simple', the jury members rank the performances in order of preference, with no discussion. 'It is a good jury – no mafias,' Hoppe says.

'And it is good to have a lawyer to settle disputes,' Heinemeyer adds hopefully.

Van Pagee gulps at his wine backstage. 'It's difficult when you feel quite passionate about the outcome,' he says. 'You hope the judges will make the right decision.'

Soon the audience is asked to return to its seats, and Julian Burnside steps on to the stage. 'I will speak for only a moment,' he says, 'because I have only one thing to say that is of interest to all of you.' He scans the audience like a startled owl. 'Three quartets have been selected for the finals. The Ardeo, Navarra, Badke. The piano trios are the Morgenstern, the Tecchler and the Atos.'

There are six groups with genuine smiles in the room, and ten that are just pretending or not even bothering to do that. This is the brutal mathematics of a competition. Hoppe hugs von Hehn. 'Where's our little man?' he asks, and finds Heinemeyer and embraces him, too. Trio Fridegk starts to weep. 'I don't care at all,' insists the pianist from the Manhattan Piano Trio, a surprise omission. Australia's TinAlley String Quartet is gracious but a little stunned. They played well and could easily have been in the final.

I have a little first-aid kit for failure, a selection of clichés for topical application. None of them helps, but there is nothing else to say. 'What doesn't break you makes you stronger,' I offer TinAlley's cellist, Michelle Wood.

'We got out of it what we put into it,' she trades me.

Van Pagee shakes his head grimly. 'That's competitions,' he says, as if he has always known they were the worst things in the world.

There is a drafty, post-apocalyptic feeling in the hall as the ABC crew takes down the microphones and volunteers disassemble the floral arrangements. The losers drift off; the finalists have to stay for a photo shoot. A girl plays a ditty on the violin. 'What's that noise?' asks Hoppe. 'Enough music already!'

A competition official steps up to make a speech. 'Congratulations,' she says, 'you must be very pleased.'

'We are very thirsty,' Hoppe calls out impatiently.

Later that night Hoppe puts his arm around the violinist from the Manhattan Trio. 'How are you doing?' he asks.

'Fine,' says the violinist, and shrugs him off.

'The difficult thing is knowing how to act,' Hoppe says afterwards, 'around all these disappointed people.'

He organises a subdued celebration in his room and pulls out his laptop to cheer up the disappointed. First he shows a slideshow of photos of funny cats. Then he plays a recording of a disastrous performance of Ravel's *Bolero*. The assembled company chuckles, but the pianist from the Manhattan Trio laughs and laughs, and then laughs more, until she is rolled up into a ball on his bed and is suddenly crying.

*

The competition finals, on Sunday, are held at the Arts Centre's Hamer Hall. It is an unkind venue for chamber ensembles: its vast spaces destroy nuance and reduce music to a series of loud gestures. Clusters of speakers hang from each side of the large stage; out of the corner of my eye they turn into lynched men.

The Morgenstern Trio begins with a game, committed Brahms C Major, but in the Shostakovich that follows a breeze moves through the hall and worries at the violinist's music. The audience gasps; the violinist's face becomes blotchier. At the end of the first movement she turns urgently to the pianist. The page-turner runs backstage for a moment, and the whistle of the air-conditioning descends a tone. In the second movement the violinist gives a thrilling performance, playing like a woman possessed. But the breeze still teases at her music, and in the last two movements she is again unsettled. 'Did you see what happened?' she asks afterwards. 'My mind was lost; it was too late. How could this happen?'

It happens again during the Teccher Trio's performance of Frank Martin. The cellist swats at his music with his bow, but then it blows shut completely. He turns to the violinist with a rueful smile and plays on by memory. The Brahms B Major that follows is not as emotionally fraught as the Morgenstern Trio's performance, but nor is it as interesting.

The final performance is by the Atos Trio, and the zephyr leaves them alone. Von Hehn is beautiful as she steps on to stage, with her hair pulled back in ropes and a diaphanous blue train that billows behind her as she walks. Heinemeyer's hair is gelled back, gangster-style, but will not remain that way for long.

Earlier, Hoppe had spoken to me about the violinist Ishtak Perlman, for whom he used to work. 'Perlman was a big influence on me in the absolute joy in his playing. If you see his face on stage, it is radiant. I know for a fact this is not show. This is inspiration.'

The Atos Trio is radiant now on stage, and its radiance fills the hall. Perhaps Heinemeyer amps up his gestures a little for the scale of the venue, but the joy of their playing is real. In Beethoven's Op. 70 No. 2, Heinemeyer and von Hehn lean into each other and smile; I glance around and see an entire audience smiling back at them. Sometimes it is this simple: music is alive in an ensemble or it is not, like love in a marriage. The audience knows it and can only hope that the jury does, too. After its final work, by the Spanish composer Cassadó, the trio is summoned repeatedly back to the stage. Finally, von Hehn and Hoppe take their leave. Heinemeyer is not yet ready to part with his audience and remains for another bow.

The trio is too nervous to stay for the quartet finals. Instead, the three of them go to a restaurant where they try, unsuccessfully, to eat. They then return to their rooms where they try, unsuccessfully, to sleep. These are difficult hours, filled with portent. During the meal Hoppe fingers a meticulously folded five-dollar bill in his pocket for luck; von Hehn counts the number of sips it takes to finish her wine, as if this might tell her something.

At one competition in Osaka, I invested my own trio's fate in a giant inflatable elephant on the roof of the skyscraper adjacent to our hotel. On the morning of our first-round appearance, it was proudly inflated, taking up much of the sky. It remained buoyant for the second round, which went well, but became a grey, inauspicious puddle before the announcement of the finalists. 'I knew we hadn't made it,' said Helen, our violinist, as we flew home, 'when I saw that they had deflated that elephant.'

We hadn't spoken once about the elephant. To articulate it would look foolish, as well as destroying its magic. Instead we had achieved something notable as a trio: a perfect ensemble of magical thinking.

*

That night, after the announcement of prizes, a weary Hoppe calls his family. At the after-party at Cookie, a fashionable city drinking spot, Heinemeyer holds forth to a cluster of groupies. Von Hehn sits at the bar, beaming. She no longer has to count the sips in a glass of wine. 'I'm very happy,' she says. 'I can't believe how many prizes we won.'

Perhaps it was van Pagee's 'suspiciously simple' voting system, but for once the jury got it right. The Atos Trio won the Piano Trio Audience Prize, the Piano Trio first prize, the Primus Telecom Grand Prize and the Musica Viva Special Prize. Second prize was awarded to the Morgenstern Trio; the ABC Listeners' Award went to the Manhattan Trio. As the pianist strode on to the stage to collect it, her defiant, vindicated footsteps echoed through the hall. The string quartets were more disappointing. Second prize went to the artistic, inaccurate Navarra Quartet, and first prize to the English Badke Quartet. 'We feel a little strange about winning,' the Badke Quartet's violinist admits at the after-party, 'when we didn't think we played our best.'

Other ensembles are still wounded, and remain huddled in groups, trading conspiracy theories. *This competition has never liked Russians. Is there any chance that breeze might have been engineered?* After a few drinks, some of them will summon up the courage to approach the jury members for feedback.

Four years ago, my own trio was one of these wounded groups. The Melbourne International Chamber Music Competition was the last competition we entered as a trio. Two years earlier, we had won the Piano Trio and Audience Choice awards at the national competition, but the international competition had always been our raison d'être. We had spent the previous two months in Germany, rehearsing for eight hours a day. We were eliminated after the first round.

I can't remember if I wept or not, but I had my driver's licence renewed the following day and a photo was taken of my astonished face. Each time I present my licence I am reminded what disappointment looks like. It is cadaver-white, unseeing.

'I think it's hilarious that people come to competitions and expect them to be fair,' says juror Caroline Henbest at the after-party. 'I don't believe in competitions, but I believe in what Marco van Pagee is trying to do with this one, which is to encourage chamber music.'

I thought it might be painful to revisit the site of such disappointment, but this has been a joyous week. Never again do I want to hear that we are all winners, or that music is the winner, but in this competition van Pagee is creating something profound. There is an intimacy to chamber music that is perhaps as close as humans get. At its best, it expands to include the audience; van Pagee's vision is that it might expand to include a country, too.

After the competition, the disappointed and the triumphant return to their homes. Neither winning nor losing changes things as much as expected. Hoppe paints his house; von Hehn visits her parents. What remains in Melbourne is an audience hungry for chamber music, and a legion of young ensembles inspired to work.

After my trio's disappointment four years ago, the three of us sprang apart and barely spoke to each other for six months. Then we remembered that we loved each other, which is not too strong a way of putting it, and that we loved chamber music. We tucked our CVs of failure into our back pockets, and we kept on playing.

The Monthly

* * *

In Shiraz

Don Walker

Imam Khomeini International Airport, Tehran, and within minutes of the luggage belt lurching to life we know that Emirates has failed to transfer our suitcases in Dubai. We have a domestic flight booked on to Shiraz in a few hours. In the airport lost-luggage office they advise us to catch that flight, that our suitcases will find their way to Shiraz after us, God willing.

The 'God willing' outlook is common here, though not universal. It provides a thread of patience, fatalism and calm to civic affairs. Problems aren't attacked, they're allowed to unravel. Aligned with entropy, not against it. It's the opposite of the Western world's 'God helps those who help themselves.' Nobody invents and produces mobile phones, space shuttles and tunable lasers 'God willing.' On the other hand, none of these toys would exist without the immense Persian contribution to abstract mathematics and philosophy over the last three thousand years, concepts only available to patient minds, unfussed, un-anchored by the trivial. We decide that God might be too busy in Gaza this week to be bothered with our luggage, we're going to re-book the Shiraz flight a day later, plant our feet in Tehran and make the luggage thing happen.

Tehran is fifteen million people, a first world freeway system, two million cars. The car emission controls that were legislated in Australian cities decades ago are unknown, and gasoline is the equivalent of US10 cents a litre. The resulting pollution is lethal, and hasn't improved since we were here four years ago. All else is as I remember it, the density and energy of the crowds on the corners and cutting through the traffic, the rickety street fronts of brick and scaffolding, every surface hand-painted with advertising in the fluid Persian script so that the whole city at street level has the dusty sheen of an antique poster.

The hotel is almost generic western four-star, but there are a few touches that make it clear this is a different civilisation. Tea, coffee and sweets are served to the fifty or so people doing business or socialising in small groups across the lobby, but no alcohol. A remote corner is roped off for non-smokers. I keep out of sight while my wife books accommodation at Persian rates. We get a small suite on the top floor for the equivalent of US$100. One glimpse of me during the booking process and the price would triple. Twenty hours out of Sydney, we shower and sleep.

The luggage comes in on the next Emirates flight around 8 p.m. It's a four-hour round trip back out to the airport through traffic like Manhattan peak hour only on a vast scale. By the time we get back to the hotel my face is beginning to swell from the fumes, but we have our suitcases, all is well with the world. In the gardens behind the hotel there are tables set for dining, and seated there with fountains cooling and cleaning the air we begin to re-integrate body, mind and location.

*

Imam Khomeini International is like mid-size modern airports anywhere – clean, steel, glass and lots of space. Mehrabad, the old airport, an hour away by car, is chaotic, third world and under construction. Today is the annual holiday mourning the death of Fatima, the daughter of the Prophet, and the check-in areas are packed to the walls with families from across the region, from Sudanese to Uzbeks, tribal families from the south-west to Azerbaijanis. We are not, as we had been led to believe, booked on the single flight to Shiraz today, and neither are a list of about seven hundred others who need to catch the same plane. The only functional Farsi speaker in the family repeatedly fights her way to crowded counters and is shunted through offices to try and move us up this list while the other two of us guard a baggage trolley. Finally she suggests I give it a go, playing the dumb naive Australian lost in an alien world. Within half an hour I have us booked on.

The plane is a Tupolev 154. Like most Russian aviation it's beautifully designed and constructed. With a needle-like fuselage, clipped wings and three powerful tail-motors, the Tupolev takes off and flies like a rocket, so long as no bits fall off. When I was in the Soviet Union in the '80s this was the main domestic commercial aircraft, but they were old then, and I approach this one in fear. The cockpit is curtained off from the cabin with what looks to be a camel blanket. Like most Westerners I do most of my praying in the air, the older the plane, the more fervent the prayer, and it's a pretty fervent hour and a half to Shiraz, but we land safely in the end, to a joyful reception of friends and family who haven't seen us for too long.

*

A few facts to set the picture:

Iran is bounded by Iraq and Turkey to the west, Pakistan and Afghanistan to the east, the Caspian Sea to the north and the Persian Gulf to the south.

Iranians, otherwise known as Persians (a Greek word), migrated into this region from central Asia four thousand years ago. They are not Arabs.

A succession of Persian empires has spanned this area of the world for most of the last two and a half thousand years.

Iran is not an artificial state cobbled together by colonial powers. Iran has been here since our ancestors, as the saying goes, were wiping their arses on the trees.

The Persians were conquered by Alexander the Great (who they call Iskander) in 330 BC, by the Arab armies of Islam in the sixth century AD, and by the Mongols in the thirteenth and fourteenth centuries AD.

They have always been a literate and philosophical people, and from the beginning made a powerful contribution to the evolution of Islamic thought and art.

Iran today is an Islamic country of seventy million people.

Shiraz is the capital of Fars province in the south of Iran. The city is probably four thousand years old, but really began to flourish after the Arab conquest. Wine may have originated here.

*

The Vakil Bazaar in Shiraz is several kilometres of twisting and intersecting tunnels, mostly re-built in the 1700s by Karim Khan Zand, but with some sections much older than that. The grander hallways run straight for up to four hundred metres, with arched ceilings of intricate brickwork, closing to a ventilation hole at the apex of each square vaulted section. The older passages are narrower and lower, the ceilings still vaulted, but of mud and straw, patched in places. In other passages the ceiling has been replaced by corrugated iron and logs. The booths that line these tunnels are six to ten feet wide and up to twenty feet deep. The floors between are now tiled or asphalt. That's the architecture, but it's the people and the goods that make the Bazaar an orientalist's wet dream, a setting beyond the wildest laudanum-hazed yearnings of Aubrey Beardsley, packed with drifting rivers of humanity from impossibly wealthy Arab families to the desperately poor, tribal women in gold masks, messengers on motorbikes cleaving the crowds and filling the halls with two-stroke exhaust fumes, barrow boys pushing wide flat barrows piled with cherries, Shirazi grapes and apricots, the stall owners and their wares of fabrics, clothes, rugs, freshly hammered kitchenware from nomadic to apartment use, gold and silverware, antiques both rubbish and priceless, every kind of wood, inlay, enamelling, precious thread embroidery, leatherware, illumination, crusader-era weaponry and armour only from the other side, stalls of vegetables, stalls of sweets, and the stalls of spices and medicinal teas. The spices are piled into hills of every colour above rows of burlap bags of the petals of flowers that'll put you to sleep, wake you up, clear your chest or keep it up for days. This is all real, there are no tourists but me. If I stand still for long I attract a little crowd, milling around in earshot, glancing sidelong at my weird skin and hair, hoping I'll say something in English like Tupac. On another day I come face to face with a Westerner, maybe a German, our eyes brush past each other and we quickly turn away. I know how he feels. I resent him in a realm I thought I had to myself.

At the centre of the Bazaar is a large courtyard surrounded by shops at ground level and offices above, built around a still pool to staunch the heat of the day. My daughter's ancestors used to own this part of the Bazaar, until her great-grandfather donated it to the city. Angling off this courtyard is a section where the globes are in light-fittings and the booths are glazed into tiny shops selling handmade chess and backgammon sets, masks and Ahuru Mazda amulets, cheesy paintings and carvings of Hafez, Ali, the Archaemenian kings and the Virgin Mary.

We've been searching for the tinkers' corner, the area of the Bazaar where craftsmen make pots and pans and kettles with a deafening racket of hammers on tin and pewter and brass and steel, but when we find it the tunnels are filled with no more than the murmur of commerce. The goods are there, every conceivable container for brewing tea or cooking jams and stews or boiling dyes, some five feet across, but now they're made elsewhere.

We take a break in the cool of a basement teahouse, tiled walls and floor, medieval furnishings, eating *faludeh*, a frozen confection like fine white spaghetti with fresh lime juice.

*

One block away from the Bazaar is the Vakil Fortress of Karim Khan Zand, who made Shiraz his capital and ruled Persia from 1750 to 1779 AD. He is regarded as a wise and benevolent ruler, who did much building during a peaceful reign, but he made a small mistake early on. He never controlled more than 75 per cent of the country, and felt the pressure of rivalry from a powerful tribe in the north-east called the Qajars, so he had the young heir of the Qajar tribe, Aaghaa Mohammad Khan, castrated when he was twelve.

When the old king died peacefully in his sleep, he was succeeded by his nephew Lotf Ali Khan, but by that time the Qajar heir Mohammad Khan had reached maturity and gathered a large army. Lotf Ali was defeated everywhere, and finally took refuge in the city of Kerman. The Kermanis protected him there and kept Mohammad Khan at bay for eight months, mainly because they could not stomach the idea of losing to a gelding. When Mohammed Khan finally broke the city and sent Lotf

Ali off to Tehran to be tortured, he rounded up all the male Kermanis and had a high tower built from their gouged-out eyes. Then he had the old king Karim Zand dug up and re-buried under the front steps of this palace in Shiraz, so that the general public and even tourists from Australia would forever walk on the man who had had his balls.

Mohammed Khan founded the Qajar dynasty, which united and ruled Iran until the 1920s. He was succeeded by his nephew, who more than made up for his uncle's infertility with the help of one hundred and thirty wives.

*

We've set the alarm so an aunt can take us for an early morning walk in the park several blocks away. At this time of the day traffic is light and the air is still crisp. A few others are out exercising and walking, a street sweeper, a few soldiers. There's a queue to a small counter on the way, and several men are throwing and peeling flat bread from the inside of a tandoori oven. The park a block further on is fifty acres of lawn, paths, pine and mulberry trees, fountains and modern benches. It was built in the Shah's time from barren land on what was then the edge of town. In those days Shiraz was a dreamy little city of 400,000 people, but that changed with the Iran–Iraq war. For those caught in the war Shiraz was the closest population centre to the north, and the streets became tent cities of refugees. When the war ended many of the refugees settled into new suburbs and stayed, but the city infrastructure never quite caught up with the new reality. At this time of the day, however, in this park, you can almost see and smell the old Shiraz: sumptuous shade, dry desert air that intensifies the perfume of any tree and the backdrop of the bare baked mountains.

Two details set this place apart from any similar park in the West. There are no dogs. Dogs are unclean under Islamic teaching, and public dog ownership is rare. Cats are everywhere, though, and on quieter streets it's common to see them playing, flickering from hide to hide or soaking up the sun. The second difference is the permission granted anyone from out of town to camp in a city park. Here and there families are wrapped in and on blankets, either under the open sky or in the kind of three-man modern tents commonly used by families camping in Australia.

We cut round and across the park, passing men and women of all ages walking briskly or exercising. The women are covered as always from chin to wrists to ankles, with their hair in the Bruegel-style hood seen commonly in Shiraz, only with trainers on.

On a paved area twenty or so young men play a pick-up game of soccer. A young girl, dressed in what we would see as a nun's costume, walks by. Their game intensifies, their shouts become more urgent.

Whether by law or convention, women in Iran are required to cover their hair and limbs, and as far as possible disguise their shape, from the day of their ninth birthday, so as not to distract the minds of otherwise righteous men, but of course it doesn't work. To restate a central theme of early rock and roll, it ain't the shape it's the moves.

The young girl doesn't even glance at the soccer game, but there's clear laughter in the body language radiating through all that drapery as she sways off between the trees, more sensual than all of Hollywood.

*

When I first drove into Shiraz some years ago, I noticed that the civic statues are not of statesmen, generals or kings, but of poets. Shiraz, they say, is the city of wine, poets and roses, although they sometimes forget to mention the wine these days. The roses that filled the median strips of Zand Avenue a generation ago are gone, but the tombs of the poets Hafez and Sa'adi will always be two of the main cultural attractions. Hafez's tomb is in a garden in the centre of the city, a massive block of stone sheltered by a delicate stone cupola, surrounded by paths, gardens, trees and colonnades. Teenage Shirazis dress up and lounge or stroll around here to impress each other.

Sa'adi's tomb on the outskirts of town is a grander affair, a single towering room, impossibly elegant, with a single colonnade to one side leading to a smaller tomb. We approach it on a wide path, almost a causeway with gentle steps. Around and behind it are pine and citrus groves, their dark leaves cooling the breeze, stark against the massive sun-baked hills that frame the city. A stair leads down from the gardens into a teahouse surrounding an underground pool, high vaulted ceilings of mosaic tiles overhead. While we're there, sharing tea and frozen desserts, a beautifully dressed young man enters and meets with another the same. In Sydney two gay men in a teahouse don't attract a second glance, and it's the same here for the opposite reason. In this culture, under this legal system, homosexuality is unimaginable.

Sa'adi was born in 1189 AD, and left Shiraz while still a student to study at the Al-Nizamiyya University in Baghdad, then the finest in the world. He was in Baghdad when the Mongols sacked the city, a traumatic event that haunted him through thirty years of wandering across the savaged northern remains of the Caliphate, through India, and to the West, where he was captured by Frankish crusaders and put to work as a slave labourer in Tripoli. He returned to Shiraz late in life and began to write, firstly *The Bustan* (The Orchard), an epic poem, and then a collection of prose and poetry called *The Golestan* (The Rose Garden), stories he had gathered in the teahouses and inns and trader's camps of his travels. Three lines of his poetry, in Farsi, mark the entrance to the Hall of Nations at the UN headquarters in New York.

Hafez, a mystic as well as a poet, lived a little over a century later. His life is much less well documented, and much more encrusted with myth and legend. He probably never left Shiraz.

*

In the early evening we go walking to a shopping area two blocks away. Many others are out walking as the air cools. Outside a walled area a young revolutionary guardsman sits on a chair beside a gate with an assault rifle across his knees. The barrel is aimed squarely at my crotch until I draw level when, watching me, he puts his two hands together, Christian prayer style, and nods solemnly. Caught by surprise, I do the same back and move on. The citizenry are out strolling rather than hurrying, browsing past shops of office furniture, shoes, stationery, gold work, mobile phones, audio equipment, pharmacies and little internet cafés. The shops are small and shabby, but there is life and energy everywhere. The young men are whippet thin and wear tight shirts and slim trousers, belted high. There's a lot of polyester going on, and a lot of colour combinations like, say, brown and orange. When I first arrived, before I got my eye in, I thought, 'These blokes have no idea,' but now I'm re-considering. I have to admit there's a certain greasy cool going on here, a '70s black movie pimp style of cool, without the afros. Persians have straight or wavy hair, and the young men wear it in a kind of Chuck Berry quiff and sideburns. I'm thinking I should blow a hundred dollars and take home a whole new look. The older men often do the socks and sandals, and make it look very cool. Although I'm the right age, I'm not going to even attempt that one. On the way back the guardsman with the assault rifle suddenly appears from across the street and holds out a box to me with some delicate pastries in it. He's big, for an Iranian. He's big for anyone anywhere, and very hard looking, not a gram of fat. He'd fit right into the Penrith Panthers' second row, and I'd lay money on him to go the full eighty minutes. I take a pastry and introduce myself, he shakes my offered hand and goes back to his post.

*

I haven't had a drink, alcohol that is, since I left Sydney. I don't miss it and I never think about it. In fact I feel refreshed and clear-headed, freed from the inevitable beer or glass of wine at the end of the day. One night my wife asks her mother if she might have a bottle of wine stashed in the back of a cupboard, but all she gets is an astonished no. Of course, like any prohibited goods anywhere, there is illicit alcohol in Iran. There's gossip going around town of a recent wedding party where alcohol was served, but it's like cocaine in Sydney, something a society hostess might flourish at guests to prove to them and herself that she's edgy and a little bit naughty. In general, this society believes alcohol to be a senseless evil, religiously forbidden, a source of stupidity, and it's sobering to consider that not just in Iran, but for a whole vast swathe of humanity, from Gaza to Nigeria, from Morocco to Java, everybody goes to bed with a lucid mind, nobody wakes up with a hangover. In general the advantages to society are clear and formidable, but I wonder. Is a man wiser who is always sober? Is a man more alert when he's deprived of sleep? George W. Bush is of course a teetotaller.

In Shiraz

One afternoon we are invited for tea to another house and I converse with a Shirazi who is highly educated, who did his high school and his medical degrees in Texas. He is also a devout Muslim, and talks to me about it politely but patronisingly, until he realises I know a little of these matters and I'm open to know more, then the conversation becomes more interesting. He's talking about Hafez. There's a lot of love in Hafez's poetry, of God, of women and of wine, and he regularly urges his readers to drink until they are drunk. My friend over tea is certain that Hafez wasn't being literal, that the drunkenness he was referring to is the ecstasy of being close to God.

And he's right, in that Hafez often writes of wine and intoxication symbolically rather than literally. But not all the time. During a two-year period in his lifetime when a conservative ruler introduced prohibition to Shiraz, Hafez wrote mourning the loss of his occasional tipple.

I do no more than listen, interested in the conflict in his words, his love of Hafez, his avoidance of the idea that a Muslim poet could contradict religious law. He is a courteous man, very earnest, very sincere. His wife is completely covered in black apart from the oval of her face. Although she too speaks English, she sits carefully on the other side of the room, apart from when she serves him with the succession of fruits, sweets and tea. There's a feeling in the room, an old, familiar, creepy feeling, and it's only later that I identify it – small-town Christian devotion, Bible groups meeting in people's houses on Tuesday nights to parse scriptural verses, St Paul's letters setting out the subservience of women to the will of their husbands, the women offering tea and cakes, bearing the burden and the blame for the sin that stalks the night outside, some poisoned into a fundamentalism of their own, others burning with hidden resentment and rebellion. These are good people, the middle-class devout family in Shiraz, the middle-class devout family in Grafton or the Hills District of Sydney, men and women of goodwill trying to follow and apply their conception of God's will. They just sometimes follow each other a long way wrong.

A widely quoted Iranian aphorism, derived from the poetry of Homa Esphanie:

Mey bokhor, manbar beh sozan, In doh rooz, omre kotah, ra del azari makon.

Drink wine, burn down the pulpits, But in this short, two-day life, don't break hearts.

*

Every religion has its inoculation clause, the bit that says 'there are other religions, but no matter how beguiling, they are false because ...' For Muslims the inoculation clause is the whole Qur'an, which they believe to be, every word, the direct unfiltered word of God to Man. Along with Muhammad they believe that Ibrahim (Abraham), Musa (Moses) and Isa (Jesus) were also legitimate prophets of God, but that the message these men brought has been misinterpreted and corrupted.

The words in the Qur'an do have a much clearer provenance, straight from the mouth of the Angel to Muhammad, recited by Muhammad to those around him, inscribed by some of those onto whatever materials were handy, and some of those inscriptions survived, I've been told, at least until the 13th century AD in Syria. Islam has the advantage both of being six hundred years more recent than the competition, and of being a political state with the means to preserve important relics within Muhammad's lifetime. Unlike the followers of any other major religion, Muslims can visit the resting place of their founder, in the Al-Masjid al-Nabawi mosque in Medina. Nearby is a plaque that reads 'Inside here is bones and nothing more,' nevertheless there he is. Just there. He talked to God. Or at least face to face with an Angel. My wife asked me if the Cross of Jesus exists anywhere. I said if they collected all the pieces of the True Cross scattered across Europe and Russia, there'd be enough wood to build a Brisbane suburb.

Muslims believe that Jesus was perhaps the greatest of their four main prophets, but they believe he was, like Muhammad, no more than a man. They believe the Christian Bible was partly written by the Roman Emperor Constantine, a pagan, and his bishops at the Council of Nicaea three centuries after Jesus' death. They regard with anathema the idea that God could have a 'son,' or that God could be a Trinity, not One. They'd be surprised to know there are Unitarian Christians who feel the same way. The Christian Gospels weren't written at Nicaea, of course, they were written by people who knew Jesus first-hand. They are the words and memories of men and women, reporting what they'd seen and heard, and struggling to figure out what it meant. They are not the direct words of God, except where Jesus is quoted, if you believe the quotes are accurate.

By the fifth century AD the Christian Church had settled on the four canonical Gospels that form the core of the Christian Bible. The latest of these four, the Gospel of John, was written perhaps by the Apostle John, anywhere between 50 and 100 AD. In that Gospel Jesus is quoted as saying, 'I am the way, the truth and the life. No-one comes to the Father except through me.' (John 14:6) For Christians beguiled by Islam, this is their inoculation clause. For Muslims, who believe that Jesus was a true messenger of God, this quote should present a problem. Some Muslims say that the quote is authentic, but Jesus meant no more than that he was a prophet of God's truth. They say that Muhammad is the 'Comforter' promised by Jesus in subsequent chapters of the Gospel of John.

Others say that the Apostle John was also just a man, his memory confused by the years and the Devil, and go back to what they believe is the direct word of God in the Qur'an.

*

Ayatollah Khamenei is on television tonight. He is seated comfortably in a big chair with two microphones in front of his face, on a stage in a huge auditorium full of people. The majority are men, but there are women and children seated in a separate section, the women heavily covered. Onstage to the right and below Khamenei is the elected president of Iran, Mahmoud Ahmadinejad, cross-legged on a kind of mattress with a cushion behind, like an obedient schoolboy singled out to sit in front of the class, and in fact Khamenei, with his huge spectacles, has exactly the manner of a headmaster, wise, patient, a twinkle of humour now and then as he addresses the assembly below, but with absolute authority. How can America, he says, this most powerful nation in human history, with their vast economy and invincible armies, how is it they face defeat on every front, in Iraq, in Afghanistan, in Palestine, in Lebanon? Because people hate them, he says. Everywhere they go ordinary people all over the world hate them. And those thousands in the auditorium, now standing, say a phrase back to him, repeated with quiet determination: Death to America thunders softly around the auditorium, Death to America.

*

Beh shir shotor, khordan o' sousmar, Arab are bejai residast kar keh Tage Kiani konad arezoo. Tofoo bar to ey charkhe gardoon. Tofoo.
These drinkers of camel's milk, these eaters of lizards, these Arabs now aspire to the Peacock Crown. Spit on the wheel that turns. Spit on it.

Thus wrote the Persian poet Ferdowsi in the 10th century AD, in despair at the Arab conquest of his civilisation. The eaters of lizards, though, had a book, in Arabic, dictated by the Angel Jibreel in a cave in the desert, every word like a tongue of fire, and no earthly throne could withstand that. Islam swept through the rotting Sassanid Empire in 641 AD like a bushfire through a dry thicket of souls. Fourteen centuries later Arabic is compulsory in Iranian primary schools, as it was under the Shah.

*

It's difficult, as a travelling tourist, to gauge how popular or otherwise a government is. You hear about a lot of grumbling. One acquaintance comes in laughing that a taxidriver said, 'If Muhammad had known these mullahs are coming he'd never have introduced Islam.' But a lot of it is grumbling, such as goes on against any government anywhere at street level. There isn't the slightest vestige of an alternative government here, and the Americans have demonstrated in Baghdad what happens when a regime is overthrown with nothing to replace it. I don't believe anyone here, no matter how hostile to this government, would accept an alternative government parachuted in by the Americans from among opposition groups in exile, and I believe a physical threat from outside would unite Iranians behind the mullahs like nothing else. Satellite dishes are illegal here but most people have them, and Voice of America is available among many other satellite channels. It's very slick, but anyone I know watches Iran TV or occasionally news from Germany.

In Shiraz

I should state here that I love America and I always will, not just the coasts but the heart. I cheered for Reagan, and later cheered for Pat Buchanan. I reckon any country that kicks off its Olympics with Little Richard has got it caned. But it's important for there to be a part of the world that is Not America, and in 2007 this is how far you have to come.

*

Tonight is our last night in Shiraz, and we're going back to the Bazaar to buy small presents for friends and family back home. On the way down Zand Avenue I hear the call to prayer, and this is the first time I've heard it in Shiraz. Four years ago we were wandering through the courtyards of the Golestan Palace, the home of the Qajar emperors in Tehran, when the call to prayer opened up through the over-driven tannoys of a mosque a block away. It was the loneliest and most primitive sound I've ever heard, a gasping cry to God in the desert from a swollen tongue. For pure chill up the spine it made Howling Wolf sound like Donnie Osmond. This Shiraz call to prayer is a lot tamer than that, barely floating above the noise of the traffic.

The Bazaar seems to be busier at night, more exciting, now that the energy-sapping heat has gone out of the sky outside. The passages are floodlit and festooned with naked bulbs, the smell of the spices hits from the street outside, stinging the nostrils and cleaning the blood. My wife and daughter buy some tiny boxes, carved from camel bone, exquisitely etched and painted in Isfahan, and hand-knitted tribal slippers. I buy a very old handmade knife for a mate of mine in Nashville, because he likes that kind of thing.

*

The music begins with a struck chord. A long hanging silence, then another, like a last cough, then a single-note trill building out of the distant haze. Gradually the landscape is revealed by the *tar* alone. Only after eight minutes, when the listener is totally drawn into this world, does the singer appear, a long parched note, quavering then straightening, circling like a bird before expanding into language, a word, a phrase, silence, then an answer from the *tar* again.

It's six days later, our last day in Iran. We're driving south from the Caspian Sea into the Aldorz Mountains, surrounded by mist and vast interlocking planes of slanted stone. 'Who's that?' I ask the driver, indicating the CD player under the dash. 'Banaan,' my wife translates back, 'the greatest of the traditional Persian singers' and she and the driver continue to talk. 'He must be quite old, but he's still alive, and often performs sold-out concerts in Tehran.'

*

We arrive at Imam Khomeini International Airport, an hour and a half south of Tehran with hours to spare, having allowed for possible landslides. I try to buy any CD by the famous Persian singer Susaan. Three girls behind the counter start to giggle and tell us she's illegal. I buy all the CDs they have of Gholaamhossein Banaan, knowing it's my sacred duty to keep them out of the hands of 'world music' thieves, because this stuff doesn't need beats, pygmies or dolphins.

The security check-ins of Iranian airports are segregated, and the partitioned women's check-in always has a female official who monitors the clothing of female passengers. Hair covered, body shape disguised etc. I'm reading the first English-language translated newspaper I've seen for weeks, the *Tehran Times*. On the front page is a piece celebrating National Women's Day in Iran:

'As in Western countries, before the Islamic Revolution, women [in Iran] were regarded as commodities and their social activities were not respected. However, the revolution took a compassionate, Islamic attitude toward women.

'Unlike certain Arab and Muslim countries, where a woman is viewed as just a housewife and a bearer of children, the status of women in Iran is in some regards higher than men.

'In the Islamic Republic of Iran, a woman is one of the country's vice-presidents, women are members of parliament, lawyers and university professors, and there are no hindrances preventing women from assuming high-ranking political posts.

'The Iranian Constitution grants women equal rights with men, and this can be a model for all Muslim countries.'

*

In Shiraz

My wife has gone into the female security section to put her hand luggage through, wearing loose trousers, a cotton shirt buttoned to the collar and the wrists, and a large headscarf. She is ordered to unpack her luggage and find an overcoat to put on before she will be allowed out of the country.

A few hours later we take off and climb south. Long before we leave Iranian airspace we sit watching the female passengers, most of them Iranian, queuing at the aircraft toilets to change into clothing of their choice.

*

In Dubai the next day we learn that as we flew out of Iran, Madonna headlined a series of concerts across the Western world to 'raise awareness' about climate change. A more vacuous, bloated event is hard to imagine, a massive fart of celebrity carbon that raises awareness of nothing but itself and is gone with the Sunday papers. I read that al Qaeda has issued a deadline to Iran: cease all support for and contact with anyone in Iraq within two months or al Qaeda will be declaring war and taking that war to the streets of Iranian cities.

I'm in the front seat of a taxi in Dubai City having a conversation with the Pakistani driver. We both think we're speaking English, but at least one of us is mistaken. 'How far is it to Iran across the water there?' I say. 'Fourteen per cent,' he says. I'm looking at the Persian Gulf across a beach as wide and beautiful as any in Australia, although the surf is a little flat. It stretches south-west to the Burj Al-Arab, now the most famous hotel in the world, like a spinnaker in the haze twenty kilometres down the coast. The pace and scale of construction here is staggering, there wouldn't be this many cranes on any horizon outside China. I assume Sheikh Mohammed bin Rashid al Maktoum is racing to convert his gas and oil revenues into a metropolis that will have enough critical mass to survive their exhaustion, but the fact is that gas and oil already account for only 3 per cent of an economy that has diversified into tourism, finance and service industries for the region and beyond. We've just passed the Burj Dubai, already the tallest building in the world, with a few hundred feet still to be constructed. The Emirates Mall, with its indoor ski run, is now the world's preferred place to shop.

Suburbs are rolling out over sand dunes, new cities on artificial land laid out into the gulf, every apartment and every villa architect designed by the best firms on the planet competing, every few blocks a new and more beautiful mosque, and all in stone with hedges, lawns, borders and gardens where there was nothing five years ago. It all looks a little bit like Beverly Hills, only much, much bigger, and with an Arab twist, like Disney does Islam. Everything is clean and superbly efficient, there are sit-down toilets everywhere, everything works, but everything is just a little bit fake. We book a dinner on a dhow cruising up Dubai Creek, and eat a buffet while they play The Eagles, The Bee Gees and The Captain and Tennille. Back in the hotel room a half-litre of Johnnie Walker Black is displayed next to the TV. I leave it sealed and put on Banaan instead.

From a longer account of a trip to Iran

Blow-ins on the Cold Desert Wind

Kim Mahood

Each year I drive from my home near Canberra to the Tanami Desert and spend several months in an Aboriginal community that has become my other home. The trip takes a week or two, allowing for the incremental adjustments that make my arrival one of recognition, pleasure and ambivalence.

There was a year I did it differently, flying directly to Alice Springs and travelling the thousand kilometres of corrugated and sandy desert track squashed into the back of a troop carrier with nine or ten elderly Aboriginal artists. We arrived in the early hours of the morning, less than twenty-four hours after I had left Canberra. The vehicle headlights lit a disorderly world of damaged houses, broken cars, lean furtive dogs and accumulated rubbish. This was a number of years ago, when I was still sorting out the uneasiness of my relationship to the place and people, and I felt the rise of old anxieties and discomfort. It seemed that, having departed from the orderly, over-planned surrealism of the national capital, I had arrived at its sinister twin. As I helped to drag tattered foam mattresses and assorted bundles from the back of the troop carrier, I thought of the plans and policies manufactured in the tidy hill-fort of Parliament House, and imagined them on their trajectory across the nation encountering a zone of refraction somewhere in the upper atmosphere, arriving as a mess of shattered fragments on this windy plateau. This image has stayed with me, a visual metaphor for the sustained capacity of remote Aboriginal Australia to subvert the best intentions of successive state and federal governments.

One of the results of moving on a regular basis between predominantly white urban Australia and predominantly black remote Australia is an awareness of the gulf of perception between those people for whom Aboriginal Australia is a reality and those for whom it is an idea. An idea can tolerate a number of abstractions. Reality, on the other hand, must tolerate a number of contradictions. The way in which these contradictions are bridged by both white and black is largely through humour, irony and a well-honed sense of the absurd – qualities generally missing from any public representation of white and Aboriginal interactions.

*

The whites who work at this interface talk about Aboriginal people all the time. The trajectory of every conversation, no matter where it begins, ends up in the same place. These conversations are full of bafflement, hilarity, frustration, admiration and conjecture. They are an essential means of processing the contradictions with which one deals every day.

The Aboriginal people talk about the whites too, but I doubt that it is in the same sustained and obsessive way. I can't be sure of this, and it is something I will probably never know. What I do know is that the western desert word for white person, *gardiya*, runs like a subliminal refrain under the currents of ordinary conversation. No matter how much time one has spent or how strong one's relationships with Aboriginal people, the word follows you about like a bad smell. It is not intended as an insult; it is simply a verbal marker to underline the difference between *us* and *them*.

It becomes an insult, however, if one is Aboriginal. In the volatile world of family and community politics, it is the greatest insult that can be levelled at anyone who is suspected of harbouring *gardiya* aspirations and values. To take on any form of authority over your peers opens you to such an accusation, as does the refusal to share vehicles, money and possessions. People of mixed descent are continually reminded of their compromised status, and children with white blood are frequently referred to as *gardiya*.

To be white exempts you to some extent from the network of responsibilities and obligations. It is accepted that you belong to an inexplicably cold and selfish branch of the human family, and refusals to share what you have are accepted with equanimity. However, the boundaries become more difficult to hold as relationships deepen, and negotiating one's place in all of this is a continuing process.

By the standards of white Australian society, the life I lead is extremely provisional. I don't have a regular job, I don't own a home and my annual income is in the bracket that attracts a low-income rebate on my tax return. In the eyes of the Aboriginal people among whom I work, I own a reliable vehicle, I can buy fuel when I need it, I always have food in the house, I am allowed to run up an account at the store. These are indicators of wealth. Sometimes, as I weave my evasive course through a web of subtle and overt demands, carrying only small change in my pockets, walking instead of driving so my car is not commandeered as a taxi to ferry people home with their shopping, making continual small adjustments and compromises against my better judgment, I catch a glimpse of the truly provisional nature of people's lives. When I buy diesel at $2.20 a litre, when I pay $5 for a carton of soy milk that would cost me half that in a southern supermarket, I appreciate the mirage-like nature of money in this world. I understand why the fortnightly pension cheque is converted to cash and lost in a card game an hour later. Paul Virilio, in *The Aesthetics of Disappearance,* says 'number games, like lotto or the lottery, with their disproportionate winnings, connote disobedience to society's laws, exemption from taxes, immediate redressment of poverty.'

*

If I was of an academic turn of mind, I would be tempted to pursue a thesis on the role and meaning of money in Aboriginal communities. There is no apparent logic to its availability. Acquiring it is a serious preoccupation, with none of the social prohibitions that disguise the same preoccupation in non-Aboriginal society. It is easy to become cynical at the manoeuvring to prove traditional links to mining land and thus access to royalties. It is easy to be appalled by the ruthlessness with which elderly painters are milked by their extended family, or to be exhausted by the relentless pursuit of payment for the smallest snippet of cultural knowledge.

These are the cross-cultural tensions nobody talks about, except in those *gardiya* enclaves within the communities, as one tries to find ways to dissipate the frustrations and misunderstandings. I found an explanation that took much of my own cultural distaste out of the equation when I made an analogy between hunting and gathering for food and hunting and gathering for money. It may not persuade others, but it works for me. One has only to listen to accounts of traditional itineraries to notice the preoccupation with food. Desert society evolved in the boom and bust economy of one of the hardest environments on the planet, and survival was predicated on the efficiency with which its resources could be utilised. My theory – not entirely frivolous – is that the same energy once spent on getting food is now spent on getting money.

To be white is to be seen to have mysterious access to money. Sometimes I think we are perceived by the Aboriginal people as money guards, standing at the door to vaults full of wealth and doling out pocket money to them while we take all we want for ourselves. The government supply lines that support remote communities are poorly understood by the recipients. In the tightening political environment, there is a growing emphasis on accountability and effective governance, with a number of training programs and workshops designed to assist communities. Earlier this year I was co-opted to assist in the trial of one such program.

'The Australian Governance Story' has been designed in response to a request from Aboriginal communities to explain how government works in Australia. Its purpose is to give the people an overview of where they fit into the larger structures of government, where the money that supports their existence comes from, and their rights and responsibilities in managing these funds and services.

Over the years of my involvement with the community, I have deliberately avoided the Gordian knot of bureaucracy, working instead on cultural mapping projects to record the stories and knowledge people still hold about their country. A fortuitous encounter with a deeply committed and imaginative public servant called Kerrie, one of those people without whom the really hard challenges would never be attempted, resulted in us throwing ideas around about how our different enterprises might assist one another. My brief assignment as a public servant was an experiment, to see whether my work could be married to the daily business of people learning to manage their communities effectively. My reasons for taking it on were self-interested. I try to spend several months of every year in this place, and it is a constant financial struggle to find ways of doing so.

*

This is how I find myself with the task of explaining 'The Australian Governance Story' to the community members and persuading people to attend a workshop – a proposition that more or less cancels itself out. I am up against the deeply embedded suspicion of and resistance to white government-driven agendas, even when those agendas are in response to requests and proposals from the communities themselves.

The workshop is planned for July, the time of year when the congestion of visitors is at its most intense. One of the major disadvantages of belonging to a disadvantaged minority, particularly one that is central to our sense of national identity, is the relentless stream of government officials whose job it is to assess and redress those disadvantages. On any given day between May and September (after the wet season and before it gets too hot, which happens to coincide with the southern winter), a number of spanking white four-wheel drives, doors decorated with logos, will be parked in the dusty quadrangle outside the office, while the government officials they have brought compete for the attention of the community residents. It's not uncommon to find a disconsolate government rep hanging about with a satchel of information and no-one to deliver it to.

In any small community, there are a limited number of people who take on the responsibility for its social and practical maintenance. This is especially true of an Aboriginal community. Whether the issue is governance or child care or aged care, social security, substance abuse, sexual health, store committees, education and training, tourism development, environmental management, fire control, dogs, housing or garbage management, it is the same seven or eight people who are in demand. Meeting fatigue is endemic. Burn-out is a recognised syndrome among white staff in communities, but little notice is given to the same phenomenon among the Aboriginal people. When the pressure gets too much, they simply disappear for extended periods.

A three-day workshop is a big ask for people on whom the daily functioning of the community rests. It is a fine line I have to negotiate between the requirements of the government agency (I will call it ACRO) and the potential workshop participants. There are bureaucratic formalities to be met – numbers, names, the demographics of age, gender, literacy and language, signed agreements from participants that they will attend and complete the workshop.

This last requirement presents particular difficulties. It is as likely to scare people away as it is to commit them to coming. Signed pieces of paper are whitefella business, implicit with danger. I know that I can count on the core group of older women with whom I usually work, unless family business intervenes. They will come because I ask them to, because over the years we have established a relationship of mutual trust and exchange. But family business takes precedence, and signed papers will not alter that. Among the younger, overburdened community members, the risk of getting them to sign up lies in giving them too much time to plan their escape.

I re-read the list of selection criteria that applies to my temporary position as an Australian public servant: At 'no. 4 – Innovates' I find what I am looking for: 'able to develop solutions that are outcomes focused and informed by a strategic perspective'. I interpret this to mean get bums on seats by whatever means necessary.

*

Since Rebecca has discovered that we have the same-sized feet, she has been humbugging me relentlessly for the slip-on shoes I wear, unimpressed by my refusal on the grounds that they are the only shoes I've brought with me.

'What am I supposed to do, go barefoot?'

She looks pointedly at her own bare hard-soled feet and says nothing.

'You're a blackfella, you go barefoot all the time. I have to wear shoes, my feet are too soft.'

She throws me a grin that is knowing, charming and manipulative. 'I got some old ones you can have.'

'I don't want your old shoes. I'm quite happy with these.' I beg a cigarette from her. My resolve not to smoke is folding, as it always does within a few weeks of returning to the community.

'Where's that thing you got for not smoking?' She's referring to the nicotine inhaler I've been sucking on since I arrived. I take it out of my pocket and show it to her.

'Doesn't work?'

'Not under pressure.'

'Buy me a packet of cigarettes.'

I agree to do this. That way I can beg one from her whenever I need to.

Rebecca is smart and literate, one of the people in constant demand to interpret the two worlds to one another. She fits the profile of the target workshop participant perfectly.

'You can have my shoes if you promise to come to the workshop.'

'That's, what do you call it … coercion.'

'Fuck off. Do you want the shoes or not?'

'OK, I'll come. Can I have them now?'

'No way. After the workshop. And you have to come all three days.'

She gives me a deep, resentful frown, one of her stock array of expressions, all bordering on parody, which crack into broad grins of amusement at the absurdities we are obliged to play out. The self-satisfied crocodile grin appears; she has established that the shoes are negotiable. Whether she comes to the workshop or not, we both know which foot the shoe is going to end up on.

*

Enlisting men was always going to be difficult. So many of the arenas in which their identities as men are formulated have been undermined. The radar alert for coercion is set at a hair-trigger.

In any case, there are very few young and middle-aged men in the community, a fair proportion of them being in jail for various misdemeanours and crimes, mostly alcohol-related.

My key target is Patrick, a man of standing in the community and a member of one of the strong families. He is a short, square, suspicious man with a flaring temper, and has just returned from a stint in prison for cutting someone with a tomahawk. A few days ago I gave him and his wife a lift back to the community from a broken-down car. Later that evening I encountered him with his son and brother-in-law trying to get the same vehicle going, and loaned them my torch and tools. I have also loaned him jerry cans of fuel on several occasions.

'Patrick, I need you to come to this workshop. It's to teach people about how the government works, to help you to look after the community properly.'

Patrick's expression is sceptical, mildly amused. Most of what is important in the encounter is unspoken. There is genuine liking here, and also an understanding that the situation is improvised, because neither of us has more than a bare glimpse into the other's thinking processes.

'You're strong. People respect you. If you come, some of the other men will come too.'

The appeal to his vanity works. I get him to sign the paper. We both know that this is no guarantee that he will attend the workshop. What it does mean is that he will put in an appearance and that this will help to swing a few of the men and boys to at least consider attending.

*

Payment is an issue. People are used to being paid for attending meetings. For those on the work-for-the-dole scheme, the hours spent in the workshop can be claimed, but for the rest there is nothing I can offer except the suggestion that it's in their own interests to participate. This does not wash with Fatima, who has the profile and character of a Roman potentate.

'You *gardiya*,' she says, 'always coming and telling us what to do. You want us to come to meetings and then you won't pay us.'

Attack is the best form of defence with Fatima, who is one of the community powerbrokers. 'Listen, if you were white you'd be expected to pay for a workshop like this, not be paid to come.'

She leans her bulk back in the chair and smirks, satisfied that she's made me say something she can hold against me later.

'Anyway, it's about how to manage things yourself, so you don't have to put up with *gardiya* telling you what to do.'

'You shouldn't get upset, Napuru. I'll come, just to help you out.'

*

And so it goes for the weeks leading up to the arrival of the training team. Kerrie wants a guarantee of twenty participants, preferably the younger, more literate members of the community. I tell her I can't guarantee anything, but I'm doing my best. Rebecca checks every day that the deal with the shoes is still on.

I receive a list of questions from the trainers:

- Do people understand what it means to be a COAG site?
- Do DOTARS, DEWR, ICC and OIPC have regional reps?
- What is the current status of SRAs in the community?
- Do people have an understanding of how the CDEP changes will affect them?
- Will they come under an RAE?
- How will it impact on NAHS, HACC and FACS?
- Who is the local RSP?
- Is the IPA funded by DEH or DIA?
- What is the role of the KLC? Does KALACC come under the same umbrella?
- Has anyone in the community accessed the ISBF?
- Should one approach KLRC or KIC for interpretive services?

With the help of Rebecca and her sister Julie, I decode most of this curious document.

When the training duo arrives I am mending a flat tyre. They are called Bob and Deborah, and have been refining and delivering workshops to Aboriginal organisations for many years. They are experienced, good-humoured, flexible and tough. In the face of their professionalism I feel awkward and incompetent.

Kerrie and her ACRO team arrive the next morning. Things look moderately promising. The weather isn't too cold and most people have stayed in the community in spite of it being school holidays. This has also made it possible to hold the workshop in the school library, which is comfortable, well resourced and away from the distractions of the community. It is also potentially intimidating for people who don't usually sit at desks, but there's no better alternative. I have a list of seventeen possible participants, about half of whom I can be confident will turn up.

The workshop is due to start at nine. At eight-thirty I begin my rounds. There's a recognised protocol to this, which is to drive your vehicle as close as possible to people's houses and keep your hand on the horn until someone appears. After a few circuits I've roused most of the community and extracted promises that they will come down to the school after they've been to the shop. No-one shows any enthusiasm. At nine I do another round and catch Fatima trying to climb into the Indigenous Protected Area (IPA) troop carrier, which is taking a group of young rangers away to a training workshop. I work her over with shameless emotional manipulation, payback for the many times she's done it to me.

'How can you do this, after you promised me? I thought I could trust you. This makes me really upset.'

She casts a backward glance at the troopie, which is too crowded to fit her in, and pats me on the arm. 'Don't worry, Napuru. I was going to look after these kids but you need me, so I'll come with you.'

By ten-thirty about twenty-five people have wandered down to the school to see what's going on. The trainers give their introduction and we break for morning tea, after which the numbers drop to sixteen. Patrick has put in his promised appearance, lurking just inside the door and ducking outside after half an hour for a cigarette. I join him.

'What do you think?'

He shakes his head. 'That stuff make my head hurt.' He finishes his cigarette, gives me a nod and leaves.

After lunch the numbers are down to nine. By my reckoning the drop-out ratio is one-third per session, which doesn't bode well for tomorrow. But the afternoon session becomes animated.

Bob and Deborah know their stuff. They get people to unpick the network of organisations that service the community. Rebecca and Julie spearhead the group of women who reveal a sound grasp of the organisational network, which is astonishingly complicated. I am in sympathy with Patrick – it makes my head hurt too.

The challenge on day two is to get people to the workshop before the Tanami bus comes through on its bi-weekly run into Halls Creek. I collect them in twos and threes and drop them at the school. Half of them circle around behind the toilet block and beat me through the gate. They wave as I drive past, and someone calls out 'Taxi', at which they all hoot with laughter.

I drive to Fatima's house to see whether she is coming today. Yesterday there was a nasty domestic incident involving her youngest daughter, who collapsed after being beaten by her husband and has been flown out on the doctor plane. This incident accounted for most of the absentees from the afternoon session. There's no response to my horn, but I see the curtain flicker in the front room. In attempting to get out of the car, I discover that the door lock is jammed. Fatima appears in the doorway to watch me climbing out of the window.

'What you doing, Napuru?'

'I can't open the door.'

'You should get that fixed.' She gets into the car. 'What we doing today?'

On the way to the workshop, several of my previous passengers flag me down for a lift back to the school. They inform me that the Tanami bus has broken down and there's no run to town this week.

*

I am impressed by the training team, who adjust seamlessly to the changing dynamics of the group, and keep everyone fully engaged. The day is spent outlining the structure of the federal government and the lines of communication from the community through to the various departments responsible for delivering services. Most people are not aware that there is both a state and a federal government. The most pertinent piece of information they absorb is that the Budget is passed by law, and that once a certain amount of money has been designated it can't be altered, and must be delivered through the appropriate channels. At the community level, money is an arbitrary and unpredictable resource, so the notion that it is a finite and regulated commodity is novel. The trainers tell them that the money is provided by taxpayers. 'Your money,' they say. This bothers me, since I know that no-one in the community apart from the white staff pays tax, although I appreciate the need for people to feel empowered. It's another of those irreconcilable contradictions.

At the end of the day, everyone agrees to come at nine the next morning. They say I don't need to drive around and pick them up, although they enjoy seeing me climb in and out of my car window.

'You should get that door fixed, Napuru.'

That evening, on the downward haul, there's an air of hilarity among the workshop team. I remark that I feel like a hapless victim of fate, and we discuss the need for more hap to deal with events like this. This leads to reflections on being gormless and feckless. The next morning, the team are sporting name tags that say Hap, Feck and Gorm.

At eight-thirty the wailing begins and my stomach drops. Someone has died, and I feel the fear we all live with that it will be someone you know and love. Life is so precarious here, death frequent and sudden. But it is Wendy's sister who has died in Derby, a woman whose life has been violent and troubled for many years. I join the group of people offering condolences, and sit with Wendy while the older women join her in the protocols of sorry business. So much for the nine o'clock start. It's out of my hands now; people will decide their own priorities.

Evelyn comes by to tell me she is going out with her family to kill a bullock. She says she will keep some rib bones for me, indicating that she feels I need to be compensated for her withdrawal from the workshop. She's learned as much as she wants to know about the 'guvment'. Her own concerns are closer to home, in the refined and complex politics of family and country. Rebecca has also dropped out with the excuse that she has to get organised to travel to her father-in-law's funeral. She wants to know if she can still have my shoes. We negotiate a debrief on the workshop when she gets back.

By ten o'clock there are ten people in the library. The new name tags of the training team members pass without comment. After all, people here go by names such as Rimikus, Spieler and Blah Blah. There is an air of empowerment among the stayers. They carry out enthusiastic role-plays of how to present a request to their state or federal minister. They have a far better grasp than I do of the labyrinthine structures at the lower levels of bureaucracy, which I have come to appreciate bear some resemblance to their own convoluted family and political structures. At the end of the day they are pleased and happy with what they have learned, and eager for follow-up sessions. The training team has a substantial list of adjustments to implement from the trial. Everyone but me seems to think that something has been achieved.

*

The next day, Bessie comes to the office and asks me to ring Peter Costello to ask him about funding for her outstation. I find the number of the Treasurer's office and tell her to ring him herself. Monica appears with a photocopied paper which shows the line of funding support for the Indigenous Protected Area.

'You can help me?'

'What for?'

She shows me the paper. 'This for money in't it?'

'Only for the IPA.'

She throws the paper in the bin.

Julie comes in and asks me when I'm going to pay her for her work as interpreter for the workshop.

'That's ACRO's business. They haven't paid me either. Where's that list telling us who to ring up?'

Fatima comes in and parks herself portentously in the chair beside my desk.

'Napuru, you know I'm always working to help people, old people and young people together and *gardiya* too. I should get paid for that.'

Evelyn comes to tell me she's got some rib bones for me in the freezer at her daughter's house.

During a lull, I lock the office and make my escape. The community is quiet; today there are no visitors from the other world.

The cold desert wind that seems to rise in agitation at the influx of too many outsiders has dropped, and the day is clear and sunny. I climb through the car window into the driver's seat, avoiding the broken mirror stem where the rear-vision mirror has been pulled off by a child doing chin-ups.

'You should fix that door, Napuru,' someone calls out. 'It looks like a Aboriginal car.' Fatima appears at the passenger door with her shopping.

'You can give me a lift home, Napuru?'

In the car she says: 'That was a good meeting. We should have more like that.'

Griffith Review

What Is a Tree?

Tim Flannery

Animal, mineral or vegetable? Whenever our parents bundled us into the car for a long journey my sisters and I kept ourselves occupied with that guessing game. At its heart is the puzzle of how things should be classified, the more ambiguous the better. My inventive youngest sister came up with 'a cow's moo.' Through its astonishing revelations about what is related to what in the plant world, Colin Tudge's *The Tree* reawakens the pleasure of those childish games. But *The Tree* is a far deeper book than this might suggest, for its author has a remarkable ability to ask fundamental questions about trees and their world – questions that, much to our detriment, most of us stopped asking as we grew up.

Humans are innate classifiers, and our earliest efforts were doubtless classifications of convenience: edible and inedible, for example. Despite this predilection, our workaday world is filled with appalling classifications. Consider the forester's venerable division of 'softwoods' for the conifers (including the remarkably tough parana pine of South America) and 'hardwoods' for the broad-leaved trees (which include the very soft balsa). Despite its obvious potential to mislead, it's so convenient for common lumber that it's used by almost everyone.

And yet we instinctively recognise a good classification. Perhaps it comes from our sense that the natural world has a true orderliness. Birds, for example, are instantly recognisable as such, as are mammals and frogs; and so with smaller groups like kingfishers, hawks and doves. In pre-Darwinian Europe natural philosophers hoped that by comprehending the 'true classification' of nature they might glimpse the mind of the Creator. Yet in the absence of divine revelation, how could they hope to discern the one and only 'true' classification from less perfect models?

In the mid-eighteenth century the Swedish botanist Carl Linnaeus provided natural philosophers with a hierarchical scheme that classified living things into kingdoms (of which he had just two – plants and animals), classes, orders, genera and species. It is these final two categories that provide the scientific name. Linnaeus, for example, classified himself and other humans as *Homo sapiens* (though at first he dubbed us the rather less appropriate *Homo diurnis* – daytime man). The first part of the double-barrelled name is the generic part. It is shared with a group of similar species, and so acts rather like a surname in a family. The second – the species name – is unique in the genus to that individual species, and so acts like a Christian name.

Linnaeus's scheme was brilliant in its simplicity, and it is the basis of the universal scientific classification used by all taxonomists (classifiers of living things) today. When it came to higher levels (the classes and orders) of plants, Linnaeus turned to vegetable sex. And this scheme, carried on by botanists down the centuries, really has, to borrow from Andrew Marvell, grown 'vaster than empires, and more slow.' Linnaeus's highest plant categories – the classes – were arranged according to the nature of the plant's male genitals (stamens), while his next level down – the orders – was based on the female genitals (pistils). This 'male on top' approach had some unfortunate consequences: the castor bean tree (a flowering plant), for example, ended up in the same class as the pines (non-flowering plants), and his scheme did not account for the 'plants' that had no obvious sex organs at all, such as algae and fungi.

All of this, however, might have passed as a minor flaw had the Swede shared the prudery of his age. Instead he was quite the opposite. We still have a genus of creepers called by him *Clitorea* (the beautiful blue flowers of one species really do bear a remarkable resemblance to female human genitalia), and botanical classification is besieged by copious 'phallus' something-or-others (though here the resemblances are I think more imaginative). In Linnaeus's day botany was considered a fit occupation for young ladies, and such provocatively named plants caused professors throughout Europe to obfuscate, or – as Linnaeus's contemporary Johann Siegesbeck did – condemn the entire Linnaean scheme as 'loathsome harlotry.'

*

The scheme's misfortunes only increased when it was introduced to the English. The man who undertook the translation was Erasmus Darwin (the grandfather of Charles), a ponderous, pockmarked and ungainly man whose principal interests were plants, poetry, sex and ingenious mechanical devices. Darwin was a wild romantic and despite his Johnsonian appearance and stammering speech, women loved him. To court his second wife (who was married when they first met) Darwin landscaped an entire valley, damming streams and planting bowers of exotic trees and meadows of flowers. It evidently worked: from his two marriages (and a governess in between), he fathered twelve children.

Darwin revelled in sex in all its manifestations – from marital to masturbatory – and perhaps homosexuality as well (he certainly had many homosexual friends, whom he never condemned). Indeed, he believed that sex was health-giving – it cured hypochondria, for example. One wonders, incidentally, whether this had anything to do with the first Mrs Darwin being sickly, overly fond of the bottle and inclined to smoke opium.

Because of his interest in poetry, it seemed entirely natural to Darwin to translate Linnaeus's dense scientific work into rhyming couplets, so as to create a romantic epic. *The Loves of the Plants* was published in 1789 by the radical publisher Joseph Johnson. One of the most unusual scientific tracts ever written, its botanical classification is enlivened with alarmingly anthropocentric descriptions of the goings-on of male and female genitals in their 'nuptial bed,' as Darwin refers to the calyx of the flower. Because some flowers have many male parts (some of which can be sterile – and thus liable to be characterised as 'beardless youths') and they share the nuptial bed with just one female part, some of Darwin's 'scenes' resemble the interior of a sultan's bedroom – or a Roman orgy – more than they do a violet or pansy.

Erasmus Darwin was working at the dawn of the modern era of classification, and throughout the late eighteenth and first half of the nineteenth centuries interest in botany grew apace. It was during this period that many of the world's great natural history museums and herbaria were founded, their collections forming a vast system that allowed the classification of the world to go on ever more expeditiously. And yet still no-one could demonstrate that their particular classification was nearer the 'true classification' than anyone else's. It was Erasmus's grandson Charles who provided the answer to that age-old riddle. Evolution by natural selection helped explain the orderliness of nature, and more importantly, it provided the mechanism that had given us the family tree of life. Yet for a century after the Darwinian revolution, most taxonomists continued with their task of classifying the world without fully absorbing the message evolution held for them.

What many taxonomists did was to say that if two organisms looked similar, then they must be related. It took a German entomologist, Willi Hennig, to change that. He saw that only some similarities tell us who is most closely related to whom. To illustrate the nature of Hennig's breakthrough, we can imagine a family whose members have always had black hair. But then a child with red hair is born, and she gives birth to more redheads. These offspring are more closely related to their black-haired cousins than they are to more distant black-haired relatives. Yet anyone using black hair to understand relationships might misclassify all black-haired individuals as close relatives, and the redheads as more distant. Red hair, however, providing it breeds true, would be an accurate indicator of relatedness, at least within the redhead family. Hennig's work gave rise to a new scientific method called cladistics, and it is this method that underpins Tudge's book.

*

Scientific classification had come a long way between Linnaeus and Hennig, yet despite the great advances, before the 1980s

What Is a Tree?

many botanical classifications bore little resemblance to the true evolutionary relationships of plants. One final discovery was required before such classifications could be improved – the deciphering and use of DNA. Is the mushroom animal, mineral or vegetable? Most non-scientists I'm sure would place it in a classification of convenience – perhaps with the cauliflower in the vegetable tribe. Indeed traditional classifications place the fungi alongside the plants. Yet modern evolutionary studies using DNA reveal that mushrooms are more closely related to human beings than to the cauliflower. Given just the three choices the child's game allows, the mushroom is an animal.

It's not that DNA provides some sort of divine revelation about who is related to whom, for it too is prone to convergence in evolution and errors of interpretation. But as botanists combine the results of DNA studies with more traditional methods such as the study of wood structure, and seed and leaf type, ever more robust classifications (ones that are increasingly difficult to find fault with) are emerging, and they reveal just how far astray our classifications of convenience can be. Who, for example, would ever have guessed that plane trees (sycamores to many Americans) and members of the protea family, such as South Africa's proteas and Australia's banksias, are close relatives? Even more mind-stretching is the newly published finding that the mighty teak is intimately related to herbs such as mint, oregano and basil. Even as I recount it, I'm astonished that botanists now believe cucumbers are close relatives of oaks and beeches – far closer, indeed, than oaks are to sycamores.

This new knowledge, along with an ever-improving fossil record, reveals that the evolution of trees has been more epic than Erasmus, Darwin or Linnaeus could ever have imagined. As Tudge puts it:

> It is a wonderful thing to contemplate a living tree, or a fossil one, or any other creature. It is even more moving when we add the fourth dimension, of time, and see in our mind's eye how the ancestors of the tree that grows in the field next door first saw the light in some remote corner of the globe millions or hundreds of millions of years in the past, and floated on its respective bit of continent as the continent itself circum-

navigated the globe, and skirted around the glaciers of the ice age, and perhaps sweated it out in some primeval, long-gone swamp, with alligators around its feet and the world's first hawks and kingfishers scouting from its branches.

As rich as the new discoveries are, *The Tree* is about far more than plant classification, and it begins with a question: 'And what, pray, are trees, that anyone should presume to write a book about them?' As you might have already guessed, one of the most challenging lessons of *The Tree* is that the entire concept of 'tree' as a classificatory category has no evolutionary reality whatever, for the things we call trees have arisen multiple times from humbler vegetation, and trees have repeatedly been transformed into vines, shrubs and herbs. Some tree species, indeed, can exist as either shrubs or trees. As Tudge says, 'Nature was not designed to make life easy for biologists.'

*

At this point, rather than becoming bogged down in elaborate evolutionary explanation, Tudge gives us a child's definition of a tree as 'a big plant with a stick up the middle,' and the 'stick up the middle,' it turns out, is one of the most fascinating and useful objects in nature. Some woods can be made as sharp as steel and cannot be worked except with tools of tungsten and diamond. Others, such as the Japanese cedar, can be buried in the earth until they become deep green in colour, and are then regarded as a kind of semiprecious stone.

The key ingredient in wood is lignin, a chemical compound that binds together wood's celluloid fibres. Plants without it, which are called herbs, use water pressure to stay upright. Real wood only exists where the lignin is laid down in an intricate and meticulous manner; and wood, according to Tudge, 'is one of the wonders of the universe ... remarkably complex ... minutely structured ... lovely to look upon, and infinitely various.' 'If humanity had only one kind of timber to draw upon it could think itself blessed ... But in practice we have many thousands – a tree for every job, and for every decorative caprice.'

Tudge's documentation of the specialist uses of timber opens a world of craftsmanship and acute observation which is unknown to most of us. Why, one wonders, is the katsura tree of East Asia especially suitable for the manufacture of pencils and Japanese shoes? And who discovered that the lignum vitae of Central America makes splendid rollers and wheels in pulleys that are hard to get at, because the wood is self-lubricating; or that abura wood is excellent for battery boxes, because it resists acid? There is something about the timber of the coachwood of New South Wales that suits it to the manufacture of gunstocks and musical instruments, while tropical American snakewood makes marvellous violin bows and umbrella handles. Snakewood would not do for xylophones, however: for them one must seek out the wood of a *Dalbergia* tree. Presumably someone knows why the wood of the African ekki tree was used to support the tracks of the Paris metro. In view of the present sad state of Africa's rainforests, one wonders where replacement timbers will come from should the existing ones wear out.

Familiar trees sometimes have mysterious uses. Who for example would have guessed that elm is favoured in the manufacture of 'buttock-moulded seats,' or that basswood was the best timber for the fronts of pulpits? And why is it that the jacaranda is favoured for making pianos – but only in Egypt? Tudge has seen cogs made of hornbeam at work in a century-old brewery near his home, where they perform better than cogs of iron; such sights perhaps inspired him to write: 'The intricate knowledge that our forebears had of each kind of plant and its caprices and possibilities never ceases to astonish me.' It is 'knowledge now largely lost, or at least confined to academic tracts of whimsical accounts like this one. Maybe when the fossil fuels run out and heavy industry has run its course, such wonders may be rediscovered.'

Of course trees have mysteries far deeper than the functional qualities of the material composing their 'stick up the middle.' Despite all of his botanical knowledge Tudge does not know why the Indian rain tree goes out of its way to encourage epiphytes – plants that grow on other plants – when most trees seek to discourage them. Some indigenous people possess enormous botanical knowledge. Tudge writes of Brazilian Indians known as *mateiros* whose expert knowledge of tree species and their uses outstrips that of the wisest professor. Not all indigenous knowledge of trees, however, may be correct. Tudge is unable to confirm whether the asoka tree (a close relative of the Indian rain tree) does in fact blossom more vigorously if kicked by a young woman, as reputed in Indian folklore. In the botanical world, however, scientific facts can be more fascinating than folklore: who would have imagined that alder trees accumulate gold in their tissues, or that their near relative the birch accumulates heavy metals in its leaves, and so can be used to clean up toxic mine sites? *The Tree* is full of similarly wonderful scientific facts and folklore.

After leading us through such diversions Tudge asks again – but this time from a functional point of view – what is a tree? His answer, which pertains to all life including ourselves, is profound. Living tissue, he says, 'is constantly replacing itself, even when it seems to stay the same. It is not a thing but a performance.'

The performance that is a tree is in fact an interaction between the four elements recognised by the pre-Socratic Greeks: air, fire, earth and water. Air is the principal ingredient, for trees are quite literally made of air, or at least the carbon dioxide (CO_2) it contains. For this gas, combined with the hydrogen wrested from water (H_2O) by photosynthesis, is what makes those great trunks, arching bows, and leafy canopies. (Photosynthesis occurs when the green pigment chlorophyll assists in combining carbon dioxide, water and light, thus transforming the sun's energy into a chemical form.) Next time you look at a tree, think that it was, not so long ago, CO_2 wafting about in our atmosphere. It's a thought that has great import for our battle to control global warming. For all our ingenuity, humanity has never devised a machine that can so efficiently and elegantly convert greenhouse gases into the most wondrous natural sculptures known.

*

There are 'around' 60,000 species of trees and still counting, which prompts Tudge to ask, 'How on Earth can anyone – the most astute of hunters and gatherers or the most learned of professors – keep tabs on 350,000 or so species of plants including around 60,000 trees?' The answer – indeed a sort of salvation – comes in the form of D.J. Mabberley and his wondrous *Plant-Book*. From Aaron's rod to the obscure *Zyzyxia*, it lists them all in

What Is a Tree?

alphabetical order, and with such wit, elegance and compression as to be breathtaking. Indeed I suspect that it is the source of many of the more intriguing facts enumerated by Tudge.

The Plant-Book is, being all-encompassing and indispensable, the botanical equivalent of Johnson's *Dictionary*. In the acknowledgments Mabberley provides the astonishing information that 'the first edition ... was typed with the author's right index finger on a Brother electric typewriter.' The undertaking of this Herculean effort clearly required fortification, and Mabberley records his 'appreciation of the work of Philip Glass, Malcolm McLaren, Franz Schubert (1897–1828) and Carl Maria von Weber (1786–1826), which has kept me sane during some of the more tedious episodes.'

A part of just one of the hundreds of thousands of entries that compose this work must suffice to testify to its excellence:

> *Cannabis* ... more northerly cult. (in China for 4500 yrs, obligatory crop in Eliz. times in GB, where illegal since 1951) for fibre (hemp used for ropes, fibre-board, paper etc. since 4000 BC esp. in N & NE China where form. only fibre available, prob. used in first paper (AD 105) there) & subsp. *indica* (Lam.) ... more southerly cult. principally for psychotropic drugs (marijuana, marihuana (Mex.), pot (US, where allegedly the biggest cash crop worth $32 billion), dagga (S Afr.), kif (Morocco)), cannabis resin, which exudes from the glandular hairs & is used like opium (effects described 2736 BC by Chinese Emperor Shen Neng). In India, 3 common forms: ganja (dried unripe infrs), charras or churras (resin knocked off twigs, bark etc.) & bhang (largely mature lvs of wild pl). Smoked ('weed') with or without tobacco ('skunk') in cigarettes ('joints') or taken as an intoxicating liquid formed from it (hashish; Arabic for 'hashishtaker'=root word of 'assassin'), in food or drink (e.g. in comm. beers in the Netherlands) it has a stimulating & pleasantly exciting effect, relief from muscular sclerosis, cerebral palsy & glaucoma, though addictive & in excess can cause delirium & 'moral weakness and depravity' (Uphof). Seeds the source of hemp seed oil used in varnishes, food, soap, lip balm & fuel in Nazi tanks etc. & used as birdseed & to attract fishes.

Such are the uses of a single species, whose only near relative is the hops vine that gives us good beer. After reading *The Plant-Book* and *The Tree* it is plainly obvious that the extinction of even a single tree species, out of the 60,000 known, would be an immense tragedy for humanity and the natural world.

New York Review of Books

Many Me

Kate Rossmanith

On the front desk at the head office of Sydney IVF, in Kent Street, rests a marble statue of three fused figures. Two adults and a child form a clenched posy of hands, knees and feet, and the stone is so dark and smooth it's impossible to tell where one limb ends and another begins. Upstairs from reception, above appointments for couples seeking fertility treatment, are the research laboratories. Sydney IVF is one of four organisations in Australia with a licence to use spare human embryos for stem-cell research: permission to extract cells from days-old embryos and create stem-cell lines. 'Immortal lines', the scientists call them, for they divide and duplicate themselves indefinitely.

In November 2006, in an almost-split vote, members of the Senate overturned the 2002 ban on human therapeutic cloning. This year, the states are reviewing their laws to reflect the federal law, with legislation being passed recently in Victoria and New South Wales. While it continues to be illegal to grow an individual from a cloned cell, researchers will soon be able to harvest embryonic stem-cell lines from the DNA of a living person: cell lines, argue scientists, which may lead to therapies for type 1 diabetes, cystic fibrosis and other diseases. Until this year, the legislation restricted researchers to developing embryonic stem-cell lines from surplus IVF embryos that would otherwise be discarded.

Of the thousands of frozen beginnings at Sydney IVF – fertilised embryos stored by couples for future use – around 400 have so far been donated to the labs for stem-cell research. 'Half the couples are happy to donate their unused embryos, rather than have them thrown away,' Teija Peura tells me. Peura, the principal scientist at Sydney IVF's stem-cell lab, is Finnish and full-faced with seamless Nordic skin, and I can't tell her age. A framed photo of Mel Gibson sits on her desk. 'He's a hunk. He's also opposed to the research I'm doing – but then, everyone's entitled to their opinion,' she says.

Each embryo from which stem cells are derived is less than a week old; it's a hollow ball of 100 cells, a speck smaller than a grain of sand. The three trillion cells that make up our bodies can be traced back to one, a zygote, the meeting of our parents' chromosomes. But that's not when life begins, Peura explains. 'The zygote, and an early dividing embryo, is like two people living in the same house, but nothing's going on. The life of a new individual begins at the fourth cell division, when the genes of that new individual become active and take control of development.' Sydney IVF scientists extract stem cells from the centre of the ball, the inner mass cell, and allow them to grow in culture dishes incubated at body temperature.

Peura opens an oven-like door and takes out a small Petri dish. 'We just thawed them,' she says. I press my face to the microscope and focus on fine paint sprays. Embryonic stem-cell colonies, sprayed flecks carrying a couple's DNA, look like delicate squirts of spores. The groups of cell droplets, no bigger than five-thousandths of a millimetre, are bounded patches of life. And they're 'pluripotent': 'The value of embryonic stem cells is their potential to transform into a wide range of other cells. They are not yet specialised for particular functions in organs and tissues,' Peura explains. As 'blank' cells, stem cells have the ability to act as a repair system for our bodies because they can replenish other cells.

Because the ban on therapeutic cloning has been lifted, researchers will be able to produce 'embryos' with the sole purpose of creating stem-cell lines. Scientists will take the nucleus of a human cell – the DNA of one of my skin cells – and inject it into a woman's unfertilised egg whose nucleus has been removed.

Without the introduction of a man's sperm – for my DNA holds the full human complement – the egg will be stimulated in such a way that it begins to divide. If it were then implanted in a woman and left to grow, it could, theoretically, produce an individual with my genetic coding, a person who looks almost identical to me. Dolly the sheep was born this way. Instead, the egg cell will grow for five days before the inner cell mass is removed and used to create a stem-cell line with my genetic make-up.

The delicate frameworks for stem-cell research, in Australia and elsewhere, sit uneasily between science, ethics and religion, for the technology carries with it controversies around human life. While stem cells are found in adult tissues such as bone marrow, those in the early stages of an embryo are considered more malleable and therefore as having more therapeutic potential. However, in creating embryonic stem-cell lines, the embryo itself dies. *You are creating life only to destroy it,* argue opponents of therapeutic cloning. They say it is unethical to create human embryos for the sole purpose of scientific experimentation. Advocates of therapeutic cloning, however, argue that the life of an embryo is not of the same order as that of a human being. They say it would be unethical *not* to welcome research that widens the scope for the eventual development of treatment for lethal and debilitating diseases.

Politicians, patient groups, scientists, ethicists, religious leaders, the media and the public debate the slippery question, 'When does a human life begin?', but equally unsettling ones run silently beside it. Therapeutic cloning not only asks us to consider whether we are, on the one hand, 'destroying' life by extinguishing embryos; or, on the other, 'enhancing' it by potentially relieving human suffering. The research simultaneously asks us to reconsider the very boundaries of human life. When scientists extract stem cells from the embryo containing my DNA, and when they coax those cells to divide and multiply, they cultivate tiny, infinite colonies of me-ness. It's an uncomfortable thought. At the same time, stem-cell debates also ignore a question affecting millions of women: where exactly will the eggs come from?

*

Like the IVF industry, stem-cell research requires large numbers of oöcytes, or egg cells. Currently scientists use hundreds of eggs from women before they successfully create just one stem-cell line. As more countries legalise therapeutic cloning, the global demand for ova escalates, and with it, the dubious procurement of eggs.

For ova donors, egg retrieval procedures, even in countries with advanced hospital systems, are painful and carry risk. Women undergo hormone injections to stimulate ovulation, before a needle is inserted into the vagina, through the vaginal wall, to retrieve the one egg released every month. This egg harvesting practice is used in IVF treatment; however, because it is so invasive, few women outside the IVF system are willing to donate for stem-cell research. The procedure carries a 5 per cent risk of ovarian hyperstimulation syndrome, which involves pain, abdominal inflammation, possible renal failure and infertility, thrombosis and cardiac instability. It can be fatal.

In Australia, ova donation is treated like other organ donation: the eggs are a sort of gift, with donors minimally compensated. Other countries differ in their procurement of eggs, and the repercussions for women are inevitable. 'The expanding demand for research oöcytes will be most consequential for the female populations of nations that do not regulate oöcyte transfer through donation systems,' according to Catherine Waldby, an international research fellow at Sydney University. There are currently exploitative networks operating in the ova trade, 'and those same networks have already been used to procure oöcytes for stem-cell research,' she says. IVF clinics in Spain and Romania, for example, have brokered sales between poor, female vendors and rich purchasers, beyond the borders of national regulation. 'Women, desperate for money, undergo a month of major hormone treatment, followed by invasive surgery to harvest the ova.'

In the United States, where there is virtually an open internal market for ova, and where privately funded stem-cell research is unregulated at a federal level, there are no federally regulated barriers to prevent the reproductive market in ova becoming a market for research ova as well. In Boston, the Bedford Stem-Cell Research Foundation solicits women to 'donate' ova for research.

'It has recruited ova vendors from the Boston area via newspaper advertisements, paying them around $4,000 per procedure,' says Waldby. She is concerned that impoverished female populations are becoming vendors for national biotechnology industries. 'In the US, the juxtaposition of poor, ghettoised populations with high technology corridors, for example around Boston, make these kind of markets even more feasible,' she explains. 'For poorer women involved in the global oöcyte trade, an approach to oöcyte supply that combines issues of safety, consent and clinical conditions with those of workers' rights, organised representation for vendors and regulated negotiation of conditions, may yield benefits in terms of harm minimisation and transparency.'

*

Despite urgent calls for the protection of ova donors, arguments around therapeutic cloning focus heavily on the moral status of the embryo: does it have a right to life? According to many ethicists, it's a debate that is irresolvable. More than 2000 years ago, philosophers like Plato asked these very questions: when does life begin? What does it mean to be human?

A five-day-old ball of cells may or may not be *a* human life, but it is human life, with its innate intent to be and grow. It's not extinguished when the stem cells are extracted; it becomes more alive than ever, producing sprawling copies of our cells. Part of the discomfort we might have towards therapeutic cloning is not that something dies, but that something lives, and can be repeated infinitely. This may help explain why the interests of egg donors are overlooked in favour of debates about what life, what a human, is. Stem-cell technologies violently disrupt who we think we are. That colonies of our flesh – identical copies of our DNA – might multiply beyond the boundaries of our bodies questions a fundamental principle governing Western self-consciousness: our uniqueness.

The idea has survived for centuries. Twenty-six hundred years ago, when Homer wrote of the Trojan War, he was so dazzled by mortality, by the individual's irreplaceability, that he left out a critical detail: Helen had a double. 'For ten years a war raged around a woman who was not actually there, for an impalpable ghost,' writes the Italian author Roberto Calasso. In telling the story, Homer ignores the likely possibility that Helen never arrived in Troy, that Paris left her in Egypt and journeyed home with her phantom copy, perhaps a body-double, a woman just like her, or at least her symbolic presence. More startling than the existence of a copy of the Spartan Queen is Homer's omission of it. He did so, suggests Calasso, because it would have dissolved the reader's enchantment with Helen, 'the enchantment with the unique'.

This enchantment with our own uniqueness remains central to the Western imagination of the self. Therapeutic cloning not only shakes that idea; it also confronts our notion of ourselves as circumscribed individuals. As cells circulate between us, our bodies become materially implicated in each other in new and extreme ways. Our sharing of fleshy particles, beyond lovers' exchanges, or breastfeeding mothers and babies, has been a medical miracle of the last hundred years. Blood, solid organs, bone marrow can be donated from person to person. And yet an idea of the complete, discrete body has always dominated our identities. 'While contemporary medicine emphasises the individualism of our bodies, by telling us to take individual responsibility for our health, one of the major medical innovations in the twentieth century was the development of techniques to circulate biological material,' explains Waldby.

Stem-cell technologies are radical enough to challenge our notion of individuality both biologically and psychologically. In cell therapy, 'my' cells might be used some day to heal your lungs, our separateness collapsing irrevocably. While this transgression is the territory of organ transplants and blood transfusions, cell therapies stretch it further still: it's not my kidney – a discrete organ – placed in you, or a quantifiable surge of my blood through your veins, but infinite cells. Through an indefinite fusing of bodies, what disappears are the safe, certain lines where my flesh stops and yours begins.

This sense of ourselves as separate beings, detached from others, is not universal. As anthropologist Clifford Geertz famously observed: 'The Western conception of the person as a bounded, unique, integrated motivational and cognitive universe, organized into a distinctive whole and set contrastively against other such wholes, is a rather peculiar idea within the context of the world's cultures.' Throughout the Middle Ages, the carnivals which dominated European popular culture suspended the distance between bodies: revellers drank, ate, sweated, spat, fornicated and shat together, merging individuals into a corporeal mass. And in many cultures today, there exists a latent connective tissue between people and their world. The Warlpiri people, in the Northern Territory, coalesce person and country, fusing the body and the environment in terms of internal physiology. 'Thus, a sacred site is a womb, the odour of a person's sweat may evoke the aromatic sap of a particular species of tree, and a deposit of white clay may be said to be the semen of a Dreaming ancestor,' the anthropologist Michael Jackson has observed.

At Sydney IVF, Teija Peura drags a second chair to her desk and we sit. On her computer screen, she brings up a photo of a five-day-old human embryo. It takes me a beat to recognise what I'm seeing, and then I know: it's a perfect earth. It looks like the images of our planet NASA sends from space, a perfect pearly sphere. 'Embryos for almost every organism look exactly the same at that stage of development,' she tells me. Grown from tiny earths, we are already more a part of one another, part of our world's flesh, than we can imagine.

The Monthly

It's Too Easy To Say 'God Is Dead'

Guy Rundle

'Read the words,' said the angel to the man in the cave crouching over the lettered bolt of cloth. 'But I cannot read,' said the man, so the angel poured them into him. 'Take your son to the mountain and sacrifice him,' said God to the man to whom, in his old age, he had given the son as a last blessing. 'Take, eat,' said the man, 'this is my body.'

Scraps of scenes, moments of revelation, half-remembered from Sunday school, RE classes, bored afternoons in church, Sunday mornings waiting for the cartoons to start. Scenes that anyone under about sixty could reasonably have supposed, at any stage in their life, to be fading, have actually held fast, have come back to the centre of the culture. Through 2007 and beyond, God is going to be at the centre of a whole lot of discussions about who we are and what life is all about.

This conversation has been building for a long time, of course, but it started to hit a new level with Mel Gibson's *Passion of the Christ*, via Richard Dawkins's book *The God Delusion*, to the crash-course we all got in Sunni–Shia theological differences, to the relentless pressing forward of 'intelligent design', culminating – in Australia at least – in Kevin Rudd's citing of the German theologian Dietrich Bonhoeffer as the principal influence on his life and politics.

Two years ago one could have mistaken this for a blip, a hiccup, a passing fad, a knock-on for the sudden enthusiasm for yoga and Buddhism. And so it may prove, but alternatively it is possible we are on the cusp of a new era, one that puts some key and assumed features of modernity into reverse.

For decades, the assumption that we were passing into a post-theological world has been an article of, well, faith, not only for the ever broadening group of people who describe themselves as agnostic, but also for many believers as well.

Those within organised religions who continued to believe in some form of real, nameable presence, or being, called God were quietly convinced that they were entering a long, perhaps permanent period in which holders of such a faith would be in a permanent minority.

In his theological-historical novel *Sword of Honour* Evelyn Waugh – a Catholic convert – had his hero Guy Crouchback imagining himself somewhere in a catacomb as the last priest at a Mass conducted by the last Pope, as the modern age ground the truth of God between the two smooth stones of fascism and communism. The various rationalist and humanist societies – though they had acquired a distinctly crankish air even by the 1930s – had been rallying points for a militantly atheist point of view.

More recent developments, such as liberation theology, have obscured the degree to which the global Marxist movement saw the demolition of the church – often literally – as a key part of its mission.

If anything suggested that God was on the way out, it was the difficulty established churches got themselves into whenever they tried to talk about the God thing.

Before World War Two, theology had been in a prolonged crisis as the notion of an interventionist God – the idea that God is somehow like a superperson actively watching over everything – had become increasingly unsustainable in a world run on revealed scientific and technical principles.

Though people in the West had found it difficult to believe the literal truth of the Bible for decades, it was not until a range of theologians and philosophers – from existentialists Kierkegaard and Nikolai Berdyaev in the nineteenth century to Rudolf Bultmann, Martin Buber and others in the twentieth century – really began to interrogate the key notions of 'faith', 'gospel', 'truth', and ultimately the notion of a presence, that what is often called a demythologised religion came about.

While all this was going on within the higher reaches of the official churches, the literal evangelical tradition – in the 1950s largely personified by Billy Graham, whose 1959 Australian visit drew crowds of up to 200,000 in each city – was quietly gathering strength, to suddenly burst onto centre-stage in the 1970s.

The lack of attention paid to fundamentalism was not only a product of the 1960s parade going the other way – but also due to the fact that almost everyone outside it, religious and secular alike, was seeing it in exclusively sociological terms.

Born-again Christianity was the last gasp of an old literalist religion, it was held, and its appeal was substantially to people with little education or social power, to whom established churches could no longer give the guarantee of a rock-solid cosmology and a real presence.

If God could not even be defined beyond the 'ground of being', there was no way to honestly guarantee that Jesus was riding the bus with you and was with our boys in 'Nam.

Indeed, what is often taken as the single greatest text of modern theology – Karl Barth's 1922 commentary on 'Epistle to Romans' – argues that by accepting Jesus's birth as the Son of God in the world, we accept nothing else can be assumed from it and to try and fill this nothingness with human beliefs about what God would think – from gay marriage to invading Iraq – is the ultimate attack on God, since it tries to define God in human terms.

That's hardly something that the poor migrant, the lonely pensioner or the dying child wants to hear, but a very persuasive answer to the mystery of what God could be for any intelligent person in a modern civilisation.

For those of us who are philosophical materialists, there is really no mystery about God at all. Beginning with the early nineteenth-century German philosopher Ludwig Feuerbach, who was deeply influential on Karl Marx, we can say that God is the projection of humanity's growing understanding of its own powers – into an eternal and transcendent realm; with the French sociologist Emile Durkheim we can say that religion is society worshipping itself via a necessary veil that allows arbitrary cultural values to appear as grounded and God-given, thus making meaningful individual and social life possible; with Carl Jung we can suggest that gods are an externalisation of the concrete identities that form the foundation of individual selfhood; and with Sigmund Freud that our trace-memories of the experience of the deep pleasures and terrors of infantile dependency form the basis of a general idea of impossibly powerful beings capable of uplifting us – ascension to heaven as a giant game of aeroplane – or annihilating us.

All these explanations, together with a host of more recent evolutionary biological ones, can be adduced to explain it, yet none gives us a complete picture.

More useful to an understanding of religion – and particularly for the West of monotheism, the revolutionary development of belief in a single God, which more than anything defines Western (including Islamic) civilisation – is a closer reflection on its history, on the layers of separate ways of belief that went into it.

We are accustomed to thinking of the Judeo-Christian tradition as coming from the desert, of Abraham's journey to (so he thought) sacrifice his son Isaac, of the burning bush, and so on. Yet it has to be remembered that Abraham was going out into the desert from his home Ur-of-the-Chaldees that is the Sumerian city state of Ur, not far from present-day Baghdad, maybe sometime before 1000 BC.

Ur's population was somewhere between 20,000 and 50,000, a huge metropolis, with temples, palaces, money, bureaucracy, taverns, festivals – everything we associate with modern city living. Each city of the empire had its own set of gods – and the notion had not yet developed that my belief in my gods must preclude a recognition that your gods were equally real. This is completely different to the contemporary idea of relativism, whereby we simply agree to let other people have their beliefs without really taking them seriously. It was the idea that these gods were both universal and particular. It is a way of thinking that we simply can no longer fully enter into.

To the north-east, Zoroastrianism had developed as the first faith that was both monotheistic in its conception of God and dualist in its notions of two forces we would recognise as good and evil, while in Egypt there was a limited eruption of pure monotheism in the worship of the sun god, Aten. Rather than a void into which God came, it was a cosmopolitan world, built on trade, in which the market hosted competing theologies as much as obsidian. It was not out of nothing the one God came to Abraham, but out of an almost unfeasible plurality. The sheer profusion of the many suggested the one.

Yet the notion that Abraham founded the Jewish religion is another Sunday-school teaching that does not long survive scrutiny, for it is clear that the Israelite tribes continued to worship a variety of gods, that the early versions of Jahweh show him to be a particular god of war, balanced by other more pastoral deities and that Judaism as a formalised, monotheistic religion was consolidated, and then projected backwards, much later – around the time of the rise of the Greek city states, and possibly influenced by carriage of that newfangled thinking technique, philosophy.

Yet once it does develop, it marks a clear qualitative change in Western and Semitic ways of thinking, because the single God is increasingly without attributes. Unlike Zeus or other pantheistic gods, He is not of a certain general form and does not have the inclination to come down and wander the earth at will. Though man is made in His image, the notion that an image of God can be found by looking to human beings is increasingly taken as an abstract one.

All of His prophets are themselves definitively men and the central notion the Messiah has not yet come to earth serves to act as a permanent deferral, which mediates between literal and metaphorical understandings. The promise of a coming Messiah can be taken as something to be fulfilled, any day now, or it can be taken as an indication there will always be a gap between God and man, which humanity must fill, by taking responsibility for ethical action and meaning.

Paradoxically, while Christianity represents a development on from Judaism, it can also be seen as a step backward theologically. If Judaism is an absent God, served by present humans, Christianity is a Jewish sect so impatient for redemption that it must find the Messiah not only come to earth but reappearing in the mouth of every believer during communion. Christianity's great development is that it takes the tribal law of retribution ostensibly governing Jewish morality – an eye for an eye – and reverses it: not, do what has been done to you, but do as you would like to be done to, even if – as the notion of 'turning the other cheek' would have – that wish is not honoured by your enemy.

Christianity, in that respect, is a product of the intersection of Jerusalem and Caesar, of tribal reciprocity carried to the level of universal humanity as embodied in the Pax Romana. The Roman empire, uniting innumerable peoples (in subjection), makes it possible to conceive of all humanity as one.

Though Christianity always presented itself as monotheistic, the doctrine of the Trinity was offered as a deliberately paradoxical notion of it, something beyond the possibility of human understanding, even though it could be formulated in intelligible human sentences. Though early, suppressed factions of the church rejected the Trinitarian idea, it was not until the Renaissance and the Reformation that the notion of a unitary God would come to the fore.

Deep scholarship is not required to understand the fundamental difference between Islam (and Judaism) on one side, and Christianity on the other. A simple visit to their respective houses of worship will do it. Take the cities of Andalusia in southern Spain, for example, where the buildings of the Moorish empire and their Catholic successors sometimes co-exist. In Jerez, amid the innumerable detail, the saints, Mary, the leadlight windows depicting the stations of the cross etc., the surviving mosque – with its round, highly decorated, but abstract walls and a simple round hole at the top – immediately impresses us as more sophisticated, because it does not seek to represent the unrepresentable by the pure piling on of detail. A similar restraint can be seen in most synagogues.

We will have to wait until the seventeenth century and the rise of plain puritan and Methodist chapels for such a deliberate deployment of absence – of God as a negative presence – to be invoked within the Christian tradition. It is partly because of the influence of Islam within Christendom – principally through the Islamic philosopher Averroes, whose commentaries on Aristotle emphasising the role of reason over revelation in the understanding of God were extremely influential on Thomas Aquinas – that a fully monotheistic idea can eventually fight its way into the centre of Christian thought.

The importance of Islam might be that it is the last of the great religions, occurring at a point where humanity is passing out of the long era in which prophecy was possible. The psychologist Julian Jaynes in his 1976 book *The Origin of Consciousness in the Breakdown of the Bicameral Mind* argued that the rise of many new religions in this era was possible because people's minds had not yet become fully sealed – the internal voice we hear as ourselves speaking to ourselves was, before about 500 BC, perceived as an other and sometimes as the gods speaking directly to us. Culture and even evolution knit the mind together and we become individuals with an interior consciousness.

In this scenario, Mohammed's experience as the prophet – the verses of the Koran reportedly came to him with great pain and anguish, in contrast to a millennium earlier when people would tend to hear the voice of the gods coming through loud and clear – can be taken as an indication that such prophetic ability was disappearing from its hitherto central role in human life.

It is only with the Reformation and the rise of Protestant theology that Christianity begins to catch up to this more austere conception of God.

For what is most significant in the development of monotheism over the centuries is the manner in which God gradually loses all worldly character, becoming an unknowable point of love. Influential was not only Karl Barth, but also the work of Martin Heidegger, whose 1927 book *Being and Time* allowed us to get out of a few contradictions in the way we think about, well, everything. Heidegger's argument is that people – subjects – and things – objects – have very different ways of being.

Subjects exist, they are what they do, their beingness is defined by their freedom to become and to have meaning. Objects lack that possibility ('a chair is still a chair/ when there's no-one sitting there,' as noted Heideggerians Burt Bacharach and Hal David had it) but this enormous difference is covered over by the use of the same word 'is' for both states.

Given that there are two ways of being we know of, there is no reason to suppose that God would fit into either of them, is neither subject nor object. 'God does not exist, but God is real' is the way Australian Christian poet/philosopher Kevin Hart puts it. Such a position allows a theologian to concede all the material critiques of God – the social and psychological causes of the idea of the historically given idea of God – without these in any way exhausting the idea of what God might be, or what concepts such as love, prayer or origin might be.

To these critiques has recently been added Richard Dawkins's work *The God Delusion*, which has attracted a great deal of criticism (most notably a spectacular attack from Terry Eagleton in the *London Review of Books*) but which is a more effective compendium of arguments against old notions of God – i.e. those held by 95 per cent of people who call themselves believers – than many of his detractors would be willing to admit. Yet leaving aside his separate argument that the world would be better off without religion – Stalinism and Nazism were, among other things, pretty much non-better attempts to do exactly that – Dawkins has not really replied to the believers' most sophisticated arguments, of a God that is neither subject nor object, nor is it likely he would credit such a distinction with much meaning.

More importantly, Dawkins is quite unable to persuasively answer the most pressing question – why God now? The religious have an easy answer – people have turned back to Him after the disasters of a rationalist century. Atheism, the decidedly agnostic commentator John Gray notes in *Straw Dogs*, will come to be seen as a brief and odd period in human history. Those of us atheists who are less irrationally hostile to the very structure of religious belief than Dawkins might return to the point made by Durkheim in the *Elementary Structures of Religious Life*, that a society in which life is meaningful has never in human history been either fully transparent to itself or open-ended in all directions. It requires both a closed set of valued special things – the sacred – to ground the profane, i.e. mundane existence, and a sense of the eternal to ground the temporary, i.e. life.

What we have been experimenting with in the last century, and in a supercharged fashion in the last decade, is a world-society in which all that is sacred is profaned by its transformation into a commodity with a cash price, thus making it possible to render everything in terms of everything else. At the core of this the world is increasingly being radically changed by science, high technology and globalisation until nothing remains that is not transparent, segmented, disassembled and manipulable.

Once you live in such a world, the principal cultural problem becomes an endlessly expanding nihilism in which nothing, of itself, has any intrinsic value. Older frameworks of meaning are disappearing so rapidly that people are giddy with it. From quantum cosmology to Piss Christ via miles of identikit malls and the cybertundra of the internet – what was thrilling has become alarming, because one is brushing up against nothingness.

In panic at that, people reach out for whatever is the most concrete, charged and all-embracing store of meaning, a revealed God. Indeed much of the despicable hatred and fear directed at Islam from Western commentators is nothing less than a form of existential envy, directed at a culture which has retained a capacity the West has lost, to ground itself.

The success of creationism and intelligent design is precisely because of the contradiction of holding such beliefs in a civilisation in which most of what we depend on – cutting-edge medicines for example – is based on the endlessly reconfirmed principle that species evolve.

Where both Roman Catholicism and traditional Protestantism attempt to develop a faith strong in reason, fundamentalism takes absurdity – whether it be seventy-two virgins, or God designing individual bacteria – as a sign of faith.

The more gleefully you can sustain a set of beliefs that every other practice and process of a hi-tech civilisation tells you is ludicrous, the greater the bulwark against its engulfing nothingness.

The old atheist/rationalist belief was that knowledge would be its own reward, that once we realised this was all there is, we would make heaven on earth, or damn close – as captured in the old anarchist slogan, 'If God existed, it would be necessary to abolish him.'

The evidence of the last few years would indicate that we may have got it the wrong way round. We will have to change the way we live, and restore to an ungrounded world some of the more immediate and intimate frameworks, some measure of voluntary constraint and boundedness to social life – that is, guarantee through human reason what has hitherto been mediated via the idea of God – before the need for an old-man-in-the-sky starts to fade.

That would not mean the triumph of the cold and smug atheism of Dawkins, but rather – as Dietrich Bonhoeffer, man of the moment, forecast and hoped for, weeks before his 1945 execution by the Nazis – the rise of a post-religious form of belief, in which a real dialogue between theism and atheism can begin.

Australian Financial Review

Faith in Politics

Kevin Rudd

Above the Great West Door of Westminster Abbey are arrayed ten great statues of the martyrs of the Church. Not Peter, Stephen, James or the familiar names of the saints sacrificed during the great Roman persecution before Constantine's conversion. No: these are martyrs of the twentieth century, when the age of faith was, in the minds of many in the West, already tottering towards its collapse.

One of those honoured above the Great West Door is Dietrich Bonhoeffer, the German theologian, pastor and peace activist. Bonhoeffer is, without doubt, the man I admire most in the history of the twentieth century. He was a man of faith. He was a man of reason. He was a man of letters who was as well read in history and literature as he was in the intensely academic Lutheran theology of the German university tradition. He was never a nationalist, always an internationalist. And above all, he was a man of action who wrote prophetically in 1937 that 'when Christ calls a man, he bids him come and die.' For Bonhoeffer, whatever the personal cost, there was no moral alternative other than to fight the Nazi state with whatever weapons were at his disposal.

Three weeks before the end of World War II, Bonhoeffer was hanged by the SS because of his complicity in the plot to assassinate Adolf Hitler. This year marks the centenary of his birth. This essay seeks both to honour Bonhoeffer and to examine what his life, example and writings might have to say to us, sixty years after his death, on the proper relationship between Christianity and politics in the modern world.

In both George Bush's America and John Howard's Australia, we see today the political orchestration of various forms of organised Christianity in support of the conservative incumbency. In the US, the book *God's Politics*, by Reverend Jim Wallis, has dragged this phenomenon out of the shadows (where it is so effectively manipulated by the pollsters and spin doctors) and into the searching light of proper public debate. US Catholic, Evangelical and Pentecostal Christians are now engaged in a national discussion on the role of the religious Right. The same debate must now occur here in Australia. As Wallis notes in his introduction:

> God is not partisan: God is not a Republican or a Democrat. When either party tries to politicize God, or co-opt religious communities for their political agendas, they make a terrible mistake. The best contribution of religion is precisely not to be ideologically predictable nor loyally partisan. Both parties, and the nation, must let the prophetic voice of religion be heard. Faith must be free to challenge both right and left from a consistent moral ground.

*

Had Dietrich Bonhoeffer been at Oxford, he would have been one of the gods. He was at twenty-one a doctoral graduate and at twenty-three the youngest person ever appointed to a lectureship in systematic theology at the University of Berlin, in 1929. His contemporaries saw his career as made in heaven. Along Unter den Linden, just beyond the faculty walls, however, the living hell of the Nazi storm-troopers was being born.

At the core of Bonhoeffer's theological and therefore political life was a repudiation of the doctrine of the Two Kingdoms. As James Woelfel has noted:

> According to this doctrine, the proper concern of the gospel is the inner person, the sphere where the Kingdom of God reigns; the Kingdom of the State, on the other hand, lies in

the outer sphere, the realm of law, and is not subject to the gospel's message. German Christians used this argument to justify devotion to race and fatherland as 'orders of creation' to be obeyed until the final consummation.

These debates may seem arcane in twenty-first-century secular Australia, but in the Germany of the 1930s they were central to the decision of the majority of German Lutheran ministers to submit to the *Reichskirche* (resplendent with swastikas on their ecclesiastical stoles) and to retreat into a politically non-threatening quietism as the political repression of Hitler's post-1933 chancellorship unfolded. Equally, it was Bonhoeffer's theological dissent from the perversion of this Two Kingdoms doctrine that led him, at the tender age of twenty-nine, to establish in 1935 the German Confessing Church, with its underground seminary.

Bonhoeffer's seminal work, his *Ethics*, was not collated and published until after his execution. Its final essay is entitled 'What is Meant By Telling the Truth', and it represents a call to the German church to assume a prophetic role in speaking out in defence of the defenceless in the face of a hostile state. For Bonhoeffer, 'Obedience to God's will may be a religious experience but it is not an ethical one until it issues in actions that can be socially valued.' He railed at a church for whom Christianity was 'a metaphysical abstraction to be spoken of only at the edges of life', and in which clergy blackmailed their people with hellish consequences for those whose sins the clergy were adept at sniffing out, all the while ignoring the real evil beyond their cathedrals and churches. 'The church stands,' he argued, 'not at the boundaries where human powers give out, but in the middle of the village.'

In his *Letters from Prison*, he wrote, reflecting in part on the deportation of the Jews, that 'We have for once learned to see the great events of world history from below, from the perspective of the outcast, the suspects, the maltreated, the powerless, the reviled – in short, from the perspective of those who suffer.' Bonhoeffer's political theology is therefore one of a dissenting church that speaks truth to the state, and does so by giving voice to the voiceless. Its domain is the village, not the interior life of the chapel. Its core principle is to stand in defence of the defenceless or, in Bonhoeffer's terms, of those who are 'below'.

Bonhoeffer lived what he preached. The day after Hitler became chancellor in January 1933, Bonhoeffer made on Berlin radio a direct attack on the so-called 'Führer Principle', before the broadcast was cut off. In April 1933, two weeks after Hitler's enactment of the Aryan Civil Service legislation banning people of Jewish ancestry from public employment, Bonhoeffer published *The Church and the Jewish Question*, in which he urged the church to 'jam the spoke of the state ... to protect the state from itself'.

He then established his Confessing Church which, before being finally suppressed by the SS in 1941, produced much of the leadership of the German Resistance. Internationally, Bonhoeffer spent from 1933 to 1939 seeking to unite the international Christian movement into a global pacifist movement that would oppose the aggression of his own state. After the failure of these efforts, in 1940 he joined the German *Abwehr* (military intelligence) as a double agent, and until his arrest in late 1943 he collaborated with the armed forces' conspiracy against Hitler – and, at the same time, organised the secret evacuation of a number of German Jews to Switzerland.

Bonhoeffer's was a muscular Christianity. He became the Thomas More of European Protestantism because he understood the cost of discipleship, and lived it. Both Bonhoeffer and More were truly men for all seasons.

*

Where does Bonhoeffer's teaching fit within the history of Christian thought on church–state relations? This history begins with the great exchange, recorded in the New Testament, in which Jesus of Nazareth instructed people 'to render under Caesar the things that are Caesar's, and unto God the things that are God's'. The Nazarene, of course, had the good sense not to define precisely what each could lay claim to: which things uniquely belong to Caesar, and which to God. Therein lies the dilemma that has confounded Christians of all persuasions who have engaged with the political process in the intervening twenty centuries.

During the first three centuries of its history, Christianity did not just preach a gospel for the oppressed; Christians themselves were being oppressed. Christianity began as the profession of an oppressed minority, having emerged from within Judaism, Judaism in turn having had its own troubled experience within the Roman Empire. The New Testament therefore sees the world from the perspective of that persecution, as do the later parts of the Old Testament, particularly the literature of the Babylonian captivity.

All this began to change with the Constantinian settlement at the beginning of the fourth century. Once Christianity became part of the orthodoxy of the later Roman Empire, the greatest challenge of theology and politics was how to translate this 'theology of the oppressed' into a doctrine for an age in which the church was secure and legally protected through the offices of the state itself. For its first three centuries, Christianity had represented an active counterculture, but what was to be Christianity's message in a new age in which the church had become culturally dominant? This became the continuing challenge of Christianity in the Christian West for the subsequent 1500 years.

Over the last 200 years, however, we have seen an entirely different debate arise, as Christianity has sought to come to terms with a rising and increasingly rampant secularism. The impact of independent scientific enquiry, the increasing impact of secular humanism itself, combined with the pervasive influence of modernism and postmodernism, have had the cumulative effect of undermining the influence of the mainstream Catholic and Protestant churches across the West.

Where this will lead, as Christianity enters its third millennium, remains to be seen. But there are signs of Christianity seeing itself, and being seen by others, as a counterculture operating within what some have called a post-Christian world. In some respects, therefore, Christianity, at least within the West, may be returning to the minority position it occupied in the earliest centuries of its existence. But whether or not we conclude that Christianity holds a minority or a majority position within Western societies, that still leaves unanswered the question of how any informed individual Christian (or Christians combined in the form of an organised church) should relate to the state.

I argue that a core, continuing principle shaping this engagement should be that Christianity, consistent with Bonhoeffer's critique in the '30s, must always take the side of the marginalised, the vulnerable and the oppressed. As noted above, this tradition is very much alive in the prophetic literature of the Old Testament. It is also very much alive in the recorded accounts of Jesus of Nazareth: his engagement with women, gentiles, tax collectors, prostitutes and the poor – all of whom, in the political and social environment of first-century Palestine, were fully paid-up members of the 'marginalised, the vulnerable and the oppressed'. Furthermore, parallel to this identification with those 'below' was Jesus' revulsion at what he described as the hypocrisy of the religious and political elites of his time, that is, those who were 'above'.

Do these principles of themselves provide a universal moral precept from which all elements of social and economic policy can be derived? Of course not. But they do provide an illuminating principle – even a 'light on the hill', to borrow Chifley's phrase, which he in turn had consciously borrowed from Christ's Sermon on the Mount – that can help to shape our view of what constitutes appropriate policy for the community, the nation and the world.

What does this principle have to say about economic self-interest? What does it have to say about Max Weber's Protestant work ethic? Or about the legitimate theological basis for the accumulation of private wealth? On these questions we are left with the troubling parable about a camel passing through the eye of a needle. But we are also left with a parable about the proper tending of the vineyard, the diligence of those who work the vineyard, and the abundance of the harvest. In this context, Catholic social teaching has long argued for a proper balance between the rights of capital and labour, in a relationship based on mutual respect as well as legal protection.

Apart from the great questions of wealth, poverty and social justice, a second area of long-standing contention in church–state relations has been the doctrine of the just war. What is the Christian view of violence by the state? What specifically is the

Christian view of the state itself employing violence against other states? These debates are ultimately anchored in the Christian concern for the sanctity of all human life. Human life can only be taken in self-defence, and only then under highly conditional circumstances – circumstances which include the exhaustion of all other peaceful means to resolve a dispute; and if war is to be embarked upon, then the principles of proportionality must apply. On this point, for example, it is worth noting that Pope John Paul II did not support the Iraq war as a just war.

These principles of proportionality apply also to the state's role in providing, protecting or (in the current debate) circumscribing the freedoms of its citizenry. Christian teaching is sceptical about a state's demand for more and more power. We should be sceptical of that demand today, just as we should challenge the right of the state lawfully to execute its own citizens. The Christian belief in the sanctity of life should cause us to conclude that capital punishment is unacceptable in all circumstances and in all jurisdictions.

The function of the church in all these areas of social, economic and security policy is to speak directly to the state: to give power to the powerless, voice to those who have none, and to point to the great silences in our national discourse where otherwise there are no natural advocates.

*

If these are the contours of classical Christian engagement with the state, the modern forms of political engagement are in the main much cruder. Below I list five of them, of which only the fifth bears any real resemblance to Bonhoeffer's position.

1. *Vote for me because I'm a Christian*. This is the model that is most repugnant. It is the model which says that, simply on the basis of my external profession of the Christian faith, those of similar persuasion should vote for me. This is about as intelligent as saying that because I am a Sydney Swans supporter, all other Swans supporters should vote for me, because we ostensibly adhere to the same belief system. This model is alive and well in the US. Thankfully, it is much less alive and much less well in Australia, although there are some dangerous signs that for certain Christian constituencies here, it represents an increasingly

appealing message. It is a model for which there is no underpinning scriptural, doctrinal or theological authority.

2. *Vote for me because I'm Christian, and because I have a defined set of views on a narrowly defined set of questions concerning sexual morality.* Regrettably, this model has an increasing number of supporters within the broader Christian community. Such supporters tend to read down, rather than read up, the ethical teachings of the New Testament, producing a narrow tick-the-box approach to passing a so-called Christian morals test. These tests tend to emphasise questions of sexuality and sexual behaviour. I see very little evidence that this pre-occupation with sexual morality is consistent with the spirit and content of the gospels. For example, there is no evidence of Jesus of Nazareth expressly preaching against homosexuality. In contrast, there is considerable evidence of the Nazarene preaching against poverty and the indifference of the rich.

3. *Vote for me because I am a Christian, vote for me because I have a defined set of views on questions of private sexual morality, and vote for me also because I chant the political mantra of 'family values'.* That is, take models number one and two and add to them the tag of 'family values'. Regrettably, that term has become one of the most used and abused terms in the Australian political lexicon. The concept of 'family values' it involves is invariably a narrow one, and invariably leaves to one side the ability of working families to survive financially.

4. Apply models one, two and three above, and then add the following offensive play. Unleash a political fusillade against anyone who dares suggest that Christianity might have something concrete to say about the broader political, economic and social questions, and justify this fusillade with that hardy perennial, 'Religion should be kept out of politics.' This is a view which says that should anyone seek to articulate from a Christian perspective a view on the Iraq war, on poverty in the world, on asylum seekers, on indigenous Australians, or on workplace relations, then judgment may be rained down upon them from the heavens above, as in the days of Sodom and Gomorrah. Bonhoeffer's critique of the doctrine of the Two Kingdoms was, of course, a response to this.

5. In the fifth approach, the gospel is both a spiritual gospel

and a social gospel, and if it is a social gospel then it is in part a political gospel, because politics is the means by which society chooses to exercise its collective power. In other words, the gospel is as much concerned with the decisions I make about my own life as it is with the way I act in society. It is therefore also concerned with how in turn I should act, and react, in relation to the state's power. This view derives from the simple principle that the gospel which tells humankind that they must be born again is the same gospel which says that at the time of the Great Judgment, Christians will be asked not how pious they have been but instead whether they helped to feed the hungry, clothe the naked and visit the lonely. In this respect, the gospel is an exhortation to social action. Does this mean that the fundamental ethical principles provide us with an automatic mathematical formula for determining every item of social, economic, environmental, national-security and international-relations policy before government? Of course not. What it means is that these matters should be debated by Christians within an informed Christian ethical framework. It also means that we should repudiate the proposition that such policy debates are somehow simply 'the practical matters of the state' which should be left to 'practical' politicians rather than to 'impractical' pastors, preachers and theologians. This approach is very much in Bonhoeffer's tradition.

A Christian perspective on contemporary policy debates may not prevail. It must nonetheless be argued. And once heard, it must be weighed, together with other arguments from different philosophical traditions, in a fully contestable secular polity. A Christian perspective, informed by a social gospel or Christian socialist tradition, should not be rejected contemptuously by secular politicians as if these views are an unwelcome intrusion into the political sphere. If the churches are barred from participating in the great debates about the values that ultimately underpin our society, our economy and our polity, then we have reached a very strange place indeed.

*

Some have argued that Bonhoeffer provides a guide for Christian action 'in extremis', but not for the workaday problems of 'normal' political life. Stanley Hauerwas, Professor of Theological Ethics at Duke University, argues, though, that this fails to comprehend Bonhoeffer's broader teaching on the importance of truth in politics. In fact, it accepts the 'assumption that truth and politics, particularly in democratic regimes in which compromise is the primary end of the political process, do not mix'.

Here lies the searing intensity of Bonhoeffer's gaze, cast across the decades into our own less dramatic age: the need for the church to speak truthfully, prophetically and incisively in defiance of the superficiality of formal debate in contemporary Western politics. In other words, beyond the sound-and-light show of day-to-day political 'debate', what are the real underlying fault lines in the polity? Most critically, within those fault lines, who are the 'voiceless' ones unable to clamour for attention in an already crowded political space – and who is speaking for them?

In Australia today, much is being written about 'Australian values'. Much less, however, has been written about another debate, that between neo-liberals and progressives, concerning whether the balance of our national values lies with the individual or with the community. On the neo-liberal side of the debate, values of liberty, security and prosperity are taken to be paramount. On the progressive side, these values are largely shared, but to them another three are added: equity, community and sustainability.

What is the dividing line between the two? When stripped bare, neo-liberal values are an aggregation of individual interests: in Thatcher's truism, 'there is no such thing as society'. However, progressive politics argues that the mandate of the state goes beyond the exclusive celebration of self. Furthermore, we hold that a properly functioning society embraces the interests of both self and other – not just the first, to the absolute exclusion of the second. That is why the progressive values of equity, community and sustainability concern others as much as they do ourselves.

Social-democratic values are a check on rampant individualism, in part because rampant individualism, unconstrained by any responsibility for interests beyond the individual, is inherently destructive. That is why liberal capitalism, left unfettered, is capable of destroying any social institution that inhibits the maximisation of individual self-interest. That includes the family itself. A practical manifestation of this destructive impulse can be found in the radical 2006 reforms to the Australian labour market, under which the last remaining protections for preserving family time are sacrificed at the altar of market utility. In this area, at least, conservatives and old-fashioned social liberals share a common commitment to social institutions against uncompromising market fundamentalism.

This progressive social-democratic impulse is also reflected in an entire tradition in modern Western politics, now over 150 years old, called Christian socialism. Keir Hardie, the founder of the British Labour Party, was a Christian socialist, as was Andrew Fisher, the first majority Labor prime minister of Australia. For his part, Bonhoeffer was a committed social democrat, although he did not use the term 'Christian socialist' to describe his own politics. Nonetheless, his writings on 'otherness' and 'the oppressed' fit well within this perspective. It is a view of politics which seeks to enlarge society, rather than contract it into a colony of self-contained white picket fences. It also attaches a primacy to the most critical social institution of all: the family.

If we apply a Christian socialist critique to contemporary Australian politics, the precise nature of the widening values-divide in John Howard's Australia becomes starkly apparent. Mr Howard is a clever politician who often succeeds in masking the essential self-interest of his political project with a veneer of 'duty to the nation'. Mr Howard's politics are in the main about concealing the substantive truth of his policy program because – as with his new industrial laws – when fully exposed to the light of public debate, their essential truth is revealed: a redistribution of power from the weak to the strong. That is why some of the churches (consistent with Bonhoeffer's injunction to the church to boldly tell the truth to the state) have set about the task of exposing the truth of what the industrial-relations changes mean for working families. This is part of the continued prophetic mission of the church, however politically uncomfortable that may be for the state or its critics at any particular time. The purpose of the church is not to be socially agreeable; it is to speak robustly to the state on behalf of those who cannot speak effectively for themselves.

The church's increasing engagement on the environment – and specifically on global climate change – falls into a similar category. By definition, the planet cannot speak for itself. Nor can the working peoples of the developing world effectively speak for themselves, although they are likely to be the first victims of the environmental degradation brought about by climate change. Nor can those who come after us, although they are likely to be the greatest victims of this inter-generational injustice. It is the fundamental ethical challenge of our age to protect the planet – in the language of the Bible, to be proper stewards of creation. The scientific evidence is now clear, and the time for global, national and local action has well and truly come. In fact, in some cases it may have already passed. So is it ethical to engage in the deliberate sabotage of global co-operative efforts, under the Kyoto Protocol, to roll back global climate change? Or is it ethical instead to become an active, constructive part of the global solution? It is ethically indefensible for the current government to have spent the last decade not only refusing to ratify the Kyoto Protocol, but also actively working with the government of the US to marginalise it.

A further challenge is global poverty. Bonhoeffer's principle again applies: who speaks boldly to the state for those who cannot speak for themselves? Today, 1.4 billion people live below the poverty line defined by the World Bank of US$1 per day. Who speaks for them? For them, there is a great and continuing silence. In the absence of total catastrophe, they cannot capture the television sets of our collective imagination. They are, in part, victims of the great immorality of our age: if it's not on the six o'clock news, it's not happening. The UN's Millennium Development Goals represent a partial response to this. The failure to give effect to those goals represents continued ethical failure – including from Australia, where lip-service, not moral leadership, is the order of the day.

Another great challenge of our age is asylum seekers. The biblical injunction to care for the stranger in our midst is clear. The parable of the Good Samaritan is but one of many which deal with the matter of how we should respond to a vulnerable stranger in our midst. That is why the government's proposal to excise the Australian mainland from the entire Australian migration zone and to rely almost exclusively on the so-called Pacific Solution should be the cause of great ethical concern to all the Christian churches. We should never forget that the reason we have a UN convention on the protection of refugees is in large part because of the horror of the Holocaust, when the West (including Australia) turned its back on the Jewish people of Germany and the other occupied countries of Europe who sought asylum during the '30s.

How would Bonhoeffer respond to militant Islamism and the broader challenge of international terrorism today? Unlike climate change and global poverty, where there is a gaping silence in the national debate, when the topic turns to terrorism the political cacophony is deafening. But much of this noise is made up of the soundbites that are part of the colour, movement and superficiality of contemporary Australian politics. Islamic terrorism is a complex phenomenon that demands an integrated, complex response. An appreciation of complexity is not a recipe for inertia. It should instead be a recipe for effective rather than rhetorical action.

Bonhoeffer's voice, speaking to us through the ages, would ask this simple, truth-based question: what is causing this phenomenon? He would also caution against inflammatory rhetoric that seeks to gain political advantage, rather than to respond substantively and find a way forward. Of discomfort to certain elements of the far Left would be the truthful conclusion that there *is* a fundamental problem within militant Islamism, which values violent jihad in its own right and is not amenable to engagement, dialogue or persuasion. Of discomfort to the Right is the conclusion that the politics of economic underdevelopment in much of the Islamic world breeds resentment, denies opportunity and therefore provides fertile recruitment fields for jihadists. The World Bank gives us the unsettling statistic that an extra 80–100 million jobs will need to be created in the decade ahead if the *current* level of unemployment for young males in the Muslim world is not to deteriorate further.

Within settler countries like Australia, the challenge of integration is doubly complex. John Howard is correct when he says that a knowledge of the English language is an important component of social inclusion. But he is an unreconstructed hypocrite when he says that and increases the immigration intake (including from the Muslim world), while at the same time reducing the budget that funds the teaching of English to migrants. Australian sporting clubs, social organisations, churches, chambers of commerce and trade unions could be formally involved in the re-settlement process. Policies such as these would form part of an integrated, complex response to the challenge of inclusion. Such policies would produce good fruit in proper season. But they do not provide the radioactive soundbites that some in the political class deem necessary.

Radioactive language is an aspect of Mr Howard's overriding project to retain his incumbency at all costs, distracting the body politic from the reality of his faltering program for government. The substance of that program now makes for a less robust political message as he moves into his second decade in office: rising interest rates, declining housing affordability, slowing productivity growth, an Americanised industrial-relations system, a regressive consumption tax, the skyrocketing costs of university education and the steady undermining of universal health insurance. Add to these the escalating failure of the Iraq war and the deteriorating security in our immediate region, complicated by our distraction in Iraq – all compounded by a failure to tell the public the truth on Iraqi weapons of mass destruction, Iraqi prisoner abuse and the $300-million wheat-for-weapons scandal.

The role of the church is not to agree that deceptions of this magnitude are normal. If Christians conclude that such deceptions are the stock-in-trade of the Kingdom of the State in Luther's Two Kingdoms doctrine (and hence of no relevance to the Kingdom of the Gospel), then we will end up with a polity entirely estranged from truth. When the Prime Minister states that migrants should have a better grasp of the English language, while at the same time removing major funding from the program that enables them to learn English, this represents a significant prostitution of the truth. Therefore, if the church is concerned about the truth – not the politics – of social inclusion, then in Bonhoeffer's tradition of fearlessly speaking the truth to the state, it should say so.

There is a danger that John Howard's form of political statecraft will become entrenched as the national political norm. The Prime Minister's now routine manipulation of the truth poses significant problems for the long-term integrity of our national institutions, including the great departments of state. As time goes by, all are in danger of becoming complicit in protecting the political interests of the government rather than advancing the national interest of the country. There must be a new premium attached to truth in public life. That is why change must occur.

There is an alternative vision for Australia's future: one which seeks to take Chifley's vision of a 'light on the hill' into an uncertain century. This is an enlarging vision that sees Australia taking the lead on global climate change, rather than continuing to play the role of saboteur. This is an Australia that takes the lead on the Millennium Development Goals both in word and deed, and leads by example in dealing with the chronic poverty in our own region. This is an Australia that becomes a leader, not a follower, in the redesign of the rules of the international order that we helped craft in 1945, to render future genocides both intolerable under international law and impossible through international resolve. This is an Australia which takes the values of decency, fairness and compassion that are still etched deep in our national soul, despite a decade of oxygen deprivation, and breathes them afresh into the great debates now faced by our country and the international community. The time has well and truly come for a vision for Australia not limited by the narrowest of definitions of our national self-interest. Instead, we need to be guided by a new principle that encompasses not only what Australia can do for itself, but also what Australia can do for the world.

This essay began with Dietrich Bonhoeffer, who went to the gallows at Flossenbürg concentration camp on 9 April 1945, just two weeks before the camp was liberated. Hitler had personally ordered the execution of all those who had been charged with conspiracy against him. Bonhoeffer was hanged, together with his brother and two of his brothers-in-law. He died a Christian pastor, committed social democrat and passionate internationalist. I believe that today, Bonhoeffer would be traumatised by the privatised, pietised and politically compliant Christianity on offer from the televangelists of the twenty-first century. Bonhoeffer's vision of Christianity and politics was for a just world delivered by social action, driven by personal faith. Bonhoeffer's tradition therefore acts still as an eloquent corrective to those who would seek today to traduce Christianity by turning it into the political handmaiden of the conservative political establishment. Bonhoeffer's Christianity was, and remains, a more demanding challenge than that.

The Monthly

* * *

Portrait of the Monster as a Young Artist

J.M. Coetzee

In his dual biography of the two bloodiest butchers and worst moral monsters of the twentieth century, Stalin and Hitler (but is Mao not up there with them? And does Pol Pot not get a look-in?), Alan Bullock reprints side by side class photographs of young Iosif and young Adolf taken in 1889 and 1899 respectively, in other words, when each was about ten. Peering at the two faces, one tries to descry some quiddity, some dark halo, some sly intimation of the horrors to come; but the photographs are old, definition is poor, one cannot be sure, and besides, a camera is not a divining tool.

The class photograph test – What will be the destinies of these children? Which of them will go the furthest? – has a particular pointedness in the cases of Stalin and Hitler. Is it possible that some of us are evil from the moment we leave our mother's womb? If not, when does evil enter us, and how? Or, to put the question in a less metaphysical form, how is it that some of us never develop a restraining moral conscience? In regard to Stalin and Hitler, did the fault lie in the way they were reared? With educational practices in Georgia and Austria of the late nineteenth century? Or did the boys in fact develop a conscience, and then at some later time lose it: were Iosif and Adolf, at the time they were photographed, still normal, sweet lads, and did they turn into monsters later, as a consequence perhaps of the books they read, or the company they kept, or the pressures of their times? Or was there nothing special about them after all, early or late: did the script of history simply demand two butchers, a Butcher of Germany and a Butcher of Russia; and had Iosif Dzhugashvili and Adolf Hitler not been in the right place at the right time, would history have found another pair of actors, just as good (that is, just as bad), to play the roles?

These are not questions that biographers are happy to face. There are limits to what we will ever know for a fact about young Stalin and young Hitler, about their home environment, their education, their early friendships, early influences on them. The leap from the meagre factual record to the inner life is a huge one, one that historians and biographers (the biographer conceived of as historian of the individual) are understandably reluctant to take. So if we want to know what went on in those two child souls, we will have to turn to the poet and the kind of truth the poet offers, which is not the same as the historian's.

Which is where Norman Mailer enters the picture. Mailer has never regarded poetic truth as truth of an inferior variety. From *An American Dream* and *Advertisements for Myself* through *The Armies of the Night* and *Why Are We in Vietnam?* through *The Executioner's Song* and *Marilyn* he has felt free to follow the spirit and the methods of fictional inquiry to gain access to the truth of our times, in an enterprise that may be riskier than the historian's but offers richer rewards. The subject of his new book is Hitler. Hitler may belong to the past, but the past he belongs to is still alive or at least undead. In *The Castle in the Forest* Mailer has written the story of the young Hitler, and specifically the story of how young Hitler came to be possessed by evil forces.

*

The genealogical descent of Adolf Hitler is tangled and, by Nuremberg standards, not entirely kosher. His father, Alois, was the illegitimate son of a woman named Maria Anna Schicklgruber. The most likely candidate for paternity, Johann Nepomuk Hüttler, was also the grandfather, through another liaison, of Klara Pölzl, Alois's niece and third wife, mother of Adolf. Alois Schicklgruber legitimised himself as Alois Hitler (his choice of spelling) at the age of forty, some years before he married the much younger Klara. The rumour never entirely died down, however, that Alois's real father – and therefore Adolf's grandfather – was a Jew named Frankenberger. There were even dark hints that Klara was Alois's natural daughter

Once he entered political life in the 1920s, Adolf Hitler did everything he could to hide and even falsify his genealogy. This may or may not have been because he believed he had a Jewish forebear. In the early 1930s, opposition newspapers tried to discredit the anti-Semite Hitler by pointing to a Jew in his family closet; their efforts came to an abrupt end when the Nazis took power.

Through his own efforts, Alois Hitler rose from the peasantry to the middle ranks of the Austrian customs service. With Klara he had three children; he also brought into the household two children from a previous marriage. One of these children, Alois Junior, ran away from home to lead a roaming, partly criminal (also bigamous) life. Alois Junior's son William Patrick Hitler (by an Irish mother) tried ineffectually to blackmail the Führer over family secrets before emigrating in 1939 to the United States, where, after a spell on the lecture circuit as an expert on his uncle, he joined the navy.

In *Mein Kampf* (My Struggle), the book he wrote while in jail in 1924, Hitler gives a highly sanitised version of his origins. Nothing about incest, nothing about illegitimacy, certainly nothing about Jewish forebears, nothing even about siblings. Instead we are presented with a story of a bright little boy who resists a domineering (yet beloved) father who wants him to follow in his footsteps in the civil service. Determined to become an artist, the boy deliberately fails his school examinations, thus thwarting his father's plans. At this point the father providentially dies, and the boy, with the backing of his even more beloved mother, is freed to follow his destiny.

The story about deliberately doing badly at school is a patent rationalisation. Adolf was a bright boy but not, as he liked to think, a genius. Convinced that success was his due simply because of who he was, he disdained study. Once he moved from junior school to *Realschule*, technical high school, he fell further and further behind the class and was eventually asked to leave.

The world would have been a happier place if Alois Senior had had his way and Adolf had become a pen-pusher in the obscurer reaches of the Austrian bureaucracy, but that was not to be. Alois certainly chastised his son, as most fathers did in those days, and much has been made of those beatings by biographers. In the case of Stalin, beatings at the hand of his father, an illiterate cobbler, gave rise to a seething vengefulness for which the Russian people eventually had to pay. In Hitler's case, if one accepts Erik Erikson's analysis, beatings and other displays of paternal power engendered in the boy a determination not to become a paterfamilias himself, but to assume instead in the imagination of the German people the identity of the implacably rebellious son, focus of the admiration of millions of other sons and daughters with the memory of past humiliations burning in their breast. In either case, the lesson seems to be that corporal punishment is a bad idea – that a culture in which young male pride is forcefully humiliated risks provoking the return of the repressed, magnified a thousandfold.

All of the strife between Alois Senior and Adolf is present in Mailer's novel, though for a change seen as much from the father's side as from the son's. The much-maligned domestic tyrant Alois comes across sympathetically as a canny customs officer, a husband proud of his virility despite advancing years, a devoted but luckless amateur beekeeper, a man of little school-learning anxiously climbing the social ladder. The scenes in which Alois struggles not to make a fool of himself during gatherings with fellow small-town notables are worthy of the Flaubert of *Bouvard and Pécuchet*.

Mailer's Adolf is, by contrast, an unappealing, whining, manipulative child riven with incestuous desires and Oedipal jealousies and deeply unforgiving. There is a bad smell about him that he cannot get rid of; he also has a habit of voiding his bowels when he is frightened. His most shocking act is deliberately to infect his attractive, much-loved younger brother Edmund with measles:

'Why are you kissing me?' asked Edmund.
'Because I love you.'
... [He] kissed Edmund repeatedly, a boy's kiss full of slobbering, and Edmund kissed him back. He was so happy that Adi [Adolf] did love him after all.

Edmund dies, according to plan; Adolf is left in triumphant possession of the nest.

*

When young Adolf said he wanted to be an artist, it was not because he had an all-devouring love of art but because he wanted to be acknowledged as a genius, and becoming a great artist seemed to him the quickest way for an obscure youth with little money and no connections to get that acknowledgment. By the time he entered politics in the 1920s, he had dropped his artistic pretensions and found himself a more congenial role model. Frederick II of Prussia, Frederick the Great, had become his idol: in the last months of the war, besieged in his bunker in Berlin, he would for diversion listen to recitals from the biography of Frederick by Thomas Carlyle, anti-democrat, Germanophile, propagandist in chief for the great man theory of history.

Hitler was obsessed with his place in history, that is to say, with the question of how his actions in the present would be seen from the future. 'For me there are two possibilities,' he told Albert Speer: 'to succeed with my plans entirely, or to fail. If I succeed, I will be one of the greatest men in history – if I fail, I will be condemned, rejected, and damned.'

In the novels of Fyodor Dostoevsky there are two drifters on the fringes of Russian society, Raskolnikov in *Crime and Punishment* and Stavrogin in *The Possessed*, who think they can take a short cut to great man status by divorcing goodness from greatness and committing what they fancy to be great crimes: hatcheting old women to death, for example, or violating children.

The confluence of the notion of the genius – the human being of near-divine creative power, far in advance of the herd – with the notion of the great man, the man who both exemplifies and brings to their highest pitch the qualities of the age, who writes history rather than being written by it, contaminated further with the notion of the great criminal, the rebel whose Luciferian acts challenge the norms of society, had a powerful formative effect on the character of Hitler. There is a hint in *Mein Kampf* that he was first exposed to great man theory by a history teacher at school. He confirmed himself as a genius by the time he was fifteen. As for great crimes (for which, as Stavrogin recognises, little-seeming crimes qualify as long as they are squalid, mean-minded, perverse and vile enough), life in the Hitler household, at least in Mailer's version of it, provided sufficient opportunity for young Adolf to practise these.

Hitler had neither the historical awareness nor the distance from himself to recognise to what a degree he was in the grip of Romantic great man theory; nor is it likely that, had he recognised it, he would have wanted to shake it off.

Marxism famously questions the power of individual agents to impose their will on history. Finding that particular thesis of Marxism inconvenient, Stalin, who as much as Hitler aspired to be famous, restored great man theory to Marxist doctrine in the form of what would later be called the cult of personality. The route he himself took to the pinnacle of greatness was more direct than Hitler's. The verdict of history, in Stalin's eyes, pivoted on who wrote the history books. Accordingly he used his *Short Course in the History of the All-Union Communist Party*, 1948 edition, compulsory reading in schools, to pronounce history's judgment on himself. As commander-in-chief of the Soviet armed forces, he wrote, 'his genius enabled him to divine the enemy's plans and defeat them' at every turn. As for the arts of peace:

> although he performed the task of leader of the Party with consummate skill and enjoyed the unreserved support of the entire Soviet people, [he] never allowed his work to be marred by the slightest hint of vanity, conceit or self-adulation.

*

With no father around to annoy him, and a pliant mother to supply his needs, Adolf took a two-year break after high school, staying at home, reading all night (Karl May, German author of Wild West yarns, was a favourite), getting up late, sketching, desultorily strumming the piano. This is where *The Castle in the Forest* winds to an end.

According to his publishers, Mailer is planning a trilogy that will cover the whole of Hitler's earthly life. Mailer himself hints that the second volume will take us through the 1930s, and will centre on Hitler's affair with his niece Angelika (Geli) Raubal.

The affair with Geli happens already to have been covered by Ron Hansen in *Hitler's Niece* (1999), a novel that lists heavily under the weight of undigested historical research but contains one episode – on Hitler's (imagined) sexual proclivities – worthy of Mailer at his most scabrous. Mailer's second volume, if it comes to be written, will presumably take in not only Geli but also the years Hitler spent in pre-war Vienna, as well as his spell in the German army, when he underwent his political awakening. Nonetheless, the implication of *The Castle in the Forest* is that the malign kernel of the woe to be visited on the world was well developed by 1905, when Hitler was sixteen. If we are seeking the truth of Adolf Hitler, the poetic truth, Mailer would seem to say, the years from his conception and birth to the end of his schooling will provide material enough.

It is of course a truism that character is formed in our early years, that the child is father to the man. But there were thousands of little boys in Austria who loved their mothers and resented their fathers and did badly at school, yet did not turn into mass murderers. Unless one is prepared to make a leap of the kind that Mailer makes, from fidelity to the real to intuitive insight, no amount of reworking of the meagre historical record of Hitler's childhood will reveal what was special about him, what set him apart from his contemporaries.

With Hitler's move from the provinces to the capital in 1906 the picture changes. The record becomes fuller. We can follow his movements, track down the people he met, read the books and newspapers he read, listen to the music he heard. A different kind of biographical novel becomes possible.

In 1907 Hitler took the entrance examination to the Vienna Art Academy. To his surprise and annoyance, he failed. 'Test Drawing Unsatisfactory' was the verdict of the examiners; they advised that he try architecture instead. Since he lacked the technical background for the study of architecture, he could not follow their advice. So he spent the next year hanging around in Vienna, living in boarding houses, writing letters home in which he kept alive the fiction that he was a student at the academy, reading copiously, going to the opera whenever he could afford it. Wagner was his favorite composer: he claimed to have attended at least thirty performances of *Tristan and Isolde*. Sexually he remained chaste or at least self-sufficient: he had a horror of being infected with syphilis.

Called back to Linz to his mother's sick bed, he nursed her through agonising cancer. After she died, he returned to Vienna and failed the Art Academy examination a second time. There was a bitter winter when his funds ran out and he had to resort to a shelter for the homeless. Then, with the help of an acquaintance, he began to sell his paintings, and the future looked brighter. He took up residence in a working-men's club, pursuing the life of a part-time artist catering to the tourist market. In 1913 he quit Vienna in favour of Munich, where he settled in the bohemian quarter. The move may or may not have been in response to call-up papers from the Austrian military.

The Vienna years cry out for a novel of a certain kind, a novel that will do for Hitler's Vienna what the *Notebooks of Malte Laurids Brigge* do for Rilke's Paris or *Hunger* for Knut Hamsun's Oslo: blend inward and outward experience, give us not only the world in which the subject moved but also how he felt about it and responded to it. With the backing of scholarly investigations like Brigitte Hamann's *Hitler's Vienna* (1996), the novelist who takes up the challenge might not merely follow the strands of National Socialist ideology back to their origins, but enable us to understand how and why they came to be woven together in Hitler's mind.

*

Of the aspects of Hitler's Vienna period on which the historically minded novelist might build, I mention three. First, despite at times being hungry and even desperate, Hitler disdained manual labour. Second, he hated Vienna. Third, in this phase of his life he can legitimately be called an artist and intellectual, albeit an undistinguished one.

Hitler disdained manual labour because he thought it incompatible with his status – a tenuous status, considering his defective education and the fact that his parents were born peasants – as a member of the lower middle class. His hostility to socialism grew out of a well-founded anxiety about being sucked into a lumpen (ragged) proletariat of workless rural migrants streaming to the capital from all quarters of the empire.

He disliked Vienna because in Vienna for the first time he was made to realise that, as an ethnic German, he belonged to a minority – albeit a powerful one – in a multi-ethnic state. On the streets he had to rub shoulders with, and even compete with, people who spoke unintelligible languages, dressed differently, smelled strange: Slovenians, Czechs, Slovaks, Magyars, Jews. A xenophobia that was at first suspicious and defensive, a provincial youth's mistrust of foreigners, hardened to become intolerant, aggressive and finally genocidal.

Hitler may not have been much of an artist (he always had trouble with the human figure – a telling weakness), but there is no denying that, at least in his early years, he was an intellectual of sorts. He read incessantly (though only what he liked), he was interested in ideas (though only in ideas that fitted his preconceptions) and believed in their power, he involved himself in the arts (though his tastes were unshakably provincial and prematurely conservative).

From the wealth of new ideas to which he was exposed, he made a selection which he cobbled together to compose the philosophy of National Socialism. The pseudo-anthropology of Guido von List made a deep impression on him. List divided mankind into an Aryan master race, originating in the northernmost fastnesses of Europe, and a race of slaves with whom the Aryans had regrettably miscegenated over the centuries. He urged the recovery of the pure Aryan blood-line by strict sexual segregation from the slave race, via the creation of a state comprising Aryan masters and non-Aryan slaves ruled over by a *Führer* who would be above the law.

Another of the charlatans under whose influence Hitler fell was Lanz von Liebenfels, founder of the Order of the New Templars and publisher of the magazine *Ostara*, of which he was an avid reader. Liebenfels was an extreme misogynist who saw women as lower beings attracted by their nature to 'primitive-sensual dark men of inferior races.' What Hitler knew of racial science and eugenics, and later imported into National Socialist policy, came not from scientific reading but filtered through popularisers and vulgarisers like Liebenfels.

All in all, the adventures of Adolf Hitler in the realm of ideas provide a cautionary tale against letting an impressionable young person loose to pursue his or her education in a state of total freedom. For seven years Hitler lived in a great European city in a time of ferment from which emerged some of the most exciting, most revolutionary thought of the new century. With an unerring eye he picked out not the best but the worst of the ideas around him. Because he was never a student, with lectures to attend and reading lists to follow and fellow students to argue with and assignments to complete and examinations to sit, the half-baked ideas he made his own were never properly challenged. The people he associated with were as ill-educated, volatile and undisciplined as himself. No-one in his circle had the intellectual command to put his chosen authorities in their place as what they were: disreputable and even comical mountebanks.

Normally a society can tolerate, even look benignly upon, a layer of autodidacts and cranks on the fringes of its intellectual institutions. What is singular about the career of Hitler is that through a confluence of events in which luck played some part, he was able not only to spread his nonsensical philosophy among his German countrymen but to put it into practice across Europe, with consequences known to all.

*

By his own account, Hitler turned political only in late 1918, when, upon hearing that Germany had surrendered on humiliating terms, he vowed to dedicate himself at all costs to winning back for the Fatherland its rightful place in Europe. For such reawakening, he determined, Germany would need a strong leader prepared first to purge the *Volk* of Jews, Communists, homosexuals and other inferior elements. Before 1918 Hitler was one among thousands of semi-educated dreamers with their heads stuffed full of mystical racist nonsense; after 1918 he became a positive danger to mankind. Can we therefore say that in late 1918, when he made his *at all costs* vow, he entered into a pact with the devil and evil entered his soul?

To the historian this question may make little sense. Yet to anyone who searches the face of the little boy in the 1899 photograph, cognisant of the suffering this same little boy will in the fullness of time wilfully wreak upon the world, it has convincing force. 'Most well-educated people,' writes Mailer through his unnamed mouthpiece:

> are ready to bridle at the notion of such an entity as the Devil ... There need be no surprise, then, that the world has an impoverished understanding of Adolf Hitler's personality. Detestation, yes, but understanding of him, no – he is, after all, the most mysterious human being of the century.

The question *When did evil enter Hitler's soul?* thus has a most definite meaning to Mailer. His answer is *At the instant of his conception*, in much the same way that God, in Christian dogma, was present at, and entered into, the conception of Jesus. In Mailer's story, the devil had possession of Adolf Hitler from nine months before his birth in April 1889 until the day he died in 1945, to do his bidding in the world.

An answer of this form requires some theological and metaphysical buttressing, which Mailer (with a nod to John Milton) does not hesitate to supply. As there is a God, in Mailer's account, so there is a devil-in-chief, whom his underlings call the Maestro. Each has a vision of what this world of ours can be, but since neither is all-powerful neither can fully impose his vision. The twelve-year Third Reich represents one of the Maestro's triumphs; no doubt God has his victories too, though none are on display in Mailer's book.

The story of young Adolf is narrated by one of the middle-ranking devils in the infernal organisation, a functionary charged with keeping an eye on him, ensuring that he does not stray from the paths of wickedness. Adolf is not this devil's sole assignment: in 1895 he has to take a 45-page break to thwart God's benign plan for the Romanovs in Russia, and in 1898 a briefer break to oversee the assassination of Empress Elizabeth of Austria.

The kind of existence led by the immortals can never mean much to mortal beings. The account that Mailer provides, through his narrator, of eons-long low-level warfare between celestial and infernal forces, and of inter-office feuding within the infernal bureaucracy, though deftly enough done, is the least interesting aspect of his novel. But at least the answer he gives to the question about Adolf in the class photograph is a straight one. Yes, Adolf was bad even in 1899. He was a bad child before he was a bad man, and he was a bad baby before he was a bad child. Alois and Klara Hitler are convincing portraits of people doing their best as parents, given that they are human and human nature is frail, given also that they have superhuman forces ranged against them; Adolf is equally convincing as a chilling and repellent child. Despite the supernatural interventions, Mailer has not descended to writing a novel of the supernatural, a Gothic novel. Dark forces may have entered his soul, but Adolf remains unshakably human, one of us.

Mailer is now in his eighties. His prose may no longer be as electrically vivid as it was forty years ago, but he has lost none of his immoralist daring. Here are Alois and Klara in bed:

> His mouth lathered with her sap, he turned around and embraced her face with all the passion of his own lips and face, ready at last to grind into her with the Hound [his penis], drive it into her piety, yes, damn all piety, thought Alois – damned church-mouse wife, damned church! – he was back from the dead – some kind of miracle, he was all there, his pride equal to a sword. This was better than a storm at sea! And then it went beyond such a moment, for she – the most angelic woman in Braunau – knew she was giving herself over to the Devil, yes, she knew he was there, there with Alois and herself, all three loose in the geyser that came out of him, and then out of her, now together, and I was there with them, I was the third presence and was carried into the caterwauling of all three of us going over the falls together, Alois and myself filling the womb of Klara Poelzl Hitler.

*

One must agree with Mailer: helping us to understand this 'most mysterious human being of the century' is indeed a timely undertaking. But exactly how does his novel advance our understanding? By leading us into the mind of an unlovable child who gets physically excited by the sight of bees being incinerated alive and masturbates to the sound of his father's haemorrhagic coughing, is Mailer asserting that we begin to understand Hitler as we see that the evil acts of the grown man are no different in kind – though vastly different in scale – from the acts of his childhood self, both being the expression of a tangled psychopathology, ugly to the point of devilishness? Is he hereby in effect restating in different terms Dostoevsky's point that there are no great crimes, that the criminal's fantasy of grandeur is just another of the heresies of atheism? Is all evil in essence banal, and do we fall into one of the devil's cunning traps when we treat evil respectfully, take it seriously?

In other words: Just how seriously intended is Mailer's Hitler book, coming on the heels of *The Gospel According to the Son* (1997), a biography of the earthly representative of a by no means all-powerful God, a troubled young man who hears voices but is not always sure where they come from? Does the tone of *The Castle in the Forest*, which is sometimes so light as to verge on the comic, signal that we should take the celestial and infernal goings-on with a grain of salt? Why, despite the devil in him, does there seem no reason to be more afraid of young Adolf than of a sly, vicious dog? And why is the God of Mailer such an ineffectual dummy (among the devils he is scornfully referred to as *der Dummkopf*)?

The lesson that Adolf Eichmann teaches, wrote Hannah Arendt at the conclusion of *Eichmann in Jerusalem*, is of 'the fearsome, word-and-thought-defying *banality of evil*' (Arendt's italics). Since 1963, when she penned it, the formula 'the banality of evil' has acquired a life of its own; today it has the kind of clichéd currency that 'great criminal' had in Dostoevsky's day.

Mailer has repeatedly in the past voiced his suspicion of this formula. As a secular liberal, says Mailer, Arendt is blind to the power of evil in the universe. 'To assume ... that evil itself is banal strikes me as exhibiting a prodigious poverty of imagination.' 'If Hannah Arendt is correct and evil is banal, then that is vastly worse than the opposed possibility that evil is satanic' – worse in the sense that there is no struggle between good and evil and therefore no meaning to existence.

It is not too much to say that Mailer's quarrel with Arendt is a running subtext to *The Castle in the Forest*. But does he do justice to her? In 1946 Arendt had an exchange of letters with Karl Jaspers sparked by his use of the word 'criminal' to characterise

Nazi policies. Arendt disagreed. In comparison with mere criminal guilt, she wrote to him, the guilt of Hitler and his associates 'oversteps and shatters any and all legal systems.'

Jaspers defended himself: if one claims that Hitler was more than a criminal, he said, one risks ascribing to him the very 'satanic greatness' he aspired to. Arendt took his criticism to heart. When she came to write the Eichmann book, she endeavoured to keep alive the paradox that though the actions of Hitler and his associates may defy our understanding, there was no depth of thought behind their conception, no grandeur of intention. Eichmann, a humanly uninteresting man, a bureaucrat through and through, never realised in any philosophically full sense of the word what he was doing; the same might be said, *mutatis mutandis*, for the rest of the gang.

To take the phrase 'the banality of evil' to epitomise Arendt's verdict on the misdeeds of Nazism, as Mailer seems to do, thus misses the complexity of the thinking behind it: what is peculiar to the everyday banality of a bureaucratically administered, industrially organised policy of wholesale extermination is that it is also 'word-and-thought-defying,' beyond our power to understand or to describe.

Before the magnitude of the death, suffering and destruction for which the historical Adolf Hitler was responsible, the human understanding recoils in bewilderment. In a different way, our understanding may recoil when Mailer tells us that Hitler was responsible for the Third Reich only in a mediate sense – that ultimate responsibility lay with an invisible being known as the Devil or the Maestro. The problem here is the nature of the explanation we are being offered: 'The Devil made him do it' appeals not to the understanding, only to a certain kind of faith. If one takes seriously Mailer's reading of world history as a war between good and evil in which human beings act as proxies for supernatural agents – that is to say, if one takes this reading at face value rather than as an extended and not very original metaphor for unresolved and irresoluble conflict within individual human psyches – then the principle that human beings are responsible for their actions is subverted, and with that the ambition of the novel to search out and speak the truth of our moral life.

Blessedly, *The Castle in the Forest* does not demand to be read at face value. Beneath the surface, Mailer can be seen to be struggling with the same paradox as Arendt. By invoking the supernatural, he may seem to assert that the forces animating Adolf Hitler were more than merely criminal; yet the young Adolf he brings to life on these pages is not satanic, not even demonic, simply a nasty piece of work. Keeping the paradox *infernal–banal* alive in all its anguishing inscrutability may be the ultimate achievement of this very considerable contribution to historical fiction.

New York Review of Books

Lost in the Woods

Inga Clendinnen

Lately I have been pursuing novelists who seem to think they are writing near-enough history, when in fact they are making it up. Now two heavyweights have slipped into the ring: Nobel-winner J.M. Coetzee, and the long-time champ of the American Middleweight Literary Division, Norman 'Maler-Than-Thou' Mailer. This is how Coetzee opens his *New York Review of Books* review of Mailer's most recent novel, *The Castle in the Forest*, in which Mailer offers his explanation of the historical phenomenon named Adolf Hitler. Coetzee begins by brooding over photographs of Adolf Hitler and Josef Stalin as children. Then he considers the opacity of childhoods in general: 'The leap from the meagre factual record to the inner life is a huge one, one that historians and biographers … are understandably reluctant to take …' He therefore concludes: 'if we want to know what went on in those two child souls, we will have to turn to the poet and the kind of truth the poet offers, which is not the same as the historian's.' And that is the leap that Mailer has made:

> Mailer has never regarded poetic truth as truth of an inferior variety … he has felt free to follow the spirit and the methods of fictional inquiry to gain access to the truth of our times, in an enterprise that may be riskier than the historian's but offers richer rewards … In *The Castle in the Forest* Mailer has

written the story of the young Hitler, and specifically the story of how young Hitler came to be possessed by evil forces.

For that, remarkably, is Mailer's 'poetic truth': that Hitler was born evil, conceived in the presence of the Devil and in the dark stew of a family history of incest, much as the baby Jesus, conceived in purity and born of a virgin, entered this world in a state of incorruptible grace.

Coetzee's indulgence towards his fellow novelist surprised me, especially given his own sombre enquiry into the fatal burden laid on individuals by their experience of Nazism (see his recent book of essays, *Inner Workings*). Mailer's audacity is less surprising. Half a century ago, in *Advertisements for Myself*, he declared his ambitions – 'I wish to attempt an entrance into the mysteries of murder, suicide, incest, orgy, orgasm and Time' – and over the years he has attempted several entries from several different angles. Then, a decade ago, Mailer discovered that the Hitler field was still open: 'There's a marvellous book by Ron Rosenbaum called *Explaining Hitler*, where he interviews leading figures who've studied Hitler. I read the book and it was immensely stimulating, but in the end there was no explanation for Hitler.' No explanation for Hitler. Faced with so tempting an emptiness, what could Mailer do but seize the day?

The Castle in the Forest is the illicit memoir penned by a middle-rank demon occasionally incarnated as a middle-rank SS officer named Dieter and going by the nickname 'DT'. DT has been serving a term as guardian demon to a very special baby. Indeed, he had been a participant in the triply orgasmic conception of little Adolf because, according to Mailer's freehand history, and only there, this baby was the product of three generations of incest, and therefore predestined for world-historical Evil. Indications of Baby Adolf's future greatness first appear in conventional Freudian terms: his little eyes gleam when he suckles, he sometimes nips his loving mother's nipple, he sometimes makes his precious poo miss the pot. As a lad he enjoys tripping up his cute little brother; later he kisses him slobberingly, when he knows he, Adolf, has the measles; his small rival obligingly dies. Throughout, as in so much of Mailer, there is a delighted fascination with the process and products of evacuation, with the full range of bodily fluids and with what Mailer's poetical DT calls 'the hard-breathing, feverish meat-heavy run up the hills of physical joy'. Devils are routinely present on the hill-runs, with the Devil Himself likely to drop in to celebrate climaxes of world-historical moment.

The infant Hitler's wicked doings didn't much impress me. His older half-brother, lacking both the spawn-of-incest head start and the attendant demon, shows much more talent as a star evildoer. Mailer might be saying, Patience! The lad is brewing mischief! – but why make us trudge through a very long novel about the largely invisible brewing stage? Worse, when DT assures us he had been 'a charming SS man, tall, quick, blond … witty', we don't believe him. We have been listening to him for what seems several decades, and we know he is a bore and his language stilted and prissy – as if, as one reviewer said, it had been badly translated from the German.

Reviewers have done their best to ferret out artful authorial agendas to leaven the DT lump. For example: DT fusses over the reliability of the junior devils he leaves in charge while he is in Moscow, where he has been sent to observe the coming of Hitler's twin-in-evil, Stalin. Is Mailer using DT to make his own judgment on the kinds of characters attracted to the SS? Is his tedious, schoolteacherly devil a parody of tedious, schoolteacherly Himmler? Or is a different joke being played on the reader: Is Adolf's minor devil fussing over the reliability of the reports he collects from even more minor devils a parody of the fuss-budget historian fretting over his hopelessly second-hand reports, so demonstrating his inferiority to the splendid certainties of Artist-Devil Mailer? Or (I'm groping here) is the dull DT an unsubtle reminder of Hannah Arendt's regrettably adhesive notion of the banality at the core of Nazi evil?

DT does seem to be some kind of joke, but he is a most unfunny one. If you want accelerated access to the DT Experience, begin the book with the epilogue. (Why not? Mailer breaks the rules. Why shouldn't we?) After 459 pages DT is at last thinking of leaving us. Through the haze of his usual to-ings and fro-ings ('that was not wholly inaccurate'; 'needless to say') he seems to be apologising:

All that remains to discuss is why I have chosen this title, 'The Castle in the Forest'. If the reader, having come with me through Adolf Hitler's birth, childhood and a good part of his adolescence would now ask, 'Dieter, where is the link to your text? There is a lot of forest in your story but where is the castle?' I would reply that 'The Castle in the Forest' translates into 'Das Waldschloss'.

And off we go again, this time through an ersatz history of the German language, originally, we are told, 'full of the growls of the stomach and the wind in the bowels of hearty existence, the bellows of the lungs', and culminating in 'the roar that stirs in the throat at the sight of blood'. We pivot to consider the affectations imposed on this peasant tongue when its bearers migrated from their hearty barnyards to the heartless city, only to swerve again to contemplate Berliners' talent for irony: 'To every sharp German fellow ... particularly the Berliners, irony has become the essential corrective.'

Then comes the remark which made me bite my thumb in rage: 'Now, I realise this disquisition leads us away from the narrative we have just traversed, but then, this is what I wish to do.' Why? Because 'it enables me to return to our beginnings ... Needless to remark, it is my hope we have come a long way since.' And then, as we totter wearily, drearily on: 'What enables devils to survive is that we are wise enough to understand there are no answers – there are only questions.'

And so, thankfully, we part. And I have a question of my own. Having trudged through an imaginary landscape littered with blood curses and demonic presences, surely it is reasonable to ask: What possessed the occasionally great Mailer? Does he believe any of this stuff? It is seriously difficult to believe he does. Yet the novel was ten years in the making, and while Mailer jauntily promises us two more to come, to bring us through The Career and The Downfall, we have to assume that at eighty-four this will be his swan song. He has always been devoted to the maintenance and expansion of his reputation; he has tackled large semi-mythical figures (Jesus, Marilyn) before. Is he making a last grab to add metaphysical profundity to his bulging quiver? (Milton's *Paradise Lost* and all seven volumes of Nietzsche appear in his bibliography, although I failed to detect their ghostly presence in the text.) As I say, a number of his reviewers think he is joking, or hope he is, but a single piece of evidence suggests he is not. *The Castle in the Forest* is dedicated to his ten grandchildren, his grandniece and his five godchildren, with every child accorded the dignity of their full name. Therefore I think the novel is not a joke. I think Mailer means it.

What does surprise is to find a small pleasant novel buried inside the large pretentious one. With DT gone to Moscow the language changes. Mailer has shoved DT aside, and we are reading a tender pastoral about Alois Hitler, an everyday sort of fellow who, despite an innocent passion for pliable servant girls, fetches up with a good woman as wife; a customs officer turned beekeeper on retirement; a family man who struggles to hold his family together and to hold back the tides of time. There are long, leisurely discussions about bees and beekeeping, every bit of which I enjoyed (I like bees). There is a charming scene between Alois and his wife, Klara, as they discuss, with mounting urgency, the bees' ecstatic marriage flight prior to embarking on one of their own, with not a devil nor a meat-heavy uphill run in sight. I suppose it is possible that the bees are there so we can watch little Adolf watching a hive of defective bees being gassed and, later, some healthy ones being incinerated, or to allow the insertion of brief expositions on the fascistic culture of the bee state: 'our bees, all these bees, do their work by obeying the rules … They do not have patience with those who are weak or lazy.' But for most of the time the bees' appearances are occasions for wonder and delight, stimulating trusting interactions between typically untrusting members of the Hitler household. The novel-within-a-novel traces the fluctuating relationships between an impetuous, authoritarian but not unloving father and his children, and maps the trivial, tragic mistimings and misunderstandings of family life. And the language glistens. As the novice beekeeper Alois approaches his beehives for the first time he feels 'shoots of fear. Bright as rockets, they fire off in his stomach as he approaches the hive-boxes', and we think, Yes! That is exactly how it would have been. It is beautifully done, and only Mailer could have done it. To my mind his talent – his perennially fresh talent – lies not with the dramatic–orgasmic, but in penetrating the crust of the commonplace to expose the tender human flesh below. It is those qualities which suffuse the slow, sweet novel lurking inside the noisy 'historical' one.

Mailer chooses to identify his book's ontological status in magnificently obfuscating terms: '*The Castle in the Forest* is a work of fiction closely based on history.' How closely? 'A few of the names and incidents are the products of the author's imagination or are used fictitiously.' But which 'few' names and incidents? We do not know, and we have no way of telling. So there we have it: maximum freedom for invention, wrapped up in an overall claim to authenticity. My grievance against both author and book is that after invoking a question of such painful importance to humankind – What made Hitler run? – Mailer's history should prove so lamentable. He chooses to append a bibliography to the novel, including a lot of books about Nazis. Is it reasonable to complain that he has chosen to ignore the stunningly productive archival work reported by Ron Rosenbaum ten years ago, as he has ignored the work done since? Agreed, this is a novel – but a novel which makes serious claims about the possibility of historical understanding. Mailer justifies his sortie into Hitler territory on the grounds that historians have failed to explain Hitler. Hence his own explanatory fiction: that the Devil made Hitler do it. It is true that Rosenbaum was interviewing his historians for their conclusions, with evidence and argument largely excised, and that he had an interest in dramatising controversy: this was soon after the controversy over Daniel Goldhagen's *Hitler's Willing Executioners*. Nonetheless, if we read his book attentively, it is clear that a broad secular consensus had been reached as to key themes, with dispute focusing on emphases and delicate matters of timing. The Rosenbaum book clearly had a major impact on Mailer, but not, I think, intellectually. Consider: in early editions the front cover consists of two photographs: above, an adult Hitler, black-clad against a black background, ranting; below, a pensive baby, wearing white but cocooned in black. Dividing the photographs, in big blood-red capitals, is 'EXPLAINING HITLER', with 'THE SEARCH FOR THE ORIGINS OF HIS EVIL' in smaller black capitals below. It is a stunning cover, and it contains in embryo the novel Mailer would produce a decade later.

Most of the reviews of Mailer's book I have seen are either exculpatory ('this is not what it seems') or adulatory ('this resplendent novel'). Coetzee concludes his assessment of Mailer's 'poetic truth' thus:

> Blessedly, *The Castle in the Forest* does not demand to be read at face value. Beneath the surface, Mailer can be seen to be struggling with the same paradox as Arendt. By invoking the supernatural, he may seem to assert that the forces animating Adolf Hitler were more than merely criminal; yet the young Adolf he brings to life on these pages is not satanic, not even demonic, simply a nasty piece of work. Keeping the paradox infernal–banal alive in all its anguishing inscrutability may be the ultimate achievement of this very considerable contribution to historical fiction.

But for the Mailer constructing these pages nothing is inscrutable, and banal explanations of evil proliferate with no anguish attaching to them at all. I am offended by the triviality of this book and its inept metaphysical attitudinising, because it does not help us understand the Hitler phenomenon at all. I felt much the same sick anger when, as a child already terrified of Nazis, I was taken to see Chaplin's *The Great Dictator*. I knew even then that whoever this Hitler might be, he was not a self-deluding clown.

As for Mailer's explanation: Do I believe in devils? No. Do I believe in evil? No. Do I believe that incest carries a heritable moral taint? No. I would be interested to know if Hitler had a Jewish ancestor and knew it, because that would cast new light on his passionately expressed conviction of the blood-taint of Jewishness. Do I care whether he had one or two balls, or possibly four? No. By the time we can see him with any clarity he is an abstemious, vegetarian non-drinker who chooses to keep an army of devoted women at more than arm's length, save for one who transparently adored him. What matters about Hitler is his audacity, his ruthlessness, his political genius, and above all his self-belief: his ability through a period of turmoil to recruit or to destroy competing interests and to win and keep the adoration of the bulk of the German population, while sculpting first a country and then a continent to the shape he had 'in mind'. What we urgently need to understand is how a man with no advantages in birth, physique or education could have won and kept unlimited political authority through politically and economically ebullient times; how he yoked men superior to him in birth, wealth, intelligence and experience to his service. Above all, we need to know how he fabricated a political culture within which ordinary men with no experience of killing could be transported to a foreign country and there set to rounding up men, women and children, herding them to selected sites, and shooting or clubbing them to death, and to maintaining that routine of killing day after day. Those questions are too important for games.

Novelists are blessed in being free to explore imagined exemplary subjectivities, as evidence-dependent historians cannot, and by so doing they can expand their readers' understanding of other lives. Here I contrast Mailer's sorry attempt with John Banville's superb recreation out of the real Anthony Blount of the richly plausible but fictitious Victor Maskell in *The Untouchable*, or, indeed, with every one of Coetzee's South African novels, in which we are shown and made to feel the deformations visited on lives lived within a racist state. I take this penetration beyond the fully knowable to be what Coetzee means by 'poetic truth', and I honour it. Historians are obliged to differentiate at all times between speculation and assertion, and their quarry is an actual and therefore not fully knowable individual moving within an actual and therefore not fully penetrable world. It is also true that childhoods are largely opaque to the historian, as I suspect they are for the child who lives them and the adult who survives them. But despite Mailer's airy claim that the Hitler field remains open, we have richer documentation for Hitler than for most individuals, not for his childhood, but for the movement of that extraordinary political career. Recognising himself as the Führer destined to lead Germany to greatness, Hitler accepted his obligation to proclaim his heroic vision. Therefore we have not only *Mein Kampf*, libraries of letters and speeches, emblematic buildings and emblematic public rituals preserved in heroically emblematic films, but also the intimacy of his *Table Talk*: the authenticated record of what he chose to say to trusted subordinates at group meals or over the tea and cakes of late suppers. The first monologue was recorded on 5 July 1941, the last on the night of 29 November 1944, and they give us intimate access, as their editor, Hugh Trevor-Roper, puts it, to 'the self-revelation of the most formidable among the "terrible simplifiers" of history'. It is through the close analysis of Hitler's rise to power and then his terrifyingly creative use of it that we will find the secrets of his success, not in overheated fictions about his infant and adolescent transgressions.

Now I have liberated you from Mailer, what should you read instead? Since the opening of the vast Russian archive of captured Nazi documents, historians have been working to retrieve the hidden history of the Nazi party and its ruler. There are literally thousands of Holocaust historians, nearly all of them unknown to the public, and most of them good. My favourite is the American scholar Christopher Browning, because he is an uncannily sensitive reader of documents and because he writes with elegance and economy. If you want to be liberated from the fly-paper of Hannah Arendt's cozening by Eichmann's fine performance as a myopic pen-pusher at his trial, read Browning's 'Perpetrator Testimony: Another Look at Adolf Eichmann', in his *Collected Memories: Holocaust History and Postwar Testimony*. If you want to understand how individual Nazis' passion to please their Führer could precipitate competitive Jew-killing in occupied Poland, read the first essay in his *Nazi Policy, Jewish Workers, German Killers*, or, for an overview of the whole hideous process, his *The Path to Genocide*. And if you are as eager as I am to understand how family men, scarcely any of them Nazis, could be turned into the hands-on killers of terrified civilians in the course of a day, read his *Ordinary Men*. Should you lack the time or the inclination to settle to a course of directed reading, watch Oliver Hirschbiegel's 2004 film, *The Downfall*. Usually I mistrust film as too exuberant a medium to allow the critical scrutiny of evidence I take to be central to doing history, but here the focus is narrowed to Hitler's last days in the bunker, and for that period the settings, the personnel and the action, even the words spoken, have been scrupulously documented (see, for example, Hugh Trevor-Roper's meticulous reconstruction, *The Last Days of Hitler*). With Bruno Ganz playing Hitler with eerie verisimilitude, we can watch the incorrigible deference exacted by the shambling central figure, a man visibly at the end of his physical and psychological tether, even as the last vestige of the Nazi dream is pounded into dust by Russian guns.

We can work towards a flawed, incomplete because human, understanding of Hitler without appeal to derelict superstitions or to the contentless category of evil. His crimes, like the suffering they occasioned, were the fruits of human decisions and actions, not the proddings of a bored Devil. Such matters are too important to be consigned to the untestable propositions of 'poetic truth'.

The Monthly

The Innocence Manoeuvre

Anna Funder

People's ideas of beauty differ. East Germany, with all its harshness and hideousness, has always been beautiful to me. This is partly to do with personal history – the most courageous people I have ever met came from there. But it is also because the real history remained visible in the East. In West Germany, by the time I was an adult, everything was plastered over and pristine, the past put away under innocuous plaques or confined to memorial sites. But in East Berlin the buildings of Mitte were pockmarked with gunshot holes from Communist and Nazi streetfights in the 1920s; the cornices and pediments of bombed-wrecked buildings stuck out through the grass of the Volkspark Friedrichshain; the paint went only halfway up the buildings on my street – a promenade boulevard – because that's all the GDR TV cameras would show. East Germany was a regime built on lies, but it literally couldn't afford to cover up its past. I don't begrudge anyone their post-1989 renovations, but to my mind beauty and truth remain related.

Despite the discomfort of friends of mine who suffered under the regime – some of whom are refusing to see it – I think *The Lives of Others* is a superb film. It is a thing of beauty. But its story is a fantasy narrative that could not have (and never did) take place under the GDR dictatorship. The film has then, an odd relation to historical truth, a truth which is being bitterly fought for now.

The Lives of Others posits a Stasi man, Gerd Wiesler, whose task is to find incriminating material on the playwright Georg Dreyman by spying on him and his girlfriend, a famous actress. Installed in the attic of the couple's building with his surveillance equipment, Wiesler listens to their conversations, telephone calls, lovemaking. Gradually, exposed to the higher values of art and the broader thinking of his victims, his blind obedience wanes. He falls in love with the actress, and he has a change of heart: he tries to save the couple from the depredations of his own organisation. In the final scene of the film, set in the 1990s, Wiesler opens up Dreyman's new novel titled *Sonata for a Good Man*. Dreyman has dedicated it to the former Stasi man 'in gratitude.' 'That,' as Günter Bormann of the Stasi File Authority said to me, 'is hard to bear.'

No Stasi man ever tried to save his victims, because it was impossible. (We'd know if he had, because the files are so comprehensive.) Unlike Wiesler, who runs practically a solo surveillance operation and can withhold its results from his superior, totalitarian systems rely on thoroughgoing internal surveillance (terror) and division of tasks. The film alters how totalitarian systems work, in order to make room for its hero to act humanely (something such systems are designed to prevent). It's worth looking at the reality of what the Stasi did, and the current relations between them and their victims, in order to get a sense of where this beautiful fiction sits over that uglier truth.

It is now ten years since I began speaking with former resisters of the regime, and with former Stasi men for what became the book *Stasiland*. At that time, seven years after the fall of the Wall, shocking revelations about the regime were still emerging in the media: the surreptitious, deadly, irradiation of dissidents, the imprisonment of children as punishment to their parents, the loony plans to invade West Berlin. The sheer thoroughness of the regime was horrifying: it accumulated, in the forty years of its existence, more written records than in all of German history since the Middle Ages. East Germany was run on fear and betrayal: at least 1 in 50, and by CIA estimates 1 in 7 people were informing on their relatives, friends, neighbours and colleagues. People were horrified to discover what had happened, again, in their country; what human beings were capable of. And they were numbed by shame.

Now, it's a different story. Groups of ex-Stasi are becoming increasingly belligerent. They write articles and books, conduct lawsuits against people who speak out against them*, intimidate former victims, and are affiliated with the SPD (the successor party to the communist SED), which is powerful in government.

Last year in March a group of some 200 ex-Stasi protested with loudhailers outside Hohenschönhausen in Berlin, which was the GDR's main prison for political prisoners. It is now a memorial museum about the regime. They demanded it be shut down, calling it a 'Gruselkabinett' or Chamber of Horrors, as if it were not a chamber of horrors of their own making. They objected to the words 'Communist Dictatorship' proposed for plaques in nearby streets. And they poured scorn on their former victims – some of whom now take tours through the prison. They yelled that everyone here was imprisoned according to GDR law: they were therefore ordinary criminals, not political dissidents. My friend Sigrid Paul told me how ex-Stasi men sometimes insinuate themselves into the tours she conducts. As she tells the story of her persecution and imprisonment, they heckle from the back, 'Rubbish! Lies! You're just a common criminal!' Sensitivities among victims' groups are running understandably high.

The opening shot of *The Lives of Others* is set at Hohenschönhausen Prison, but it wasn't filmed there. Dr Hubertus Knabe, the director of the memorial, refused the film's director, Florian Henckel von Donnersmarck, permission. His view is, 'You can't use a place where people suffered as a backdrop for a film so remiss in its dealings with this past.'

---

* One such group of former Stasi, affiliated with the self-styled 'Society for the Protection of Civil Rights and the Dignity of Man', took offence to allegations about the behaviour of ex-Stasi in *Stasiland* and sued my German publisher. I had written about what ex-Stasi are alleged, during the 1990s, to have done to people who tried to speak out against them (threatening acid attacks, engineering road 'accidents', detaining children after school as a terror to their parents and so on). Each allegation was either true or on the public record or both, but the publisher was intimidated. The Stasi are now adept at using the tools of democracy (Germany's relatively strict defamation laws) to protect a reputation they do not deserve.

The publicity notes to the film claim 'the greatest authenticity' and 'never-before-seen accuracy' and cite many prominent historians of the GDR. It might well be the first realistic portrayal of the GDR. Earlier, kitscher films like *Sonnenallee* and *Goodbye Lenin!* might be thought of as part of the *Ostalgie* phase of the denial of the GDR reality. They minimised the role of the Stasi. Perhaps former East Germans, including eminent supporters of *The Lives of Others* such as the songwriter Wolf Biermann and the head of the Stasi File Authority Marianne Birthler, are, at some level, grateful for a film that takes the terror of the GDR seriously.

To understand why a Wiesler could not have existed is to understand the 'total' nature of totalitarianism. Knabe talks of the fierce surveillance within the Stasi of its own men, of how in a case like Dreyman's there might have been a dozen agents: everything was checked and cross-checked. This separation of duties gives some former Stasi men the impression that they were just 'obeying orders,' or 'small cogs' in the machine, and therefore that they couldn't have done much harm. Perhaps this is partly why repentance like Wiesler's is rare. To my mind, to hope for salvation to come from the change of heart of a perpetrator is to misunderstand the nature of bureaucratised evil; the way great harms can be inflicted in minute, 'legal' steps; in decisions by committees carried out by people 'just doing their jobs.'

Part of Wiesler's comeuppance is that after the fall of the Wall he is seen distributing junk mail to people's letterboxes. The ex-Stasi are vociferous in their claims of being 'victims of democracy.' But the truth is that by and large they are doing much better in the new Germany than the people they oppressed. They have the educations and solid work histories they denied their victims. Many of them were snapped up by security firms and private detective agencies eager for their considerable expertise, or they went into business, skilled as they are – to perhaps an unholy degree – in 'managing' people. Surprisingly often, they sold real estate and insurance, occupations unknown in the Soviet Bloc. (Perhaps they had a head start here because, after all, they were schooled in the art of convincing people to do things against their better judgment.)

Knabe is no doubt correct about the internal surveillance of the Stasi making it physically impossible for a Stasi man to try to save people. But in my experience the more frightening thing is that they didn't *want* to. The institutional coercion rendered these men into true believers; it shrank their consciences and heightened their tolerance for injustice and cruelty 'for the cause.'

Von Donnersmarck spent four years researching the film, and knows as well as anyone that there is no case of a Stasi man trying to save victims. He has said, 'I didn't want to tell a true story as much as explore how someone might have behaved. The film is more of a basic expression of belief in humanity than an account of what actually happened.' The terrible truth is that the Stasi provide no material for a 'basic expression of belief in humanity'. For expressions of conscience and courage one would need to look to the resisters. It is this choice, to make a film about the change of heart of a Stasi man, which turns the film, for some, into an inappropriate – if unconscious – plea for absolution of the perpetrators.

Dr Knabe objects to 'making the Stasi man into a hero.' He recounts that von Donnersmarck 'would not be persuaded otherwise,' citing *Schindler's List* as justification for what he planned to do. 'But that is exactly the difference,' Knabe says. 'There was a Schindler. There was no Wiesler.'

The system demanded such loyalty that most ex-Stasi are still true believers. Knabe describes massive events they organise in Berlin where they 'ridicule the victims.' He says, 'This shamelessness contradicts the film's story of a Stasi spy who suddenly discovers his conscience. Even sixteen years after the fall of the SED dictatorship most Stasi people are still of the view that they did nothing wrong.' A story like Wiesler's plays into the hands of the ex-Stasi as they fight for their reputation. 'There is a kind of creeping rehabilitation going on,' says Knabe. 'Germany failed to prosecute communist-era crimes except in a very few instances. This was a criminal system. But now all we're supposed to remember is the factory jobs and good day care.'

There is another crucial difference: Schindler was not a Gestapo agent, but a private citizen. The correct analogy is this: how would an audience feel if a wonderfully moving film – a film alive to nuance and contradiction and acute about the human desire for forgiveness – were made about a Gestapo officer who had a change of heart and started trying to save Jews he had been ordered to persecute? Would the director of the memorial at Auschwitz be justified in refusing permission to film there? What if this happened in an environment in which Jews were not adequately compensated and former Nazis were agitating on the streets, maligning them as criminals, scum?

Joseph Conrad had it that 'art itself may be defined as a single-minded attempt to render the highest kind of justice to the visible universe, by bringing to light the truth, manifold and one, underlying its every aspect.' But drama has its own imperatives. At the end of his 'Director's Statement' von Donnersmarck writes, 'More than anything else, *The Lives of Others* is a human drama about the ability of human beings to do the right thing, no matter how far they have gone down the wrong path.' This is an uplifting thought. But it is recognising how human beings can be trained and forced into faceless systems of oppression in which conscience is extinguished that is more likely to save us from going down the wrong path again.

It is difficult to make comparisons with the Holocaust out of respect for its victims. It is rarely even compared with the regime that followed on the same soil, with the same people subject to it, and some of the same people in positions of power over them. This is so even though the methods of political repression and of social organisation were strikingly similar.

It is the way totalitarian regimes work, and how we are vulnerable to them, and how we deal afterwards with the perpetrators that are the questions raised by the reaction to *The Lives of Others*. These questions raised in relation to the Stasi regime are still tender spots in the German psyche because of the Nazi regime that preceded it. Was a change of heart and rebellion within the ranks of the oppressors possible? If we imagine the perpetrators as good-hearted people caught in a system not of their making (i.e. victims of a kind), where does that leave the Jews, or the true GDR heroes, the dissidents?

The battle for the reputation of the Stasi men currently being waged in the media, the entertainment business, the courts, in personal intimidation of former victims, and in demonstrations on the streets of Berlin cannot be understood without understanding that it is being waged with the Third Reich in the back of everyone's minds. The Stasi men are furiously fighting so as not to go down in history as the second lot of incontestable bogeymen thrown up by twentieth-century Germany. And many Germans themselves are deeply uncomfortable about recognising the chilling inhumanity of this, the second dictatorship on their soil.

Several times on my book tour in 2004, both in the former West and former East Germany, a sad and telling question was asked. At the end of the reading, after any ex-Stasi present had left, someone would say, 'What is it about us Germans, do you think, that makes us do these things?' By 'these things' they meant the totalitarian and administrative cruelties of the Nazi and the Stasi regimes. I have no answer; I do not think they are particularly German things to do. But there is such terror and tragedy in the question that I can see why a fable of forgiveness might hit the mark.

Guardian

Born in the GDR

Gert Reifarth

Beethoven's Seventh was my favourite symphony when I was young. It must have been in the early 1980s when I heard a recording by the Sydney Symphony Orchestra, conducted by Willem van Otterloo, broadcast by a GDR radio station. I was in awe, a twelve-year-old's sort of wonder. I had never heard the piece played before with so much depth, so much fire. Whereas GDR authorities did not let too much new Western culture (decadent!) pass the border, recordings of the classics were frequently imported from the West. More than twenty-five years later, I marvel at the power of music and ponder: an Australian orchestra with a Dutch conductor – was that the GDR cultural chiefs saying that 'their' Beethoven, a staunch humanist and possibly even an early communist in their opinion, would eventually convince the West to adopt communism as well?

I was so enraptured by the recording that I decided to write a letter to Sydney to congratulate the orchestra on their performance. Back then I did not know anything about Australia, and to be honest, I had only ever encountered it as – a finger. The GDR children's organisation, 'Young Pioneers', had this weird greeting in which you stated that you were 'always ready for peace and socialism', and used your hand with each finger representing a continent to indicate the unity of all five in the not too distant future under communism. Australia was probably the ring finger.

I never expected an answer from Sydney, either because I thought they surely wouldn't care about a twelve-year-old boy from the GDR, or else because the GDR authorities would not let any mail from that capitalist end of the world reach one of its children. But a colour brochure arrived introducing the Sydney Symphony and its current season. I was enraptured yet again and treasured this brochure for years and years and still have it today. With the brochure came a letter, thanking me for my praise and also telling me that, sadly, Willem van Otterloo had died after a car accident some years earlier ... in Melbourne.

And that was that. I would never travel to Australia, as my life was an imprisoned one, or 'protected' in the official version, behind the Iron Curtain.

Then the system crumbled and the Berlin Wall fell. Then the GDR was united with West Germany on 3 October 1990, one day after my twenty-second birthday.

I finished my degree, went to work in Ireland, lived in (West) Berlin for some years finishing my PhD, and in July 2003 I arrived in Melbourne. I have lived and worked here as a lecturer in German Studies at Melbourne University since then. Although I never really missed my lost home country for many years after German unification, my being so far away here in Australia has brought about a journey, of sorts, for my identity, a resurrection of the GDR in my life, and a strong feeling of rootlessness. My former home is brought back to life for me nearly every day. There are books, films, web pages and, most important, there are questions – from students, colleagues, friends, even strangers. And I invite, even provoke, those questions, by pointing out when I introduce myself that I'm not from Germany, but from the GDR, not German but East German.

*

After school, I was initially denied the place at university I had applied for. I wanted to do German Studies, a course to which only twelve to fifteen students were admitted per year in the whole GDR. My father took action and sent a ten-page letter to a minister of the GDR government, urging him to give me the chance to serve communism by awarding me the place I had been denied. Dad dutifully and at length quoted Marx, Engels and Lenin, and sang the praises of the GDR education system so loudly I could have sworn the minister would see it for the farce that it was. But not at all: after some weeks I was summoned to the university that offered the course, three hours away by train from where we lived, and was told that I had been accepted. Today, when I re-read Dad's letter I always have to smile.

And I remember other letters that proved to be powerful tools. I wrote one to our relatives in the West with seemingly random syllables underlined, and then mailed yet another one from a different city after a while, which helped them figure out what I wanted. The underlined syllables from the first letter put together with the instructions from the second spelled 'Solzhenitsyn *Gulag Archipelago*', which was the book I wanted our relatives to bring for us on their next visit. Bring it they did, yet this affair was highly dangerous, stupid really, because not only could our relatives have been forbidden to ever enter the GDR, but also my family would have gone to prison if we had been found with that book. At barely twenty years old, Baldur Haase was sentenced to more than three years in prison for owning a copy of Orwell's *Nineteen Eighty-Four* and lending it to two friends in 1959. My family and I did not know this at the time of our Solzhenitsyn scheme, but we were very much aware of such possibilities, even if we tried not to think about them. Surely that was what I did when I secretly recorded a BBC-broadcast reading of Orwell's novel in the GDR in the mid-'80s, week by week hoping the reception would be good enough on my little GDR radio-cum-tape-recorder. A piece of communist technology bringing Orwell to me through the Iron Curtain – that gripping irony made me forget the dangers of what I was doing.

Solzhenitsyn's book, of course, was a revelation, telling us about heinous crimes committed in the name of communism. But my dad and I wanted to know more, and we embarked on another dangerous and rather stupid venture. You had to be eighteen or older to be allowed into the Deutsche Bücherei, or German Library, in Leipzig. It stores every single book ever printed in German since 1913, but GDR citizens were denied access to a great number of these. Dad created a fake ID card for me and dressed me in a suit to make me appear older. Not only did I get in, I even made it to the 'poison section' of the library, which was hidden in the depths of the building. With the supporting letter of a high-profile academic stating that it was necessary for me to go and read there for a paper I was researching on devil figures in German and Soviet literature, I managed to get clearance to read Western books on the Russian Revolution, Lenin and Stalin, breathlessly seeing more crimes of communism unfold in front of my eyes, information that I passed on to my father.

In other areas the authorities decided they should allow to a certain extent what they could not suppress. So there was a 'metal hour' on one of the GDR radio stations every week, and we would tape the music, as we had a cassette recorder that cost more than two months of an average salary (electronic equipment and cars were deemed 'luxury goods' and were incredibly expensive). Western metal records, however, we could not buy in the GDR. So I developed a little ruse. When they sent us parcels, our West German relatives would often hide money in boxes of cereal, and never once was it detected. With the money we were able to go to so-called 'Intershops' and buy Western products – a clever scheme of the GDR authorities to extract from their population the hard currency which they so badly needed. Some of the money I would give to the lead singer of an East German rock band who bought heavy metal LPs for me in the West when his band toured there. He was a nice guy, very fond of Wagner, and only after 1989 did I learn that he had been an unofficial informer for the Ministry of State Security. I'm not sure if he thought me and my LPs important enough to report to his superiors.

The other way to get Western music was to go to Hungary, where it was on sale at ridiculous prices. I went there once, and remember giving GDR authorities complicated academic reasons when I applied for a visa in 1988. Yet all I wanted was to see Metallica live in Budapest during their Justice For All tour (knowing little of the kind of justice that was less than a year away).

*

'How did you find Anna Funder's best-selling book about your country, *Stasiland*?' a colleague asked me a year after it was published in 2002. I replied that I had never lived in Stasiland.

Before his surprise managed to find verbal expression, I went on to explain how Funder describes the 'black' part of the GDR, whereas my experience was made up of 70 per cent grey, 20 per cent white – and only 10 per cent black. Black was the realm of the state's surveillance of its own people, by the Ministry of State Security, whose gruesome activity is simply not captured by its nickname, Stasi. That sounds too harmless, like a nickname for something cute and small and even helpless. White was the area of free health and child care, free and good education, heavily subsidised food items, low crime rate, and a protected life that allowed for a happy childhood like mine. Speaking of state protection, it was also protection from the capitalist world of endless choices that makes mind and senses work overtime. Grey was everything in between, the ideology that was preached to us, the efforts we made to fool the system, the boasts of economic success when it was obvious the economy was dying, the boasts of a healthy environment when nature was dying, the erection of huge and anonymous blocks of flats when old houses were rotting. Grey was also somehow the main colour of life.

So I'm worried about the possible misimpression that Funder's book describes the whole GDR, when it doesn't. Yet it's beautifully written and composed, and I said to my colleague that I cherished its view from the outside, as it is not tangled up in the continuing East–West German divide. I admire also those whom Funder calls 'heroes' – the people in the GDR who spoke up, something so brave and dangerous that I never had the courage to do it. But heroes achieve something, don't they? Whereas GDR 'heroes' would have been fully aware not only of the inevitability of the regime's merciless punishment (which suggests there was an element of masochism in their actions), but also of the futility of their protests. They did not weaken the system and, sadly, even provided the regime with opportunities to exercise their repressive devices, and thus kept the system functioning. This changed in mid-1989 when protesters were too many to be simply silenced. The growth of people power, combined with Gorbachev's new approach of openness, the lethargy of the rulers in the face of the new developments, and the dying economy extinguished communist rule in the GDR. My own first reaction to the 'peaceful revolution' of 1989 was one of utter disbelief: surely the authorities would restore order soon and force the country back to the path of communism? Amazingly, this did not happen, the Wall fell and I went to West Germany for the first time on an overcrowded train in November 1989, spending the 100DM (about A$90) of 'welcoming money', which every GDR citizen received, on magazines, LPs and beer. I remember my introduction to the West's free-market economy: having to choose between twenty or more brands of beer. I chose the cheapest. It tasted strange. And when I read the label I realised I had bought the one that was alcohol-free.

*

I'd been fortunate not to have been drafted by the NVA, the National People's Army, in the GDR. I had been seriously ill and very close to dying in 1983, and in the 1987 medical exam was deemed unfit for army service. Yet in 1989 a follow-up medical examination would have sent me to the army, had not the head doctor been a pupil of Professor Popp, who had operated on me six years earlier. Against the view of his colleagues, he protested that whoever Professor Popp operated on was to be considered genuinely unfit.

Two close friends of mine at university, however, had both served in the NVA, at the inner German border. Both of them had patrolled the border, teamed with a fellow soldier whom they mistrusted: it was a real possibility that he might shoot them and cross the border. One of my friends told me that he would have shot at anyone trying to cross the border and flee to the West, as he was afraid that otherwise he might be shot in the back by one of the people attempting to flee. (Twenty-five GDR soldiers died in this way.) My other friend, however, said he would never have shot anyone and instead fired in the air, risking serious repercussions. About 40,000 GDR citizens tried to flee the country between the erection of the Berlin Wall in 1961 and its fall in 1989, nearly three every day, with only about 2000 succeeding and 900 dying. Amazingly, my two friends were never out on patrol when someone tried to flee the country in their sector.

'How on earth did you live in the GDR, with all the control and all that communism?', a fellow guest at a dinner party once asked me. All GDR citizens, I replied, were highly talented social schizophrenics. The poet Adolf Endler says that 70 per cent of the population were against the regime, or simply not in support of it. As one of them, I had two faces, a public one that affected to endorse the system, and a private one that showed my true thoughts. This manifested itself in all aspects of my life, as I was exposed to the official glossing over of reality, and yet was familiar with the actual situation in the country. In school, I learned about the humane ideals of communism yet lived in the mess the Eastern bloc had made of those ideals. I lived behind the Wall, yet was able to cross it every night watching West German television. Carefully instructed by my parents from an early age, I held my tongue in public, yet craved and searched for critical words about the authorities in cabaret shows and between the lines of books and song lyrics. This schizophrenia was largely chosen as a strategy of conflict avoidance and survival, and enabled me and my fellow GDR citizens to lead lives that were, at their best, happy, untroubled and free from state intervention. The loyal part of the GDR population displayed traits of schizophrenia as well – just the other way around. In order to be loyal to the state, they closed their eyes to the hard facts of the reality around them. Some pretended to be normal citizens, although they were working for the secret police.

Despite this schizophrenic life, I remember a distinct GDR lifestyle, and even traditions that grew there, in art, in music. To this day I wonder how repression can produce such different things – schizophrenia, paranoia, submission, but also joy and culture. I also wonder about the absurdities that marked the lives of everyone in the GDR. Many of my memories have at their core something that I find profoundly absurd or even humorous. There was my going to a school named after Friedrich Engels in a town named after Karl Marx, though the street was for some reason not called after Lenin. While the authorities promoted FKK, or Free Body Culture, which advocated a natural relation to one's body, the country was exceptionally prudish. Then there were those small acts of passive resistance GDR citizens were so good at, such as putting one letter the wrong way around in a headline on a wall news-sheet we had to create to celebrate the GDR's latest achievements.

We used to be amused at the obvious contradictions between reality and official claims. While we were told that the egg production plan had been exceeded, there were often no eggs in the shops. The wrecking of the environment was presented as a Western problem, when the GDR's forests were half dead and when the table-tennis table left outside one night at my grandparents' was covered with a finger-thick layer of black dust the next morning. They lived near Leuna, home of the GDR's largest chemical factory, which covered a large area and had 600 kilometres of tubes.

We were rather proud of the world sporting records held by the GDR. Some of those the GDR holds to this day. When I think about them now, I can still detect a hint of pride in myself, which I dampen by reflecting that they were likely to have been achieved by athletes using drugs. Although there is (as yet) no proof of this, the fact that no-one has ever come remotely close to breaking them in all these years seems to speak for itself.

*

When the film *The Lives of Others* won an Oscar and subsequently came to Australian cinemas in April 2007, I was showered with questions on how I related to it. The movie is a gripping, haunting one that has pulled many East Germans out of their nostalgic comfort zone, and maybe Germans in general out of self-pity and denial. Indeed it is quite possible that Funder's book – much as she has criticised the film – helped prepare the ground for this to happen. The GDR depicted in the film is a dark and lonely place, yet also fascinating in its mercilessly cold approach to all things human. Any non-Germans bear in mind that the film (as with Funder's book) is *not* a portrait of the GDR in its entirety. *The Lives of Others* is less than that and more: it is set in the black 10 per cent of the country but, more important, it is about human beings in general, some of whom are villains, some good guys, some changing for the better, some losing their feet. It is a film about things human beings have to struggle with: control, power, death, love, treason, deception, hope and change. Such issues are not restricted to the GDR nor to times past.

While the film received rave reviews, some reviewers were doubtful about the transformation of an officer of the Ministry of State Security from 'Saul' to 'Paul', from a loyal servant of the state to a secret accomplice of the subject he investigates. Those who see this as unrealistic ignore the cases when officers wanted to leave the ministry. There are two cases from 1979 and 1981 when officers who had quit were sentenced to death and shot in the back of the head at close range. More problematic, for me, is that in the film the officer is shown to have a low-paid, low-class job after 1989, while the victim is now a best-selling author. This is a reversal of the real situation, where victims usually had a tough time while ex-officers of the ministry quickly found their feet in the new capitalism.

The film has triggered some events reminiscent of its story. Actor Ulrich Mühe, who plays the officer, mentioned the collaboration with the ministry of his ex-wife, Jenny Gröllmann. Owing to legal action on her part, the film company had to issue a second version of the DVD with changed audio commentary, and a German publisher had to issue a new edition of the book accompanying the film. I feel strangely uneasy when I hear Mühe, in the commentary included in the German DVD release, mention that he was under the ministry's surveillance right from the time of his first theatre engagement, in Karl-Marx-Stadt (Chemnitz). I lived in that town, and in the early 1980s, saw Mühe numerous times on stage in Goethe's *Faust*, not knowing a thing about the ministry's involvement in this theatre, with actors spying on other actors.

*

What about the GDR today? Is it gone completely? People, media and the arts inject new life into the GDR and create for it a somehow bodiless existence, slowly slipping into the realm of the mysterious. It is alive in the heads and habits of many East Germans, proving that the nature of a country is much more than physical borders and involves a resilient sense of belonging, part of a people's conception of self. Simplifying matters just a little, one could say that there were two types of East Germans after 1990. Some cherished the feeling of relief that the dictatorial regime had fallen, and they adapted to the new country and the new rules. For others, however, the demise of the GDR meant that with it had vanished the various joys of communism.

They developed a nostalgia for a glorified and neutered past, which can be quite destructive when it leads them to reject and drift away from reality.

Many of the second group seem to turn to their former schizophrenia yet again, living in two places simultaneously: the united Germany that is dominated by the West, and a new version of the GDR created in their own minds and fostered by the media. The new schizophrenia comes in various forms, most prominently as *Ostalgie*, or nostalgia for the East, the fond remembering and reviving of select features of the GDR. If any of these schizophrenic tendencies becomes extreme, it leads to a desire to live in some kind of 'past zone', or to the feeling of superiority to West Germans, or even to the desire to re-erect the Berlin Wall.

It remains to be seen if East Germans will ever be ready to leave the GDR behind. While I certainly do not pine for it, I still cherish memories of my home country. And I wonder how I'd respond should I ever hear Beethoven's Seventh played by the Sydney Symphony Orchestra in the Opera House.

Meanjin

Being There

Mark McKenna

> We give what we have. The rest is the madness of art.
> —MANNING CLARK, paraphrasing Henry James, 1967

Among the portraits and photographs that hang in the living room of Manning Clark's former home in Tasmania Circle, Canberra, there is a pencil sketch by Charles Blackman, *Drifting*. Out on the water, two men sit in a boat; no land is in sight. Another figure, completely white, stands just behind the bow: an apparition defying the current. Manning Clark saw himself as much like the ghostly figure in Blackman's sketch, as the artist-historian seeking a solitary understanding of the human condition. Clark's was a singular vision – emotive and mischievous, tortured and divine – like that of no other historian or writer of his generation.

Manning Clark relished cultivating an image of himself as the lone outsider. When he sought to place his work in the context of Australian historiography – even on the first occasion, at a Melbourne University seminar in 1954 – he dismissed nearly all the writing of Australian history that had gone before him as the product of the dead hand of British imperialism and Protestantism. He could see little cause for optimism in his own generation: the radical historians were wedded to a rigid creed that denied the mystery in human experience and lacked a great theme.

Three years later, in the introduction to *Sources of Australian History*, he wrote that Australian history after 1919 was 'like an uncharted sea'. Clark was adept at leaving himself as the last man standing, the only historian with sufficient insight and breadth of interest to rewrite Australian history. This task was made all the more noble – in his eyes, at least – by virtue of the fact that its execution was entirely cut off from conversation with his contemporaries. In private, Clark heeded the advice of his colleagues, but he chose not to acknowledge other historians in his work, continuing with the pretence that he was writing history from a *tabula rasa*.

Clark warned historians not to read what others had to say until they'd completed their early drafts, 'and maybe not then'. The duty of the historian was to create history anew from primary sources; he insisted that historians should never 'start arguing with what others have to say'. But Clark went much further than merely shying away from argument. In his histories, he could not even bring himself to discuss the research and work of others. To do so would only obscure the individuality of the historian's voice, one cast in the mould of nineteenth-century European romanticism – Beethoven, Goethe and Caspar David Friedrich – that of the artist-hero who stands alone on the cliff and gazes out to sea, seeking sublime inspiration.

In his Boyer Lectures, delivered in 1976, Clark listed the writers that had sparked his interest in writing a multi-volume history of Australia: Chekhov, Hardy, Dickens, Dostoevsky, Tolstoy, James. Not one historian of Australia – not one scholar – is mentioned, though Henry Lawson, Patrick White, Henry Handel Richardson and Martin Boyd are credited with providing inspiration. Although Clark spent thirty years within the academy, he preferred to place his work in the company of artists. And most historians who have written about Clark's place in Australian historiography seem happy to leave him there, hovering in a no-man's land, somewhere between nineteenth-century literature and an antiquated form of epic history. There is a broad consensus that Clark simply does not fit into the schema of Australian historiography in any significant way.

Stuart Macintyre and Alan Atkinson have both drawn attention to the fact that few historians have sought to engage with

Clark's work, save for one or two embarrassing attempts to imitate him. Historians have ignored Clark in much the same way that Clark ignored the work of others. In the multi-volume Bicentennial history *Australians: A Historical Library*, Clark's six-volume *History of Australia*, by then complete, received little attention. Reviewing the posthumously published *A Historian's Apprenticeship* in 1992, Geoffrey Blainey described Clark as ploughing a 'lonely furrow' and being 'deliberately deaf to many of the questions that excited social scientists'.

True to form, Clark was out of step with the intellectual fashions and preoccupations of his colleagues. He was the great generalist in a time of increasing specialisation. The revisionist history of the 1960s and '70s had little impact on his work, while his dogged pursuit of a prose style recalling Macaulay or Carlyle was already passé by 1962, when volume I of *A History of Australia* was published. Richard Waterhouse has neatly characterised Clark's work as 'a belated attempt at an Australian national history' in the mode of George Bancroft, replacing Bancroft's emphasis on progress with an unfolding tale of 'the collapse of social purpose'. As Stuart Macintyre wrote in 1994, 'in bypassing the work of others, [Clark] created a gulf that few specialists sought to cross.'

Manning Clark's audience was not the academy. Like the village parson and the local MP, he spoke often of his connection with ordinary people. Today, publishers would bid furiously for the work of a historian who saw himself as akin to 'an actor on a revolving stage'. Historians, said Clark, 'should be judged by their success in increasing wisdom and understanding and their capacity to entertain'. Clark wrote for the public gallery, and his prose is ever conscious of its presence, even to the point of inserting the applause, guffaws and shouts of abuse from an imagined public chorus into his narrative. And to keep his audience entertained, it was sometimes necessary to be flexible with the facts. Clark's eye was first and foremost on the dramatic impact of the narrative.

Humphrey McQueen once told me, 'I would never go to Manning to look anything up.' My own experience with Clark has been similar. When I first read him, in my early twenties, I did not rush off to read the work of other Australian historians.

Instead, I went to listen to Bach's *Well-Tempered Clavier*, and to the final movement of Sibelius's Fifth Symphony. If I went to Clark to look anything up, it was to find the pieces of music that he found inspiring. Years later, working on my doctoral thesis, I discovered that chasing the trail of Clark's footnotes was a fruitless task. Like many before me, I could not crack Clark's code. Quotes frequently appeared in his work that seemed to bear no relation to the sources in the notes – or, as was more often the case, they blended so seamlessly with his own prose that it was impossible to tell who was speaking. It seemed that he saw primary sources as something akin to a musical score, a mere form of notation upon which he would improvise, providing a magnificent libretto for another Clark oratorio.

All of this raises important questions: If Manning Clark's work is not seen as a reliable historical account, and is rarely used in schools and universities in the teaching of Australian history, what might we go to it *for*? What is it that makes Clark's work memorable, and how are we to understand its value?

*

> I would like to be a writer – But how! My style is poor, my vocabulary lamentably small, and my ideas indistinct. Yet I do receive inspiration, by which I mean my mind becomes filled with an idea, and I want to develop it – then I am excited … to achieve my goal I must (i) Discipline myself – no excesses – an artist should observe (ii) Note down my ideas and impressions (iii) Not be dependent on people. —MANNING CLARK, 1942

After all that has been written on Manning Clark, it seems trite to claim that his work needs to be critically understood as literature rather than history. As Peter Munz perceptively wrote in 1979, Clark's work demonstrated that Australian history was 'but a variation on the universal themes of life and death, greed and hope, curse and vengeance' – he had effectively created Australia's past as 'a series of myths'. Despite the brutalising history of convictism, frontier violence and a harsh environment, Clark showed, as Humphrey McQueen claimed in 1987, that Australia could still be 'a mythopoeic site'. Certainly, Clark's work is literary in its imaginative scope, its field of reference and its depth of feeling. In positive reviews, *A History of Australia* is described as a literary masterpiece. In critical reviews, it is condemned for being clichéd, derivative and repetitive. Still, as Michael Cathcart noted in 1995, for all the references to Clark's literary imagination, 'no-one has really managed to articulate the translucent quality in [his] work ... or quite identified how his literary imagination works, or why it gives the history a value which is not undermined by its idiosyncrasies and inaccuracies.'

One way of appreciating how Manning Clark's literary imagination functions is to examine his personal voice. It is a feature of his work that was frequently commented upon by critics, especially in the context of his literary skill. On the publication of volume I of *A History of Australia*, Max Crawford noted 'the very distinctive personal vision' that Clark brought to his subject. As each subsequent volume appeared, Crawford's remarks were replayed. Reviewers described volume II as 'personal and burning, and fascinatingly readable', 'highly personal', 'idiosyncratic' and 'highly original', but few sought to tease out exactly how Clark's voice made itself felt.

The first-person pronoun never appears in the six volumes. Yet Clark's work was deeply personal long before historians such as Greg Dening, Miriam Dixson, Peter Read, Inga Clendinnen or Tom Griffiths, among others, began to bring personal experience and reflections into their prose. Nor was Clark's voice in any way transparent or self-reflective. Indeed, he warned budding historians not to discuss the problems of writing with the reader: 'the narrator must learn to shut up', he proclaimed (this from an author whose volumes were steeped in personal comment). But if Clark's work was *political*, it was so in a unique way. Consider, for example, the bold statements of position by some of Clark's contemporaries: history is 'the struggle between the organised rich and the organised poor' (Brian Fitzpatrick, in *A Short History of the Australian Labor Movement*, 1940); 'I am for the weak not the strong, the poor not the rich, the exploited many not the select few' (Russel Ward, in the preface to the 1987 edition of his *Concise History of Australia*); 'This history is necessarily biased' (Humphrey McQueen, in the introduction to *A New Britannia*, 1970); 'This history is critical not celebratory. It rejects myths of national progress and unity. It starts from a recognition that Australian settler society was built on invasion and dispossession' (Verity Burgmann and Jenny Lee's introduction to *A People's History of Australia*, 1988).

Nowhere in Clark's histories did he seek to reveal his political sympathies so openly, yet it is he who is remembered by some as the most politically prejudiced historian of the post-war period – a memory preserved by John Howard, who has attacked Clark's alleged communist sympathies and his bleak view of 'the Australian achievement'. To a large extent, Clark earned the ire of conservatives not only because his history cast the Labor Party as the engine of Australia's national progress, but because his public statements characterised the non-Labor parties as little more than moneychangers and philistines. In its intent, however, Clark's *History of Australia* was less overtly political than the work of many left-leaning historians who were writing at the same time.

If Manning Clark's voice is personal, this quality emerges in his telling of history, in his selection of primary sources, in his presentation of conflict, and in his endless search to understand the inner life of his protagonists, a search that led him to employ emotional language which lacked the one quality that historians of his generation tended to admire: 'sober restraint'. Clark's personal voice was not grounded in political statements or in any prefiguring of postmodern scholarship, but rather in a profound religiosity, and it is this highly individual understanding of the religious – ecumenical and spiritual, in the broadest sense – that gives Clark's work its depth of feeling and its distinctive, redeeming personal quality.

It is a feature of his oeuvre that takes shape very early. Clark opened *Puzzles of Childhood*, the first volume of his autobiography, with a story he told many times. He remembered his mother telling him, when he was not yet five, 'Mann, dear, you are a very special boy. There's nothing you can't do if you want to do it.' Of course, like all his autobiographical writings, the truth of this recollection is uncertain. But it still captures an essential truth about Clark – his belief in his unique powers of perception and insight, something that was evident from the moment he began to write, in his early twenties:

> [I am thinking of writing a] short article on Australian culture ... but it is an artistic experience, not a conclusion from evidence ... My idea is: in Australia we are uncertain of everything, we feel insecure. What is the cause of this? ... First ... geography, the hostile environment, the fear experienced when alone ... second, the doubt, do we belong here, perhaps this is geography, perhaps history ... third, Australia as the harlot, raped by the Europeans, coarse, vulgar, meretricious ... I should write this when in an inspired mood.

In his early diaries – from the time of his arrival in Oxford, in 1938, until he began teaching the first full course in Australian history at the University of Melbourne, in 1946 – Manning Clark wrote frequently of the fits of inspiration that would descend upon him, the words racing through his mind 'like water with the light shining on it'. It was something that he described frequently as being received, 'images rising before [his] mind', in the manner of a painter facing a blank canvas. From the beginning, though, Clark found writing a struggle: inspiration came, but he often railed against his inability to express the thoughts that possessed him, and a sense of failure and dissatisfaction with his work remained with him until the end of his life.

Gazing at paintings or photographs, standing before monuments or historical sites, conversing with friends and colleagues, Clark was fired by inspiration that came from an unknown but implicitly divine source. He claimed that he wanted to understand what had moved men, had inspired and defeated them, believing that 'what happens and has happened in life mocks the fitness of things.' These words, echoing Ecclesiastes – 'All is vanity' – not only articulated his motivation as a historian, they also expressed the drama and conflict of his personal life.

From Clark's six volumes, and particularly his writings on history (he wrote more on the writing of history than most historians), there is the familiar refrain of Manning Clark, Historian: the seeker of the heart and soul of human beings (usually men), the worrier over the question of faith and what it meant to live in a Godless world, the tragedian, the writer who drew inspiration from art, literature and music and who, following Carlyle, saw history as the 'true epic poem of mankind' and himself as 'one of the muses' that could 'communicate a vision of the world'. What remains uncertain, however, is the extent to which Clark's highly personal historical voice was shaped by his personal life.

Several historians have hinted at the autobiographical dimension of Clark's work. Reviewing volume II, Geoffrey Serle referred to the 'depth of personal experience' that informed Clark's work. In *Suspect History*, Humphrey McQueen gives the well-known example from volume IV, where Clark has Robert Burke suffering from a 'fit of the sillies', before claiming that 'Clark carried concerns from his life and memoirs into his history.' More recently, on Radio National, Michael Cathcart insisted that the great theme of Clark's history – 'the struggle between Catholicism, Protestantism and the Enlightenment' – was really Clark's 'lifelong struggle'. Manning Clark admitted this much to be true. In 1976, he acknowledged that the central conflicts in his history – especially that of the English inheritance versus the native born – were, as he put it, 'in my veins'. Beyond the obvious tension between the different family backgrounds of his parents, the personal quality of Clark's historical voice was connected intimately with his personal life.

The polyvocal element of Clark's history (or, as Peter Craven once called it, his 'point-of-view writing') is one example. Clark's later volumes teem with voices simultaneously playing variations on a theme. Like a Handel oratorio, they rise up to take their designated role in the score, given an added touch of Clarkian drama here, an extra bit of Clarkian pathos there. The voices within his text mirror those within his mind: Clark often referred to himself as a 'polyphon', a man of many voices. He claimed to hear the future-of-humanity voice, the sceptical voice, the eye of pity, the voice of doubt about everything, the voice of 'Mr Passion' and countless other nondescript voices within 'Mr Passion'. In Clark's mind, these played constantly, usually in unresolved tension, conveying 'an eternal restlessness and discontent'.

Clark presented many of his lead characters (Wentworth, Lawson, Curtin) as divided personalities brought down by the predictable 'fatal flaw', and his private correspondence reveals that he thought of himself in much the same way. In letters to his friends and to his wife, Dymphna, he refers to 'the Double' (a description taken from the title of an early short story by Dostoevsky), the other Manning Clark who is usually saddled with responsibility for the drinking and sinful behaviour that brings the more virtuous Clark down. As the voices arose in his text, slowly taking shape and life as different characters, so the voices within his mind fought for dominance, embodying the potential persons that he might become. They also serve to displace responsibility for his behaviour.

Driven from elsewhere, by some unknown force, Clark's protagonists struggle to attain a moral sensibility and control over their own destiny. They fight to assert their own conscience, naively cling to the dream of human perfectibility, doubt the existence of God, and strain to find purpose and meaning in life. They suffer because of their knowledge of human beings' capacity for evil (a capacity which they know is also inside them), and they are confronted with the conflict between the desires of the flesh and the needs of the spirit. And, now and then, they are brought down by a fit of the sillies.

Prompted by Kathleen Fitzpatrick, a great fan of Henry James, Clark became fond of borrowing James's notion of the 'felt life'. He believed that he needed a bank of his own excitements and disappointments, his successes and heartbreaks, before he could write history as art – before he could write about the inner life of others, informing their world with the shared experience of his life. In this sense, Manning Clark's historical voice is personal in a way that few other historians' are. The past becomes the site for expressing and working through his deepest feelings. His lifelong fear of the wolves – the critics whom, he imagined, would tear his work to pieces – points to the deeply personal nature of his history. Having invested so much feeling, so much of his inner self in his work, he felt that he had laid himself open, and he trembled like a child in search of approval at the thought of his creation being subjected to censure or derision.

*

Being There

> I think that's what you've got to get over in a history – those moments, those epiphanies in human experience.
> —MANNING CLARK, 1987

In the last twenty years of his life, after his retirement, Manning Clark began to construct his own mythology as historian, writer and public figure. When he tried to tell the story of why he became a historian, and explain the personal vision that drove him to write *A History of Australia*, he often recited a series of personal epiphanies. In Clark's telling, these are moments of profound intellectual and spiritual revelation. They arrive like the words of an angel, shrouded in mystery, in a process that remains partially hidden – even from Clark himself. Through their telling, and in the contemplation of the morals they contain, Clark navigates his way through life. The epiphanies provide inspiration and, ultimately, they serve as the raison d'être of Manning Clark, Historian, informing and guiding him.

There are many Clarkian epiphanies. First, there are the epiphanies of place: visiting Cologne Cathedral for the first time, awestruck at the beauty created by man to praise God; standing on the South Head of Sydney Harbour, the sight of the turbulent sea making him want to write about what was inside the hearts and minds of the convicts; gazing at the ruins of Yorkshire's Whitby Abbey and dreaming of telling the story of how the Europeans had brought those two Great Expectations, Catholic Christendom and the Enlightenment, to the ancient continent of Australia.

Then there were the library epiphanies: discovering the Hindu fables about the world to the south of Java in a museum library in Jakarta; crying after reading that Magellan's 'black eyes wept' when he realised he had found a way through to the Pacific; seeing John Henry Newman's pencilled notes on truth in an 1864 article by Charles Kingsley, the genesis of Newman's *Apologia Pro Vita Sua*. There were also the epiphanies that came through the meeting of fellow artists – James McAuley, Patrick White, David Campbell and many others – those bonds and friendships created by a spark of unspoken recognition and understanding rather than being earned slowly over time.

Finally, there are the numerous epiphanies which relate to Clark's encounters with art, music and literature. Listening to Bach's B Minor Mass or the slow movement of Beethoven's Sonata Opus 111; hearing Henry Handel Richardson read from *The Fortunes of Richard Mahony*; viewing Sidney Nolan's *Riverbend* or Rembrandt's *Return of the Prodigal Son*; reading White, Hope, Chekhov, James or the usual suspect, Dostoevsky: all of these encounters made Clark realise that history must always run second to art as a form of human expression.

Of all Clark's epiphanies, though, there is one that stands out for its allegorical power. It is the one that he told most often, the one he invested with the most significance, especially because it explains the genesis of his life as a historian. So far as I can tell, Clark first told the story publicly in 1978, in an unpublished background piece he prepared for Rob Pascoe, who was then writing a profile of Clark for the *National Times*. Pascoe's article, 'The History of Manning Clark', led with the story, describing the 23-year-old Clark arriving at Bonn on the morning after Kristallnacht, on 10 November 1938: 'Clark made his way amid the debris throughout Bonn in a state of disbelief.' Two years later, in 1980, the background article Clark had prepared for Pascoe was published under the title 'Themes in *A History of Australia*' in Clark's *Occasional Writings and Speeches*.

Throughout the '80s, Clark was invited to reminisce about his life and career in the national media, and he told the Kristallnacht story many times. In 1987, interviewed by John Tranter on Radio National, he offered a typically powerful telling:

> What really got me going was that when I was about twenty-two or twenty-three I went to Germany to meet the woman I was going to marry, and I happened to arrive at the railway station at Bonn am Rhein on the morning of Kristallnacht. That was the morning after the storm-troopers had destroyed Jewish shops, Jewish businesses and the synagogues. Burned them and so on. And I came up out of the Bonn railway station, my head stuffed with these myths about progress and so on. And there I was confronted with these storm-troopers. Of course they didn't menace me, or threaten me. But I saw the fruits of evil, of human evil, before me there on the streets of Bonn.

Over the next three or four years, I gradually had to abandon all the myths I'd grown up with. That my world, my intellectual equipment, my spiritual equipment, couldn't cope with what I'd seen in Germany. And all the things that had meant a great deal to me and probably still do mean a great deal to me, like *Hymns Ancient and Modern*, the Old Testament, the King James Bible, the Dry Souls of the Enlightenment, as Carlyle called them, the hopes about things better, the belief in the British – all this had to go and I had to start on a new pilgrimage to see, was there anything which could replace these myths which I think I found then didn't correspond with the world as I'd come to know it.

This telling of the Kristallnacht epiphany is similar to the version in *Occasional Writings and Speeches*, as are the lessons Clark draws from the encounter, except that in the published article, Clark wrote about himself in the third person ('the author'), more consciously creating a figure of myth.

One year after the Tranter interview, the story appeared again in R.M. Crawford and Stuart Macintyre's *Making History*, in Clark's brief paper explaining his approach to the writing of history:

When I came up out of the Bonn railway station on the morning of 11 November I was confronted by men in military uniforms who had machine guns in their hands. They were wearing huge breeches. They would have made marvellous shepherd rucks for Carlton in the old days. That morning in the *Volkischer Beobachter* Dr Goebbels explained that the German people had taken their revenge on the Jews for the attempt by a Jew named Grunspan to assassinate a member of the German Embassy in Paris. Once again ... I found myself chewing over the question of human evil. There were at least two people inside me – the optimist and meliorist, and, dare one say it, the part-time messianic; and the other pessimistic, gloomy, the person who saw no answers to the problem of evil, or, as I liked to put it in those five volumes, 'the madness in men's hearts'.

After telling the Kristallnacht story on ABC TV and radio on several more occasions in the '80s, it appeared for the final time in the second volume of Clark's autobiography, *Quest for Grace*, published in 1990. At the last moment, in his ink scrawl, Clark had added the following words in the margins of the volume's final typescript draft:

> Dymphna was there on the platform at the Bonn railway station when I stepped off the train early in the morning of 8 November 1938 ... we were in for a rude shock, it was the morning after 'Kristallnacht' ... glass was everywhere on the footpath ... there were trucks with men in uniform standing in the tray.

If there is one personal experience that explains Clark's life and work, it is his experience of Kristallnacht, the point when the Nazi persecution of Jews turned towards the Holocaust. In a small village outside of Dresden, the diarist and literary scholar Victor Klemperer described his fear and sense of impending horror after the events of the night. Many of his friends 'had been arrested and taken away'. Klemperer himself was arrested but later released. He was 'free', he wrote, 'but for how long?' Like many Jews, he was 'tormented by the question ... to go where we have nothing [or] to remain in this corruption?' As the persecution of Jews spread, Klemperer, under curfew from noon till 8 pm, felt that he 'could not bear it any more – I really felt as if I could not breathe.'

For Manning Clark, the encounter in Bonn sends him on a journey to seek an understanding of the human condition. It is his creation story, taking him back to the ancient classics, the Old Testament and Shakespeare. Witnessing the aftermath of Kristallnacht, the shards of glass still on the street, Clark confronts Conrad's heart of darkness, and he doubts the capacity of the Enlightenment to deliver human beings peace and happiness. It is the 'beginning of an awakening ... the moment when the author realised that he would have to start to think again about the whole human situation. He would have to base his beliefs on something more solid than those superficial, shallow ideas picked up in Melbourne.' For Clark, history needed to be much more than an empirical or scientific endeavour: it also needed to be spiritual, a work of individual artistic expression that remained true to the personal voice and feelings of the man within. This was his credo.

In early 2006, I was reading correspondence from the '30s between Clark and his wife-to-be, Dymphna Lodewyckx. In late 1938, Clark was at Oxford's Balliol College, reading history, while Dympna was in Bonn, studying German literature in preparation for her doctorate. The two scholarship winners, deeply in love, had sailed together from Australia in August 1938.

It was late and I was tired, struggling as usual with Clark's handwriting. Reading one letter from Dymphna to Clark, dated 12 November 1938, I suddenly realised that Clark had not been in Bonn on the morning after Kristallnacht. At first, I thought I'd made a mistake. Like many others, I had taken Clark at his word. I had even quoted the Kristallnacht story in my published work. I re-read Dymphna's letter carefully, checked Clark's diary entries, and saw that it was impossible for Clark to have been in Bonn on the morning of 10 November. As his own diary confirms, he did not arrive in Bonn until 26 November, more than two weeks after Kristallnacht (which, as we know, was the night of 9 November). It was Dymphna Lodewyckx, not Manning Clark, who witnessed the immediate aftermath of Kristallnacht. She wrote to Clark on 12 November 1938, when he was still in Oxford, and she wrote again on 24 November, two days before Clark arrived in Bonn. In the letter of 12 November, she described the scene:

> The violence was over when I came – but the crowds were everywhere – following the smiling SS men, children shouting in excitement, grown-ups silent, except for children. We went along lots of streets, & saw about 15 smashed shops – mercers, frock shops, & laundry, a silk shop etc. Then we went down to the Rhein and saw the smoking ruins of the synagogue. Behind it the rabbi's house was burning ... Weitergehen! Weitergehen! [Keep moving!] from the police was the only sound to be heard except the shuffling feet of hundreds of curious sightseers, so we left the Rhein where the grey evening mist was just rising over the poplars & factory chimneys and the western sky was all rosy ... I went home but couldn't work ... on the way to

the forest, I passed a second, smaller synagogue, gutted like the first ...

Later, in the company of a friend, the Swiss student Hans Ehrenzeller, Dymphna walked the streets of Bonn to 'see the sights'. She enclosed the article by Josef Goebbels that Clark referred to in one of his tellings of the Kristallnacht aftermath, describing it as 'a gem' before remarking that 'gentlemen in uniform were not very conspicuous during the actual venting of righteous wrath,' although she did write that she had heard one girl say that 'gentlemen in black poured the oil on the synagogue here, & others set it on fire.'

I felt a sense of disbelief and disappointment at having been misled, but this did not last long. When I told two of my friends, both historians, about my discovery, the response was the same: 'Oh, no!' they said, sighing. Like me, they wished that Clark had been there; they wished that the historian, of all people, would not play with the truth in such a way. When I told two other friends, both novelists who had known Clark, the response was different: 'Isn't that fantastic?' they said. 'Typical Manning – theatrical, playful, pulling your leg. What a great subject for a biography!' It was as if they could imagine Clark laughing from beyond the grave. The novelists made me stop my rush to judgment. I began to see Clark's untruth as the most revealing parable of all.

Manning Clark not only placed himself in Bonn on the morning after Kristallnacht; he also appears to have used some of the material in Dymphna's letter, mixed it with his own recollections, and made it his own. In *Quest for Grace*, for example, he describes walking the streets of Bonn with Dymphna and Hans Ehrenzeller after Kristallnacht, as well as a later meal with two Irish students in a university *mensa*. These events seem to be taken directly from Dymphna's account.

More importantly, Clark, by claiming the story as his own, denied Dymphna the voice of the narrator. Three years after Clark died, she wrote to Carl Bridge (the head of the Menzies Centre for Australian Studies at King's College, London), trying to dispel what she called 'the myth of Manning's rejection of Oxford'. But her letter revealed much more. She wrote, 'In

December–January 1938–39 [Manning] certainly took an extended Christmas vacation to come to Bonn, but he returned willingly to Balliol and left only when the outbreak of war made it necessary for him to find a job.'

'December–January', not November. This letter demonstrates that Dymphna's memory was quite different from Manning Clark's. Dymphna Clark was not one to play with the facts. And, reading her blunt and occasionally caustic editorial comments on his manuscripts, it is difficult to imagine that, sometime between 1978 and his death in 1991, she did not question Clark's recollection. Given her nature, it is possible that one morning at Tasmania Circle, Dymphna climbed the ladder to Clark's study, confronted him and said, 'Manning, you weren't there, you know you weren't there. What do you think you're doing?' Exactly why she chose to remain publicly silent is an intriguing question. The most obvious answer is probably the right one: she was so loyal to him that she could never betray him.

There is another, related question. When Clark told the Kristallnacht tale, he did so in the context of telling his life story. He had retired and was already a significant national figure. Why could he not have told the story of Kristallnacht through Dymphna? Why did he need to reduce her to a woman who was simply waiting on the steps of the railway station to marry him? Why did he need so desperately to be the one who was there? Most likely, Clark, the great historian, needed to be there to make the parable of Kristallnacht more powerful, to draw from the events the great lessons he had undoubtedly drawn.

In this sense, there is no fabrication. The impact of Kristallnacht on Clark was genuine and profound, somehow pushing aside the mere fact that he was not physically present. In the same way that Clark felt he could not write about events in the past without visiting the places where those events had occurred, he felt he could not speak of the significance of Kristallnacht for his intellectual and spiritual development without having been present. Clark needed to be *the* witness – the only way he could make meaning of the past was to inhabit it – and he willed himself to be there. Here, another question arises: How conscious was Clark's invention?

*

> [The historian] cannot invent facts, or put into the mouths of characters words which they never used. If he does, he slides into fiction or imaginative biography.
> —MANNING CLARK, Boyer Lectures, 1976

In a life-long partnership, a couple's memories can sometimes become one, and through Dymphna, Manning Clark no doubt felt he *was* there in Bonn on the morning after Kristallnacht. He had, after all, arrived in Bonn only two weeks later, on Saturday, 26 November 1938. His diary entry for that day reveals a young man shocked by what he saw:

> I walked round the town, struggling against the oppressiveness, the sea of hostile, hard faces, and the strangeness of my surroundings ... uniforms, pictures of Hitler, notices in form of command, not of request. And yet life went on here very much the same as in England. It was very bewildering, almost frightening.

Months later, he was certainly dwelling on the question of evil. He wrote in his diary on 15 February 1939, 'I have been worried lately by the problem of evil, the existence of which we are apt to ignore in our frantic search for the ideal.' When Clark arrived in Bonn, he saw the Nazi storm-troopers and was frightened by them; he also saw and heard evidence from several people of the Nazis' persecution of the Jews; and he was torn over the best means of resolving the political crisis between Germany and England – to appease or not to appease.

His experience in Nazi Germany is the beginning of the polyphon. As he told an audience at Melbourne University in 1980, 'after the experience in Bonn in November 1938, followed by quite an epiphany in Cologne Cathedral in the same year, my mind was rather like a fugue in four voices.' For Clark, it is the beginning of his confrontation with the 'age of unbelief'. Kristallnacht, the portent of the Holocaust, is mankind's fall from grace. In this sense, there is considerable truth in Clark's account of it. The truth lies in the felt part – the emotional and moral truth – and the conclusions drawn. He did not see the glass on the street or the smoke rising from the burning synagogues on the morning of 10 November, but he certainly experienced its aftermath and the increasing terror of the Nazi dictatorship.

At the same time, there is also something typically, comically Clarkian about the whole affair. Each time Clark tells the story, he has himself arriving in Bonn on a different day. In *Quest for Grace*, he arrives in Bonn on 8 November; in *Making History*, he arrives on 11 November. On other occasions, he arrives in 'early November' or on 'one of the mornings after Kristallnacht'.

Many years later, after reading *Quest for Grace*, a friend of Hans Ehrenzeller wrote to Dymphna, noting that Hans had lived for another four years after the date Clark had given as his death. It is also highly unlikely that Dymphna met Clark at the *Hauptbahnhof* in Bonn, as he claimed. Clark's journey from London would have taken him through Belgium and across the border to Cologne. Here, Clark would have needed to change trains in order to get to Bonn, a journey of a little over half an hour on a regional train. Dymphna had written to him shortly before he left Oxford for Bonn, on 18 November, telling him that she would meet him in Cologne. Clark's details and dates, as usual, are unreliable.

But as always with Manning Clark, the dates are not the issue. He seems to have streamlined these minor details in his telling of the story, in order to dramatise his arrival. Typically, he describes it in theatrical terms: coming up out of the darkness of the underground onto the streets of Bonn, meeting his waiting lover, confronting the portent of the twentieth century's greatest horror. The scene is operatic, both romantic and tragic, like Verdi doing Shakespeare. But it is also deeply existential. In late 1938, Clark was afraid of the onset of war. He feared for Dymphna's safety, and for his own. On a much larger scale, he feared for Europe and the future of civilisation. His Anglican upbringing and Enlightenment beliefs were no match for the Nazi terror. In this sense, the desolation Clark feels as he tells the Kristallnacht story half a century later is for the sake of the future and not for the sake of understanding the past. The question he asks – Where to now? – he asks of himself and of human society. And even as he tells the story, he does not believe he has found the answer.

In the late '80s, Clark began to consult his diaries and letters as he worked on his autobiography. In the preface to *Quest for*

Grace, he explains that in writing the volume he had 'made use of diaries begun in April 1941'. This date suggests that in writing *Quest for Grace*, Clark did not have access to the first volume of his diary, begun in Bonn in late November 1938 and proving that he arrived there two weeks after Kristallnacht. But the date he gives is also odd, given that the second volume of his diary begins in May 1940, not in April 1941. Clark appears to be plucking the date out of thin air. There is no volume of his diary that begins in April 1941.

It is possible, but unlikely, that he managed to find all of his diaries from the late '30s and '40s, bar one. Yet, even if it were true that Clark did not have access to his first diary while writing his autobiography, there is no doubt that he drew on Dymphna's correspondence from the same period. In *Quest for Grace*, Clark's memory of Dymphna's visit to the home of the art historian Dr Busslei draws from a letter she wrote to him in October 1938. 'I had heard about him in letters from Dymphna,' Clark writes. At one point, recalling a belligerent outburst by Busslei, he quotes almost verbatim from her letter. That letter was kept together with others from Dymphna written in October and November 1938, including the one she wrote to him on 12 November 1938 that describes her experience of Kristallnacht. Given that Clark's account of Kristallnacht closely resembles that of Dymphna's, and that in writing *Quest for Grace*, he drew on her correspondence from the same period, it seems unlikely that he did not sight the letters she wrote to him in November 1938.

If Manning Clark chose to place himself on the streets of Bonn, knowing that he was not there, this was his inner lie. He had told the story in public and traded on his audience's trust in him as a historian. In 1997, Carl Bridge, another scholar who took Manning Clark at his word on Kristallnacht, presciently summed up Clark as 'part mystic, part fraud. He had to be. This was how he made us aware of his and our versions of the truth.' Referring to Clark's intellectual larrikinism and his penchant for preaching on the meaning of life, Bridge argued that this was part of his greatness. Clark revelled in the power of myth.

I believe that the older Manning Clark did possess some awareness of the fact that he was not present on the morning after Kristallnacht. But to claim to know the *extent* to which he was conscious of it is to claim to know the inner depths of his mind. At times, I can see his memory slipping, shifting and struggling to recall; at others, his recollections are clear. I know I can never recover what he truly remembered, the memory of his inner voice, the voice that only he heard. But it is precisely this tension and uncertainty – fed by the shadowed, fallible nature of memory – which makes the story so fascinating.

One of the most interesting aspects of the Kristallnacht story is that Clark first alluded to it in fiction. In the '60s, Clark began to write short stories 'for relaxation', as he told Beatrice Davis, his editor at Angus & Robertson. In 1966, he published 'Two Visits', a thinly veiled autobiographical story of the exploits of Charles Hogan in Bonn in 1938. The story's tone is oddly aggressive, occasionally misogynist and at times consumed by self-loathing. Like Clark in his twenties, Hogan is 'tormented by his own impotence' and frustrated by his time-wasting in Bonn. He seems incapable of producing the great work he believes himself destined to write. Hogan wanders Dostoevsky-like through the streets of Bonn. He is 'never quiet': 'Some demon inside him drove him on the whole time he was there.'

While he does not mention Kristallnacht, Clark drew similar conclusions from Hogan's experience in Germany to those he drew for himself when he first began to tell the Kristallnacht parable in the late '70s. Of Hogan, he writes:

> I think it likely that Hogan did discover things about himself in Germany; that first visit did confront him with the question: what is the source of human evil? Is the imagination of man's heart evil from the start, so that questions of social organisation, political systems, moral codes are but the scum on the pond of human life – not the well-spring?

Hogan struggles to come to terms with the brutality of Nazi Germany. He is a man without faith, an 'unbeliever' in 'Protestant Christianity' deeply sceptical of any utopian vision 'for the future of humanity'. Clark seemed to know himself better in fiction. He writes of Hogan in Bonn that his 'flair for dramatising his life' was really 'one sustained effort to draw attention to himself'. And then this: 'His flair for the dramatic often caused his memory to play him tricks.' Indeed. Clark's experience in Germany, recounted first as fiction, is fleshed out and becomes autobiography a decade later. Finally, like much autobiography, it reveals itself as ultimately a strange and unavoidable amalgamation of both fact and fiction. In Clark's case, however, this trajectory seems entirely appropriate. Whatever Clark wrote – fiction, history, autobiography, criticism, newspaper opinion or political oratory – he blended fiction and fact in his attempt to communicate feeling, insight and historical understanding.

Nevertheless, it is significant that Clark's memory of Kristallnacht is told in the context of autobiography, a notoriously imperfect and fraught enterprise at the best of times. Setting out to write her three-volume autobiography, Doris Lessing was decidedly uncomfortable with the genre. Among novelists, she is not alone. J.M. Coetzee, for example, preferred to fictionalise his autobiographical writings, believing that 'fiction has better resources for dealing with unconscious forces than discursive self-analysis.' In the process of writing her autobiography, Lessing found that it exposed 'the worst deceiver of all – we make up our pasts.' Well aware of the black holes and 'shifting perspectives' of memory, she remained adamant, like Coetzee, that 'fiction makes a better job of the truth.' But unlike Coetzee, she persisted with autobiography, largely out of her instinct for 'self-defence', given that at least four writers were then working on biographies of her.

The unreliability of memory is the unreliability of autobiography, a necessarily apocryphal genre. Distanced by time, the self who is created by the narrator becomes a character, even a complete stranger to the person who writes. Details, dates and places are lost in the fog; the felt life is often a more abiding memory than the minutiae of the lived life. The American psychologist Jerome Bruner's work on autobiography and the self best expresses the fundamental strangeness of the genre. He writes:

> It is an account given by a narrator in the here and now about a protagonist bearing his name who existed in the there and then, the story terminating in the present when the protagonist fuses with the narrator ... The self as narrator not only recounts but justifies. And the self as protagonist is always, as it were, pointing to the future.

As a historian who saw himself more as an artist than a fact-grubber, Clark showed no signs of discomfort with the genre of autobiography. Its potential for truthfulness seemed to him just as great, largely because, unlike Lessing, he rendered his life as narrative not out of necessity but willingly. As he told John Tranter in 1987, 'the only gift I had was to tell a story.' In the late '80s, with his six-volume history complete, he turned to write autobiography at a time when the genre was experiencing extraordinary popularity. Writers such as Clive James, Barry Humphries, Geoffrey Dutton, Donald Horne, Jill Kerr Conway, and Bernard Smith had all turned their hand to memoir, often, as Bruce Bennett has pointed out, tracing their life 'as part of a national allegory'. In the lead-up to the bicentenary, Clark became a celebrity and Australia's most public intellectual. Having told the nation's story, the nation now demanded Clark's story, and he relished the opportunity to tell it.

Writing autobiography allowed him to do with his own life what he had already done with his historical actors: create himself as a character, and employ the same literary devices – particularly the epiphany as a moment of 'new consciousness' – to reshape his life through literary reminiscence. In the process of recollection, and in the creation of his life as story, he was able to invest new meaning in past events. Many of the events from his past that the septuagenarian Clark saw as significant in the late '80s were not invested with the same significance at the time they occurred. Clark's diary entry after his visit to Cologne Cathedral on 9 December 1938 makes no mention of the painting of the Madonna or of the Heinrich Heine poem that allegedly moved him to tears:

> We saw the cathedral, beyond description ... we walked round the town and saw the notices ... 'Juden werden nicht bedient' [Jews will not be served] on shop windows. Everything looked very prosperous and very lovely in the soft glow of twilight, with the darkness of the buildings against the blue of the sky and the pink clouds. The dome of the cathedral seemed to cast a spell on the whole town, and the darkness came down quietly, and one felt safe.

This is a far cry from the memory of Cologne Cathedral recited by Manning Clark in 1987. In other diary entries from the late '30s, he is moved by a triptych of Rubens' paintings depicting the Immaculate Conception, the birth of Christ and his crucifixion ('Mary, in horror – that it should [come] to this'), and by Chartres Cathedral, 'which inspires that sense of awe and wonder'. 'I thought of the powers of inspiration of the Catholic Church,' wrote Clark, 'of the issues between Catholicism and Protestantism – authority & beauty against liberty of thought & dullness.' These entries reveal the traces of truth in his later recollections, and perhaps this is the best that the author and reader can hope for in autobiography: traces of truth.

For Clark, and for every writer of autobiography, there are two competing truths: one's past life as it was perceived and lived (mostly lost from view), and one's past life as seen from the time of writing, a truth that leans on the paper-thin house of memory. Despite the fact that Clark had access to his diaries as he composed his autobiography, he was more concerned with the latter truth: making his life behave as literature. The older Clark shifts the time and place of many of his early encounters in Europe, then condenses and embellishes his visions into one or two Earth-moving epiphanies as he reinvents his life before a public audience.

On every occasion in the last years of his life that he tells the Kristallnacht story, he tells it together with the Cologne Cathedral epiphany. In 1987, two months before his interview with John Tranter, he appeared on ABC TV, interviewed by the arts presenter Peter Ross. Telling the story of the two epiphanies, Clark wept:

> Clark: I went to Germany to see the girl, or the woman, I was going to marry – Dymphna – at the University of Bonn, and I happened to get there on the morning of the ninth or tenth of November ... I got there and came out of the Bonn Railway Station onto the footpath, the road, and it was one of the mornings after Kristallnacht, when the SS in Germany had conducted this savage vendetta against the Jews for the murder, or the attempted murder, of a member of the German Embassy in Paris.

Ross: You saw the broken glass?

Clark: I saw the broken glass and I saw those troops with their revolvers and their sub-machine guns and so on, on the back of trucks ... I was absolutely overwhelmed by it. I could scarcely speak, and in the long run – it's difficult to work it out, Peter, isn't it, when you're really ... But it was some time then, within the next few days or certainly within the next few weeks, that I realised that all the things I'd been brought up with ... *The Book of Common Prayer, Hymns Ancient and Modern*, and all the hopes and aspirations of those dry souls of the enlightenment ... all this was just pitiful equipment with which to face up to the phenomenon of human evil.

Ross: So the scales came from your eyes?

Clark: Yes the blinkers, the blinkers of being a member of British civilisation overseas, of being a simple boy from the Australian bush – all this had to go ... A few days after that, I went with Dymphna to Cologne, and remember I was a Church of England clergyman's son and a State school boy and a Melbourne Grammar boy, as it were, I walked up those steps of Cologne Cathedral ... I went into the cathedral ... and I ... yes ... I was overwhelmed.

Ross: You're overwhelmed now, as you recall it.

Clark: Yes, I am.

Ross: It must have been an extraordinary occurrence.

Clark: Yes, it was. I'd find it difficult to put into words.

[It was at this point that Professor Clark wept ...]

[Clark then tells the story of seeing, behind the high altar in the cathedral, Stefan Lochner's painting of the *Madonna and Child* (1450), which inspired Heinrich Heine's poem 'Painted on Golden Leather'. He translates the one line that had always remained with him: 'Inside the cathedral there stands a picture painted in golden leather and in the great wildness of my life it's always shone brightly.']

Clark: That episode in the cathedral in Cologne which had moved me so deeply – in fact, so deeply that I have never been able to speak about it since – it, I think, was germinal in writing the History, because then and subsequently I realised that I had to dispense with what had carried me through life so far, what I call my 'great expectations', either of Christian belief or the Enlightenment, and that I had to ... find another way. And that, really, in a sense the History became an account of how all we in Australia became citizens of the Kingdom of Nothingness – believing in nothing – but that doesn't mean nothing in one sense ... It's the opposite of nil. It's really giving up the great expectations and asking yourself, what then?

Clark seems to admit at one point that he is uncertain as to exactly when the encounter in Bonn revealed its mysteries to him ('It's difficult to work it out, Peter'). We see him in the act of fashioning memory anew, bringing himself to tears in the telling. He wrote to Kathleen Fitzpatrick shortly after, 'I made an attempt to talk about what I had never talked about to anyone before ... [I] am still shaken by what happened during the interview.' Clark had never spoken before about the experience in Cologne. To some extent, he was discovering its significance as he told the story to Peter Ross. In 1978, he wrote of his visit to Cologne Cathedral, but made no mention of the mystical experience he described in 1987. He seemed to create the emotionally shattering vision at Cologne in the act of performance.

When Peter Ross questioned him directly, he insisted that he *was* there in Bonn on the morning of 10 November ('I saw the broken glass'); then, at another point in the interview, he claimed that two days later, he was out cycling with Dymphna. 'It was Armistice Day,' he told Ross. In freezing cold weather, he and Dymphna came across a memorial to German soldiers. Clark claimed that this introduced him 'to the whole idea of *mittelEuropa* and German civilisation and what it had been like to be a German'. But Clark was no more in Germany on Armistice Day than he was in Bonn on the morning after Kristallnacht. Once again, he places himself in a key historical moment in order to dramatise his moment of revelation.

When he tells the story of Cologne Cathedral in *Quest for Grace*, it also follows closely behind the Bonn epiphany. ('From the day I saw evil in Bonn am Rhein there would be no putting back to harbour: I launched further into the deep when I stood in front of the painting of the Madonna and Child behind the high altar in Cologne Cathedral.') Dymphna, aware of the 'tempests' raging within her lover, retires to the back of the building, apparently unable to partake in such a shattering moment: 'inside the cathedral I was strangely moved. Dymphna, noticing what was going on inside me, left me alone to feast on it all in my heart.' This epiphany in Cologne is, in fact, almost a reincarnation of Dostoevsky's experience in Basel in the late 1860s, a fact of which Clark must have been aware.

In 1867, while travelling from Baden-Baden to Geneva, Dostoevsky visited Basel and there saw Hans Holbein's *The Body of the Dead Christ in the Tomb*, painted in the early 1520s. The painting depicted Christ's emaciated body in the tomb, the holes still visible on his blackened hands and feet, his gaunt and bearded face looking upwards in doubtful hope. Dostoevsky remained haunted by the image for the rest of his life, just as he was by his memory of Raphael's Madonna in Dresden, a painting which he described in *Crime and Punishment* as bearing a kind of 'mournful religious ecstasy'. Dostoevsky was moved and overwhelmed, unable to articulate the mystery he sensed within Holbein's work. Yet he is also plagued by the doubt that arises within him: What if Christ did not rise from the dead? Then man is truly alone.

In the back pages of his copies of *Crime and Punishment, The Idiot* and *The Possessed* (still on the shelves of his study in Canberra), Manning Clark noted the page numbers of Dostoevsky's writings about Holbein's and Raphael's paintings. Clark is drawn to Dostoevsky's mysticism and to his doubt; like him, he is eternally divided over the question of faith and belief. But even more importantly, he emulates his search for truth, cultivating (sometimes consciously) an artistic sensibility in which art, literature and metaphorical language are the one true source of spiritual revelation. Like Dostoevsky, Clark is moved but does not fully understand the experience: it is mystical, forever hinting at profound truths destined never to be resolved.

Manning Clark visited Basel in 1956 and viewed the Holbein. In 1961, during a lecture on Dostoevsky, he told ANU students how Dostoevsky's wife, Anna, had been present with the writer in Basel on the day he first encountered Holbein's work. As Clark told the story, Anna 'withdrew' from Dostoevsky: 'she knew who he was, what came up from inside the man.' Thirty years later, when Clark told the story of his own epiphany before the painting of the Madonna in Cologne, he has Dymphna withdraw in the same manner as Anna, creating the memory of his own life in the image of Dostoevsky's.

The two epiphanies, Kristallnacht and Cologne Cathedral, are spliced by Clark into an almost filmic scene of self-discovery, one representing the inadequacy of Protestant teachings and the Enlightenment to solve the problem of human evil, the other holding out the potential spiritual solace and compassion of the Catholic faith, a faith Clark would continue to dance with (but never embrace) for the remainder of his life. Like the Spanish poet Federico García Lorca, with his notion of *duende* – which Lorca described in 1930 as 'a momentary burst of inspiration, the blush of all that is truly alive … what Goethe called the 'demoniacal' [the 'dark force' that rises from within the poet] … needing the trembling of the moment and then a long silence' – Clark is rendered speechless by the visions and inspirations that rise before his eyes. 'I could not speak of the experience then to anyone,' he writes of the epiphany in Cologne Cathedral. 'Was there anyone who could understand? Many years later when I risked talking about the experience my whole body shook.'

Clark sought and depended on *duende*, flashes of inspiration that brought the pain and suffering of a deeper awareness of the human situation but at the same time served as his intellectual and spiritual guiding lights. Writing and the act of creation were not only intellectual but emotional and physical, a whole-body experience. He had no alternative but to write from the gut, to feel the physical sensation of trembling and shaking, because his was a poetic imagination. The historian's inspiration is the artist's sensibility, made real and truthful through the repetition necessary in public performance. The details of Clark's life, like Australia's past, are adapted to suit his dreams and mystical visions. Manning Clark, Australia's greatest self-mythologiser, was a daddy-long-legs spinning his thread.

Far from being out of place or shocking, Clark's misrepresentation of his presence in Bonn on 10 November 1938 is entirely in keeping with the spirit and intent of his life and work. Rather than diminishing Clark, it reveals him. He fictionalised his life, just as he played with primary sources in writing his histories. He lived out the life of his greatest character, himself, the historian whose potential greatness was constantly undermined by his fatal flaws. Both his *History of Australia* and his autobiographical writings are unreliable as historical sources. But this should come as no surprise: where Manning Clark's life is concerned, the last person we should trust is Clark himself. He created himself as myth, cultivating a theatrical persona of the people's priest and sage, telling history as parable. And as the Kristallnacht epiphany reveals, the moral of the parable always mattered more than the facts.

The true story of Kristallnacht reveals the true nature of Manning Clark's voice: the voice of the heart and mind, the inner man seeking 'higher truths'. Voices spoke to Clark – from within him, from the past, from the present – and he struggled to play them back to us, mediated through his unique emotional intelligence and sensibility, so that we might hear them, too, as if for the first time. Clark's *History of Australia* is a flawed attempt to write history as a revelation of the human condition. It is a search for the time when the veil, for a brief moment, is pulled back, and life is seen for what it is. This is the translucent quality of Manning Clark's work.

The Monthly

Bons Mots No Match for Nazi Bullets

Clive James

'A liberated woman,' said Karl Kraus, 'is a fish that has fought its way ashore.' Even at the time there were women, some of them among his cheer squad of beautiful mistresses, who thought he was talking through his hat.

Agree with him or not, however, you wouldn't mind being able to say something that sharp. Kraus (1874–1936) was famous for being able to do so whenever he wanted, but eventually, as with his hero Oscar Wilde, his fame as a wit was there instead of the full, complex, tormented and deeply contemplative man.

As a writer and practitioner of the higher journalism, he is still up there with all the other great names of literary Vienna – Arthur Schnitzler, Robert Musil, Joseph Roth – but up there for what, precisely?

The risk run by the aphorist is that people will grow restless between aphorisms, because they aren't getting enough of what it says on the label. Even while he was alive, most people didn't want any more of Kraus's world view than would fit into a fortune cookie.

Though he had no computer on his desk, Kraus was essentially a blogger before the fact: his basic technique was to write a couple of hundred words about something silly in the newspaper. He sometimes wrote at length, but his admirers preferred him to keep it short. The kind of thing they liked best from him might have been designed to pop up on a BlackBerry today.

'An aphorism can never be the whole truth,' he once wrote. 'It is either a half-truth or a truth and half.' Yes, but that's an aphorism. So is it true?

Outside German-speaking lands Kraus is known mainly for having been the Viennese café pundit who brilliantly fulfilled a self-created role as the scourge of loose language.

Serious readers, even if their serious reading does not often include him, know that Kraus, from before the turn of the twentieth century until a couple of years before the Anschluss in 1938, was the linguistic health inspector who searched through what was said for what was meant, and was particularly scathing about the jingoistic propaganda that helped drive a generation of young men irretrievably into the mincing machine of World War I.

Kept out of it by his distorted spine, he was the pacifist on the warpath, the libertarian grammarian. Whether in the pages of his magazine *Die Fackel* (The Torch) or by means of his celebrated readings on stage, he constantly pointed out the connection between official bombast and the suffering of the people, between journalistic mendacity and political duplicity, between fine writing and foul behaviour.

Some of those serious readers also know, or think they know, that Kraus finally fell silent because, on his own admission, Adolf Hitler had left him speechless.

Not true. The facts say that Kraus, immediately after confessing that the Nazis left him with nothing to say, went on to say quite a lot. There are thousands of facts such as that in Edward Timms's biography, *Karl Kraus: Apocalyptic Satirist*, a two-tome desk-breaker that can be taken as the instigation of the piece I am writing, because such a big, factually precise yet historically approximate biography brings to a focus some of the problems that Kraus's brilliant career exemplified.

Such a biography can also be a problem in itself, if its interpretations come to define its subject. Something like that, I believe, has happened in this instance, and it might be worth attempting a short historical account of Kraus's career without wasting space by decorating the narrative with the usual sprinkle of aphorisms. There are a dozen different anthologies of those, quite apart from the compendiums of his writings that Kraus put together. What we need, however, is a picture of the mind behind the fragments. Was that fragmentary too?

Timms's first volume, with its Margaret Mead-sounding subtitle, *Culture and Catastrophe in Habsburg Vienna*, covers 1874–1918 and was published to acclaim in 1989. The second volume, *The Postwar Crisis and the Rise of the Swastika*, covering 1918–36, came out in late 2005.

I had meant to write about it before this, but first I had to read it. As with its predecessor, ploughing through it took time. Timms has done a lot of reading, and takes a lot of reading in his turn, far more than most non-academic students will ever give him.

It should be said that he makes that demand with good credentials. Though his hulking double-whammy of a book is further burdened by an ultra-postmodern vocabulary and by his apparent conviction that having become an expert on the European politics of the early twentieth century has somehow given him automatic insight into the world politics of the early twenty-first century as well, he has done a good job of bringing subtlety to the accepted picture of Kraus, the picture we thought was adequate.

It wasn't. But it wasn't all that untrue, either. Kraus, in the end, might not really have run out of things to say, but he did run out of hope that they might be relevant. His business had been to criticise high-flown speech that concealed base motives. Now, with the Nazis mouthing off in all media, he was faced with gutter talk that concealed nothing, or else with lies so blatant that they were clearly weapons in verbal form.

There was nothing to uncover. Like Othello's, his occupation was gone. Although Timms has the smaller facts to say otherwise, the larger fact remains: Kraus spent a lifetime thinking that euphemistic talk led necessarily to evil, as exemplified by World War I, which he had thought the most evil thing imaginable.

But the Nazis, who largely said exactly what they meant – and even their euphemisms were meant to be decoded as the threat of murder – brought an evil even worse than that. Though it's a conclusion Timms doesn't reach, his facts reach it for him: Kraus had been wrong from the start. This, however, is a conclusion we should not reach too early. Today there is no excuse for failing to see that the avowedly irrational doesn't yield to reason. Kraus had every excuse, because total irrationality was not yet in charge of a modern European state. Even before World War I broke out, Kraus had ample cause to think that he was already dealing with enough madness to keep him busy.

Kraus was a Jew, but if he had not sought baptism in 1911 he would have faced a lot of closed doors. He wanted those doors to be open. He wasn't against the Austro-Hungarian social order, he merely wanted it to be less stupid, and indeed it wasn't until quite late in World War I that he began blaming the empire for having driven its various constituent populations into a slaughterhouse.

As we learned from the first volume, he preferred to blame the newspapers. He blamed them no less if they were owned and/or edited by Jews. Indeed, he seemed to blame them more, a fact that left us obliged to deal with the question of Kraus's anti-Semitism.

Timms deals with it in torrential detail, but seems to be in two minds when dismissing the usual accusation against Kraus of *jüdische Selbsthass*, Jewish self-hatred. Timms can only partly dismiss it, because Kraus really did seem to reserve a special virulence for Jewish artists he didn't admire – the list went back to Heinrich Heine, on whose grave Kraus regularly danced – and really did seem to go out of his way to accuse the Jewish bourgeoisie of money-grubbing, especially if they had taken baptism in order to increase their opportunities. (Kraus found it convenient to forget that he was living on an unearned income: it flowed copiously from the family firm in Czechoslovakia, a source that made it inflation-proof.)

The question was already omnipresent in Timms's first volume, and in the second, which takes up the Kraus story from the end of World War I, through the disintegration of the old empire and on into the various phases of the new Austrian republic, the question attains something worse than mere omnipresence: a focused virulence that takes it out of culture and society and puts it into the heart of politics.

Timms might have reached an answer on the subject more easily if he had realised, going in, that it was Hitler who gave the question new life – or, rather, new potential for death. Before being Jewish became unequivocally an issue of race rather than of religion, any Jew who vilified another might indeed have been aiding and abetting an institutionalised prejudice. But he wasn't complicit in mass murder.

Very few Jews, no matter how clever, even dreamed that such a day could ever come. At the turn of the century, Theodor Herzl had guessed it, but most Jews thought he was just a nut. Schnitzler had half-guessed it, but most Jews thought he was just a playwright.

Freud, the master of dreams, never dreamed of it. Kraus, whom Freud admired for his insight, never dreamed of it either. The multi-zero deaths of World War I were racially unspecific. That there might ever be, in modern Europe, such a thing as a racially specific extermination was unthinkable.

It should be said, however, that Kraus sometimes sounded as if he might be trying to think of it. In 1916 he wrote a poem naming Israel as the 'cosmic enemy'. You can strain to believe that he was using Israel as a symbolic analogy for Germany, but it seems more plausible to take it that by Israel he meant the Jews.

And in 1918 Schnitzler was surely right to complain that Kraus, when denouncing the war profiteers, seemed only to notice them when they were of Jewish origin. The fact awkwardly remains, though, that a Jew could as yet flirt with anti-Semitism and still convince himself that he was being merely rhetorical.

For a man nominally at war with rhetoric, this was a strange flirtation to indulge, but no doubt the causes went deep. It could have been that like so many Jewish *rentiere* intellectuals living on incomes they had never had to work for, Kraus just despised the bourgeoisie for their materialism, and that the bourgeois people he knew most about were Jews.

In Germany during the 1930s, the same lofty distaste drove Walter Benjamin to become a Marxist, even as the Nazis were busy proving all around him that their views on the Jewish question were free of class bias, in no way theoretical and immediately effective.

In post-war Austria there were all kinds of contending views among the Jewish population about who they actually were, how they fitted into the state and what kind of state they should favour. There were even Jews who backed the idea of Austria's joining itself to Germany (Anschluss) as soon as possible. Kraus never really made his mind up on the subject of what the state should be.

Even as he lost faith in the ability of the old social order to revive, and began to favour socialism, he still wasn't sure, under his crisp air of certitude, that democracy could bring about a reasonable society.

Like young radicals almost fifty years later, he began to nurse a fantasy about China. In his case there was no sweet smoke involved, but it was the same pipe dream. In a letter to his great love, Sidonie Nadherny, he said 'but really there remains only China'. It scarcely needs saying that he had no idea of what China had been like, was like then and might be like in the future. He just wanted a cloud-cuckoo-land to console him from the stress of living in his actual surroundings. Sidonie had already gone a long way towards providing him with that.

The baroness Sidonie Nadherny von Borutin was elegant, sexy, clever and loaded. Her country seat, Schloss Janowitz in Bohemia, was the full Arcadian dream. Kraus was no hick – several great ladies had been among his mistresses – but he was still pleased by such lavish access to gracious living at top level, whereas Sidonie, with the delightful charm of a Euro-aristo bluestocking whose malapropisms came in three languages, enjoyed having her grammar corrected by the man who could make her laugh.

In private, Kraus had a sweet nature to ameliorate the biting sarcasm he deployed in public, and he had the key element of a way with women: he found them interesting. Under the style and gloss, the baroness had a wanton nature and Kraus knew how to set it loose on the overnight train from Vienna to Trieste.

Well aware that he was a great man, Sidonie was as flattered by his attentions as he by hers. Timms began to tell the story of their long, on-and-off romance in the first volume, but in the second he could have told us more about how it petered out.

In a work whose chief characteristic is to tell us more than the doctor ordered on almost every topic, this is an annoying deficiency, because the romance between Kraus and Sidonie was something much bigger than a love affair: it was a meeting of history running at two different speeds. Sidonie stood for inheritance, for noblesse oblige, for a longstanding social tradition that contained all its contending forces in a recognised balance, if not a universal harmony.

Kraus stood for intellectual merit which, in a rapidly developing political explosion, was only one of the contending forces, and possibly among the weakest. Even if the crisis had never come, the two lovers would have been star-crossed enough. Sidonie was one of the rulers of a Bohemia with a capital B. Kraus was a different kind of bohemian: no capital letter.

However brilliantly, he lived outside the walls she owned. There have always been liaisons between the two realms but it works best if the participants respect each other's individuality even when their physical union is intense. Sidonie quite liked his possessiveness, but the day came when she found herself gasping for air.

Kraus somehow overdid it. He got all the love she had to give but wanted more. The dynamics of the breakdown are hard to specify because his half of their correspondence is missing. But we should be careful not to underrate the significance of the part played by Rainer Maria Rilke, who warned Sidonie, at a time when she might have been considering marriage to Kraus, that Kraus was essentially a stranger.

Possibly Rilke, a schmoozer de grand luxe, had his eye on a solo guest spot at Janowitz: his talent for scoring free board and lodging from titled women was up there with his talent for poetry. But there can be no doubt what Rilke meant by his warning word *fremd*. He meant that Kraus was a Jew.

Timms is well aware of this, but doesn't make much of it. And possibly it doesn't tell you much about Kraus and Sidonie who, after all, went on being loving friends. But it does tell you an awful lot about Rilke.

And Sidonie's tolerance for what Rilke said tells you an awful lot about the insidious prevalence of anti-Semitism even among the enlightened international beau monde.

There is no reason to think that mass murder would ever have got started anywhere in Europe if the Nazis hadn't come to power in Germany. But the Nazis, on their way up, had a lot of prejudice to draw upon, and it doesn't need a very big minority to look like a majority when it comes parading down the street.

Military force transferred to civilian life was the revolutionary new element that would eventually paralyse conventional political expression and Kraus's critique along with it.

After World War I, Kraus realised almost as soon as Hitler did that if the war's unfettered violence were to be unleashed in peace-time politics, private armies could enforce a new and criminal legality. Unlike Hitler, however, he had little idea of what to do about it. He can scarcely be blamed for that. Apart from the psychopaths, hardly anybody had. Sticking with the old legality looked like the only civilised option.

The realisation that the civilised option, even with a professional army at its command, had little hope of prevailing against the uncivilised one was slow to dawn. By the time it did, the sun had set. Comprehension came after the fact.

Kraus saw the menace, however, and should be respected for his insight. From 1923 onwards he had no doubts that the Nazis were out to wreck everything. He just had trouble believing that they could. On the eve of World War I, Kraus had said 'violence is no subject for polemic, madness no subject for satire.'

Here was a new and madder violence, a reign of terror. When it came to power in Germany, in 1933, Kraus was faced more acutely than ever with the question of what form of government in Austria might stave it off. His Social Democrat admirers were horrified when he failed to condemn the authoritarianism of chancellor Engelbert Dollfuss, but Kraus was choosing the lesser of two evils: a choice that evil always demands we make, revealing itself in the demand. In his long paper, *Third Walpurgis Night*, Kraus pilloried the Social Democrats for not realising that only Dollfuss's illiberal measures could keep the Nazis out.

Timms gives a long and valuable analysis of *Third Walpurgis Night* – it was the speech about the Nazis that Kraus gave after saying they had left him speechless – but doesn't make enough out of the fact that Kraus never published it. It was meant to appear as a special issue of *Die Fackel*, but it didn't.

In effect, Kraus was already retreating from his public role. After the assassination of Dollfuss by Nazi agents in 1934, he gave up altogether. He was through with politics. The sophisticated reasoning of a lifetime had come down to the elementary proposition that anything was better than the Nazis.

After Kraus's death, the plebiscite that Dollfuss's successor Kurt Schuschnigg called for would probably have shown that the majority of Austria's population thought the same. Aware of this, Hitler terrorised Schuschnigg into calling off the plebiscite, and the Nazis duly marched in. A lot of them were already there. Austrian citizens put on swastika armbands and set about their vengeful business.

Kraus was lucky enough to breathe his last before they took power but he already knew that his long vigilance over the use of language hadn't changed a thing.

The dying Kraus could congratulate himself that he had at least, at last, seen things clearly. He had discovered the limited effectiveness of telling people they are fanatics when they think fanaticism to be a virtue.

The full force of totalitarian irrationality had become plain to him: the real reason why *Third Walpurgis Night*, pace Timms, was not only unpublished, but incoherent. It was a piece of writing that knew that it was useless.

Kraus might have reached the same conclusion about all his previous satirical writings had he lived long enough. His German equivalent, Kurt Tucholsky, had the same trouble sinking to the occasion. Asked why he had not said more about the Nazis, he said: 'You can't shoot that low.'

In exile, before he committed suicide, Tucholsky was heard to wonder whether being satirical about the Weimar Republic had ever been a particularly good idea, in view of what was coming next.

But even the brightest people – in fact, especially them, and especially those who were Jews – had been slow to form a view of what was coming next until it actually came. Even then, some of them still couldn't believe it. Rational people expect rational outcomes. In exile in London, Freud said in a letter that there was still a chance the Catholic Church would straighten the Nazis out. Not long ago I heard that letter read aloud, at a literary soirée in his old house at Hampstead, now a museum. If one of the great analysts of the human mind was capable of that degree of wishful thinking, we can only imagine what drove him to it. But imagining that, of course, is still the hardest thing.

World War I had confirmed Kraus in his pacifism, but by the

time he died he knew that peace, in the face of Hitler, had ceased to be credible as a principle and could be espoused merely as a desirable state of affairs. He had been blindsided by events, but at least he changed his mind.

Many of his admirers were to prove less flexible. Kraus preceded George Orwell in the notion that the lying language of capitalist imperialism was the cause of all the world's evils. Orwell also was obliged to change his mind in the light of events, but once again there were epigones who never gave up on the idea: it was too attractive as a catch-all explanation.

And there is something to it, after all. But the idea has an imperialism of its own, which we can now see most clearly expressed in the assumption that nobody would behave irrationally unless driven to it by the dominant West, with the US to the forefront.

In its extreme form, this mass delusion of the intellect comes up with brainwaves such as the one about George W. Bush having arranged the September 11 attack on the World Trade Center. Since it was always clear that Bush was barely capable of arranging to recite his own name with the words in the right order, it seems a bizarre notion.

It is quite possible to imagine Kraus having a fun time with Bush's use of language, although first it would have to be translated into German, and before that it would have to be translated into English. Commentators who amuse themselves today with the verbal output of Bush are following Kraus.

If Kraus were here, he might point out that their target is a sitting duck. Kraus, before Orwell and even before H.L. Mencken, was the ancestor of many of our best sceptics, and almost all of our best bloggers. (The blogger technique of glossing some absurdity highlighted in a mainstream publication was what Kraus did in every issue of *Die Fackel* and even in his enormous play, *The Last Days of Mankind*, which consisted almost entirely of citations from newspapers and periodicals.)

But his biographer, who has gained a dangerous authority by the sheer magnitude of his labours, takes a lot on himself when he assumes that Kraus would have been against armed intervention in the Middle East as an example of our being led into folly by 'propaganda for war'.

The phrase is of Timms's coinage, and rings like pewter. By the time Kraus died, he knew that there could be an even bigger danger in propaganda for peace. Some of the brightest people in Europe, up to and including Bertrand Russell, preached non-violence up to and beyond the day Hitler invaded Poland.

The British Labour Party, sitting in Opposition to the Conservatives, denounced fascism but also denounced any proposed armed opposition to it as warmongering. In service to the great analyst of cliché, Timms is hampered not only by his cultural studies jargon (the leaden word discourse riddles the text) but by an untoward propensity for not spotting what a current cliché is. The two drawbacks are connected, by his tin ear.

Kraus, whom Timms tacitly invites to join in the widespread practice of putting jokey quotation marks around the phrase war on terror, might have pointed out that the quotation marks are a cliché in themselves, helping as they do to disguise a brute reality: terrorists are at war with us, and don't care who they kill. The reason terrorists don't use those risible cosmetic terms of ours such as collateral damage is that they not only have no intention of sparing the innocent, they have no more desirable target in mind.

The terrorist can talk a pure language: it's purely violent, but still pure. His opponent is bound to equivocate, and sound silly doing so. That was the point Kraus missed because it had not yet become apparent by contrast with something worse.

A liberal democracy, of any kind or degree, is bound to deal in hypocrisy and lies, simply because it has a measure of real politics, and is not unified and simplified by an ideology. Totalitarian irrationalism can say exactly what's on its mind. Hitler had genocide on his mind, and said so. But only his nuttiest colleagues believed he would actually do it.

Samantha Power, in her excellent, Pulitzer prize-winning book *Genocide: A Problem from Hell*, reached a conclusion she didn't want to reach, as the best analytical books so often do. After showing that no genocidal government in the twentieth century had ever been stopped except by armed intervention, she reluctantly concluded that the armed intervention usually had to be supplied by the US.

Those among us who sincerely believe that the Iraqis are killing each other in fulfilment of an American genocidal plan might think that her conclusion is no longer true. We would have to ignore the implicit opinion of the 11 million Iraqi adults who voted in the last election, but most of us would rather do that than be taken for suckers.

The Vietnam War dulled the Stars and Stripes in our eyes. But Power's idea was certainly still true when Kraus was alive. And there can be no question that he would have eventually spelled out the same conclusion himself.

In effect, he had already reached it. In 1930 he published a piece called *SOS USA*, predicting that the US would have to step in if Europe were to be saved. And in 1933 he renewed the provision in his passport to include travel to the US. Timms, who makes little of that development, could safely have made more. He could have said, for example, that in making of itself a refuge so difficult to reach, America had abetted the efforts of the maniacs. It would have been true, or at any rate half-true.

Kraus had no particular love for America – it wasn't China – and he definitely underestimated what the US would have been able to do in the short term, when its armed forces were still considerably inferior even to those of Czechoslovakia.

But he guessed how the balance of forces was shaping up. Can there be bad violence and good violence? But of course there can. It's a tragic perception, though, and the day is always sad when a comic perception must give way to it.

Kraus had a comprehensive sensitivity to all the abuses of society. Injustice angered him. He was way ahead of the game on questions of race. Nobody ever wrote more powerfully against capital punishment. Despite his famous pronouncement about the fish that fought its way ashore, he understood what women were facing and why they had to fight. He was their champion.

He was a serious man, and a piercing satire was his weapon. But it worked only because he was funny. And then, first gradually and then suddenly, being funny wasn't enough.

The Australian's Review of Books

Hard Cases and Hearts of Darkness

Nicolas Rothwell

Much like the savage art of war, the craft of the war correspondent has, over the past generation, metastasised with all the fatal vigour of an end-stage cancer rampaging through some afflicted organism. The changes in the way Western nations and their armies conduct military campaigns stem from advances in weapons technology, from the growing economic resources of the modern state, and perhaps even from a rise in the value generals and politicians place on preserving the lives of the soldiers they command. The changes in war writing, though, are more elusive and more profound. They descend not only from the changing nature of contemporary conflict, and from the immediacy of today's communications, but are also linked to our need, and our willingness, to peer beyond our civilisation's well-kept rampart lines, to a shift in our appetite for death and horror and to the ever-increasing role of televisual images in forging our narratives of the wider world.

For a long time, the history of war corresponding follows a simple evolutionary arc. It begins in earnest with the first participant-observer, Athenian historian Thucydides, a general in the Peloponnesian War, who failed in a military operation, was banished from his city, and used the status of exile as a means to collect testimony from all sides.

In Thucydides, war is drama and the model is always tragedy: the most poignant moment in his austere eight-book record of

Athenian eclipse comes when a group of soldiers on the ill-fated Sicilian expedition watch the destruction of their fleet in Syracuse Harbour. As the ships are pulverised, the spectators on the shore let out a lamenting cry like that of the chorus in a tragic drama. But there is an epic shadow, too: the historian writes in the shadow of the great poet of war, the Homer of *The Iliad*, who first fixed combat as the path to eternal fame.

Epic and tragic: those are the registers that have illuminated war writing down the centuries and they are still current, if in somewhat distorted form. There are exemplary and educational aspects to these two modes: the epic account preserves the names of brave men, while the tragic narrative seeks to offer insights into human nature. This twofold line of conflict writing stretches more or less unbroken through the set-piece disasters of Western warfare up to a crescendo in World War I, the most barbaric and most widely described of history's gladiatorial campaigns.

Writers such as Robert Graves, in his memoir of the front, *Goodbye to All That*, or serial novelist Henry Williamson, or Wilfred Owen, the poet of the trenches, as well as the various official war correspondents dispatched to the front line, all found themselves inclined to focus on the conditions of the battle as much as on the goal of the struggle.

Fighting became ordeal, passion, nearness to death. War took on the aspect of suffering and spiritual quest. But by mid-century, the age of written war, of war experienced initially or primarily through printed words, was done.

The stage was also wider: it was planetary. New channels carried the message. The fight against Adolf Hitler was cast, and scripted, very much as epic but the plot was disseminated by means of radio waves and cinematic newsreel.

CBS newsman Ed Murrow, broadcasting his descriptions of bomber raids, might serve as the epitome of this phase in the evolution of war reporting. As was only fitting in such a conflict of good against evil, the field correspondent filed his dispatches very much from our side, alongside our troops, with a clear intent to downplay the nightmares of battle and to maintain morale.

After the Western victory of 1945, the four decades that ensued, of Cold War and ambiguities and proxy conflicts, changed the landscape, for in the age of nuclear weapons war was no longer something that would be fought to save civilisation; it was something that must be avoided in order to preserve civilisation.

The moral lustre was stripped from conflicts, which became regional, limited, often covert and tactical in nature. And this also changed the way wars were covered and how they were placed in the flow of history.

Vietnam can stand for this process, just as that name stands for so many ineffable things, for Vietnam marked the deconstruction of war writing and of Western war itself. It was regular army versus ghost-like guerrillas; it was war as soundtrack, war as theatre of the absurd, force against concealment. Entire battles were fought out on sensors and television screens, for viewing each night on the home front.

Reports from correspondents travelling with American units conjured up a jungle world of suspicion and paranoias, of secret projects, of glitter and darkness, of rhythm and sweat. War was a trip. The journalism of the time hovered near the edge, where words give way and consciousness fragments. Again, a single writer most embodied this era: the restrained, self-concealing Michael Herr, whose Vietnam memoir, *Dispatches*, based on his pieces for US magazine *Esquire* but published only a decade after his years in-country, defined a conflict and a time: 'Vietnam, Vietnam, we've all been there.'

Herr's text has also shaped the enduring memory of that conflict. It is the guide rail and inspiration for each haunting Vietnam movie: Stanley Kubrick's *Full Metal Jacket*, Oliver Stone's *Platoon* and Francis Ford Coppola's myth-encrusted *Apocalypse Now*. This is almost certainly the last time in our era that a piece of printed reportage will play such a role.

Let the clock tick on. Let a generation pass. Now it is the post-Cold War age, the age of unequal wars, of embedded TV crews and fine-tuned media management. The power and precision of military hardware has reached surreal heights; 9/11 has provided a new fault line for the world, given birth to an open-ended war on terror and spawned its series of aftershocks.

Conflict and the coverage of conflict is measured by sensation: offensives tend to last no longer than a few days, enemies are often destroyed at long distance, in the space of hours, the doctrine of choice is shock and awe. Network reporters covering this electronic battlefield are themselves dusted with a short-lived celebrity as heroic witnesses appearing live on screen in the thick of battle, the angel companions of the troops at war.

And naturally this latest phase in the evolution of war corresponding has thrown up its own emblematic figure – only, by the perverse logic of contemporary life, he is as far from the 'embed' as he could be. He is a rebel, an anti-hero, the extraordinary, quite uninventable Anthony Loyd.

An old Etonian, a descendant of celebrated war heroes, once a serving British officer in Northern Ireland and now a freelance war specialist for *The Times* of London, Loyd is a slave to adrenalin and paradox, a reformed, if relapse-prone heroin addict and a writer capable of the most ecstatic flights of yearning, questing prose.

Eight years ago, after Loyd had completed his journalistic apprenticeship in the Yugoslav civil wars and emerged as a hard case in the thin ranks of modern war correspondents, his first book, *My War Gone By, I Miss it So*, a bleak record of his Bosnian days, appeared to reviews of shocked admiration.

Its newly published sequel, *Another Bloody Love Letter*, is not just the gore-spattered, self-tormenting memoir of Loyd's subsequent progress through the last of his heroin days and through war-zones in the Balkans, west Africa, Afghanistan and Iraq, it is also a kind of manifesto for his particular way of seeking out and reporting war.

These startling books mark a new twist in an old field: the reverence and esteem with which they have been received, by the critical establishment and by Loyd's professional colleagues, say much about the nature of the times.

Loyd begins his *Letter* with a bang and a challenge: we are in Iraq's Anbar province, with Bravo Company, moving forward, beside the reedy banks of the wide Euphrates. The day's fighting is done, the soldiers are weary, the vibe is heavy.

Loyd's own mind is drifting, to the past, the impossible future. He glances at the young men beside him and swiftly sketches the derived, mediated nature of their sense of battle:

> Some barely out of college and experiencing their first foreign country, many of the younger American soldiers were living

their own war films, life and art enmeshing in a freakish coupling to a contemporary soundtrack of thrash metal and gangsta rap, unaware that war seldom has a clear end, and never a final credit.

Then, as in every story, something happens: ambush! There is a sharp exchange of fire: a US soldier falls dead.

'Hey,' says a senior non-commissioned officer, some time later to Loyd, who notes the Airborne flash on the older man's shoulder, 'you get what you were looking for?' The scene soon dissolves, much like a music video.

Over the next 300 pages, on front lines in three continents, Loyd agonises over this question and the broad ethics of war reporting, a profession wholly dependent on observing the deaths of others. For we have moved on, in theme and treatment, since Herr's Vietnam; in the work of many writers it is not the weirdness of modern war that is the subject of choice so much as the weirdness of the act of witness. Loyd's focus is precisely himself and as a result we come to know a great deal about his life, his world and his subjective states during his advance through the battle zones.

In fact, he sets out his credo repeatedly and it jumps each time from the page: for the familiar mechanics of war coverage interest Loyd relatively little. He is not, in this memoir, greatly concerned with the individual combatants he meets or with the generals and political leaders. The complex chains of cause and circumstance that lie behind and influence the outbreak of wars, the negotiations to bring them to an end, the struggles for political authority that may lurk within the feints of battle, all these things bore him, almost to incoherence. The long expository segments of *Another Bloody Love Letter* read as though they were drafted on autopilot.

No, the only thing that excites him is war, the moment of battle, and the sight of it, and those like himself, war reporters, war junkies, who cannot keep away.

He worries at war from many angles. First, there is the anthropological-historical:

War by its nature sets out to be the very negation of civilisation, an experience which has the quintessence of killing and destruction and is designed to extinguish the most sacrosanct of all human rights: life. The front line is thus both a precipice and an altar, and the details of those who live, fight and die there are vital knowledge for anyone wishing to get a glimpse of the caved beast lurking beneath society's thin topsoil.

Then there is the epic-poetic:

Every war is a secret war, known only to those who were there. Whatever you say, however you say it, you can never explain that despite the fire, the fear, the smoke, the chaos, the killing, the madness and the loss, there exists something far beyond the trite accounting of collective risk and mortality: the best-kept secret of battle – the shared and terrible love of it all.

But if Thucydides and Homer are present in the mix, there is something else as well, for like most addicts, whatever their fix, Loyd is mesmerised by his private struggle and spends much time trying to justify what he does.

And he very often deploys the addict's most sublime, convincing tactic: perfect understanding of his circumstances. In a hotel in the run-down Kosovo capital of Pristina, he gives this unblinking delineation of his colleagues:

Men and women versed in the currencies of violence: dramatic and self-dramatising; concerned and callous; mostly white and middle-class and angry and childless; selfish through circumstance but often kind by inclination; sometimes brave; invariably great pretenders. Us. War correspondents, to use the professional term.

This is the seductive club Loyd elected, as a youngish man, to join and now chronicles. *Another Bloody Love Letter* is in truth a love letter to his colleagues, to his calling and to the hectic, refining violence of the wartime world.

At one point, Loyd goes so far as to offer a utilitarian account of his profession. Truth, he contends, is fugitive and hard to track down in a fighting zone.

It is never to be found in press conferences, briefings or a military contact's private phone call, 'Which is why war correspondents exist: intrinsically flawed characters prepared to take a chance and push through the breach to deny the propagandists their prisoners.' This claim, though, betrays a peculiar understanding of the reporter's task and its importance in the scheme of things. A moment's cool reflection discloses its wild, unreal optimism. For it is hard to summon up from the campaigns of the past 100 years too many instances where heroic correspondents on the spot have uncovered large-scale deception or brought forward facts that have changed history and transformed the reading or watching public's understanding of the deeds being done in its name.

The My Lai massacre was revealed only by congressional investigation; the mass executions at Srebrenica unfolded despite extensive reportage; the single greatest outrage of the Soviet occupation years in Afghanistan, the Red Army's persistent use of chemical weapons, remains unacknowledged despite repeated journalistic coverage. Rather, the role – and the unique power – of correspondents is to describe the human face of war: the fate of soldiers and civilians, the look of conflict, its feel, its cost. This is their duty of witness.

The great war reporters of the post-war era have built their lives around this calling. Two of this company, newly dead, come to mind: Ryszard Kapuscinski, the Polish news agency reporter who first explored the dark, near-forgotten wars of post-colonial Africa in his detailed, meticulous prose, and Anna Politkovskaya, chronicler of the Russian destruction of Chechnya, murdered last October outside her Moscow apartment.

Writing changes nothing but it colours thoughts and enters hearts. It does so most succinctly and effectively when it is lean, prompt and free from the baggage of introspection.

Loyd, though, is proposing something very different in this memoir. In his eyes, war, in all its hallucinatory strangeness, sometimes comes close to serving as an escape: a hit. Intensity and drama bequeath the truest sense of life.

Correspondents who have felt the lash of battle often know this fearful temptation and must seek to balance the grievous, intoxicating taste of danger with a sense of responsibility to their descriptive tasks.

One of the first figures to initiate Loyd into this domain was veteran Reuters correspondent Kurt Schork, the central presence of this book. Schork was killed in an ambush in Sierra Leone in May 2000; the portrait Loyd gives here of this substitute father-figure is also a sketch of his ideal war reporter:

> War both completed and complemented him. It soothed his frustration, jousted his impatient will, and he found no better soil to nurture his acute sense of right and wrong than that which lay beneath the shadow of the gun. Under his ascetic, cerebral exterior swam delight, fury and compulsion. The friction made him a brave, focused man with a hunger for the testing ground of action.

After the funeral, and almost a year of mourning, Loyd went in search of Schork's killers and the place of his death. This journey forms his narrative's emotional core; it unfolds in abrupt sequences, much like an animated version of *Heart of Darkness*, leaping from voodoo ceremonies to high-octane road trips.

There are more disasters, more moments of enlightenment and even a touch or two of grace. Loyd both finds and fails to find the instigators of the shooting of his friend. Perhaps the peak of bizarrerie is reached in his visit, accompanied by a Nigerian intelligence officer, to a bush nightclub in the shanty town of Makeni on the twentieth anniversary of Bob Marley's death:

> Inside, the dance hall boasted a bar and real-time rebel DJ. The air was a deoxygenated fug of humidity, sweat, beer and marijuana as some 200 rebel guys and dolls from the most heinous guerilla army in west Africa bumped and ground on the floor to War and Rebel Music like they meant it and it meant them, their numbers swollen by a posse of hookers, Sierra Leone's notorious night-fighters, and the lovers of Nigerian officers who had moved up to Makeni to chance the ceasefire with their men. Neither group appeared mutually exclusive.

This Conradian sortie over, the love letter unspools in assignments to Afghanistan and northern Iraq, complete with a poignant lesson in the scales of life and death.

Loyd's beloved mother, a shadowy presence in the preceding

decade of adventures, is diagnosed with cancer and, in the months between the invasion of Iraq and the start of the insurgency, she dies. Loyd's grief and sense of loss puts him in tune, he feels, with the grieving Iraqis all around him as he stares across the roofs of Baghdad. But inside himself he notices a new emotion, which he describes with the rapturous, near-clinical fascination he lavishes on all his inward states. It is, he decides, hope:

> Death seemed diminished, friendship undimmed. A feeling of profound fortune emerged to cloak me; an awareness of sudden prize and intense gratitude. Though not what I thought I had been looking for when it all began so long ago with that first war, and not what I had expected to discover in that city of all cities, on that day of all days, as an inheritance it was inestimable. No venture has richer reward. As unquantifiable in its essence as love, I had been bequeathed with life's great defiance, the unwinnable struggle's only possible victory: hope. I lived in hope.

And so, after this long, savage trip through wars and mayhem, punctuated by ever more brutal encounters with inhumanity, Loyd passes abruptly from his readers, a new and, as he would have it, a wiser man.

There are lines and scenes in *Another Bloody Love Letter* that linger in the mind for their shock value alone: the moment when Loyd snaps a photo as he drives by a dying Taliban fighter serves as adequate proof of the lesson in his own moral ambiguities that he is so keen to share.

And there is another, rather different-textured moment, when a group of Nigerian soldiers stand beside him, in shared lament over the body of a dead friend. As one man, they all sigh, and in their voices Loyd hears 'a sound loaded with deep understanding of sorrow, the echoed communication of the universal nature of death and loss'.

Rather than seek to make some assessment of these pages, with their rhythmic repetitions and their constant, looping returns to the author's innermost obsessions, it seems natural to pull back the focus from Loyd's chamber world of front line and risk, and to consider what lies ahead for war writing.

What future can there be, at a time when the West stands once more at the point of exhaustion in its pursuit of yet another missionary conflict on distant battlefields?

We know, of course, how swiftly and profoundly technology has changed the word's role and given the image its primacy. But the watching gaze of the TV camera has also shifted the balance of what the viewer seeks to see, and, by extension, the reader's operative field.

Film and video, instantly transmitted, breed a taste for excitement over emotion, sentiment over reflection. The Western viewer's visual vocabulary for comprehending Iraq includes, for instance, these key components: bomb plumes over Baghdad; twisted corpses; weeping men and women. The society's style and mood, the lives and fates of its people, all these elements remain out of shot.

When the print journalist becomes a supernumerary and news becomes drama alone, the writer has few choices left: he or she must run before the TV crews or turn his thoughts upon the baroque tone of the conflict or, ultimately, upon himself.

Something has got lost here, and it is hard not to draw a connective line between the narcissistic elements in much of today's war reporting and the Western world's deep lack of interest in the societies where it wages its wars. This gap of empathy has more than merely moral significance, it goes some way to accounting for the systematic failures of policy-making that have beset the linked enterprises of the ongoing, open-ended war on terror.

As one glances back at the long tradition of war writing, from its Homeric and tragic wellsprings to its latest and most extreme journalistic incarnations, it is hard not to feel that we have come, after a voyage down roads of utter darkness, to a full stop.

This may go some way to explaining the paradox of today's most highly written reports from the front line, a-glitter as they are with immediacy and intelligence, with the pain and pity of war. They have the pulverising, fragmenting effect of some up-to-the-minute cluster munition: reading them leaves the sensation of peering into a void.

The Australian's Review of Books

Love Me Tender?

Anne Manne

It is a story for our times. The amateur DVD boasting the exploits of the self-described 'teenage kings' of Werribee looked like any other. It had an R rating on the cover. The credits listed its 'stars': 'Boofa', 'Choco', Brendan and the rest. In a homely note, it thanked one boy's mother for the use of her video camera. What the DVD contained, however, horrified a nation. Among teenage pranks like burnouts and throwing eggs was the centrepiece: the abuse, sexual humiliation and degradation of a sixteen-year-old girl with a mild intellectual disability.

Through an internet chat room, the girl agreed to meet two of the boys at the local shopping centre. There, she was surrounded, overpowered by up to twelve young men, and forced down to a nearby secluded riverbank. Her clothing was thrown in the mud; she was made to expose her breasts and perform oral sex while the rest of the gang watched and jeered. She had a cup of urine tipped over her; several of the young men urinated on her. They set her hair on fire three times. Called 'The Victim', the teenager is pointed at and mocked. One youth turns to the camera and says, 'What the fuck; she's the ugliest thing I've ever seen.' At another point, the boys discuss pimping her. As one urges the others to give her a Brazilian wax, he says, 'We've got to make this bitch look like a slut … get with this whole deforestation thing.' Throughout, the girl cowers, terrified but smiling pitifully.

The story gets worse. Segments of the film were displayed for over three months on YouTube, a website which posts video clips. One segment of the DVD, called 'Pimp My Wife', was viewed by almost 2500 people without anyone finding anything amiss. As viewers around the globe snickered over its content, as the DVD was sold in Melbourne high schools for $5, the young female victim was shattered. Overnight, her father said, she changed from a 'happy-go-lucky' kid to being withdrawn and terribly ashamed. Over the next three months she quietly disintegrated. She is now seeing a psychologist.

It was only when excerpts from the DVD were shown on *Today Tonight* that the full moral weight of the crime was felt. The victim finally made statements to police, and the boys came under investigation for rape. Even then, amid widespread outrage, messages of support for the lads were posted on the internet. The girl's anguished father was told by Channel 7 that the parents of some of the youths involved in the crimes had laughed it off as 'a bit of fun'. Other parents, while not endorsing the DVD, nonetheless knew of its contents but did nothing. Some local teens interviewed were sceptical that anything much wrong had occurred. 'Daniel' thought it was 'just like in the movies'. 'Alissa' said, 'You can't make someone go down on their knees. You seriously can't do that … no-one is going to admit to giving a guy head in front of people.'

As in the Dianne Brimble case, it was not just the actions themselves which were so horrifying, but the fact that they were photographed. As Brimble lay naked on the cabin floor, dying from an overdose of the date-rape drug Fantasy, no hand stirred to help her. Instead, those hands were holding a digital camera, capturing lurid photographic trophies to circulate. As with the Werribee DVD, no-one realised or acted on the moral horror of what they were viewing. Some of the women on the cruise ship, to whom the photos of Brimble were shown, actually giggled.

Susan Sontag has written about another 'bit of fun', the porno-torture photos of Abu Ghraib prison:

> For the meaning of these pictures is not just that these acts were performed, but that their perpetrators had no sense that there was anything wrong in what the pictures show. Even

more appalling, since the pictures were meant to be circulated and seen by many people, it was all fun. And this idea of fun is, alas, more and more ... part of 'the true nature and heart of America'.

After Dianne Brimble, after the Werribee 12, is Australia any different? Some commentators noted the continuities between what the Werribee boys did and the contemporary version of what Barry Humphries' Sandy Stone character once called 'A Nice Night's Entertainment'. Even the milder versions of reality TV – the weigh-ins on *The Biggest Loser*, or Kyle Sandilands insulting young hopefuls on *Australian Idol* – depend upon ritual humiliation, and often upon group aggression against an individual in the form of expulsion. Other programs, such as the US show *Bumfights*, which paid homeless people to fight one another for the amusement of the viewer, carry more than a whiff of the sadism of the Roman circus. The Werribee DVD, too, shows a homeless man being harassed. As the British cultural critic Paul Taylor says, 'Everything becomes a potential image for the voyeuristic gaze and less and less is ruled out on grounds of taste or any other consideration.'

There has been less discussion of the intersection of our present taste for displays of aggression with the new culture of sexual liberalism. Yet the Werribee DVD is hardly an isolated sexual incident. Earlier this year, the *Atlantic Monthly* published an article called 'Are You There God? It's Me, Monica'. It concerned what one might call the Monica-isation of America's teenage girls. 'The Great Fellatio Scare', as one cynic dubbed it, was that teen girls were casually servicing teen boys with unrequited oral sex. A new generation, it seemed, was giving new meaning to Germaine Greer's memorable comment that women were men's 'sexual spittoons'. Similar concerns were at the centre of Ariel Levy's *Female Chauvinist Pigs*, published here in late 2005. In a swingeing critique of the new and nasty turn that the commodification of sex has taken, Levy also took aim at female complicity with the new 'raunch culture'.

In Australia, we have had our own worries on the girls-gone-wild teen-fellatio front, as well as allegations of serious sexual assaults and 'gangbangs' levelled at Rugby League players. The month of October opened with one kerfuffle, the left-of-centre Australia Institute's report on the sexualisation of children in advertising, and ended with another, over the Muslim cleric Sheikh Taj Aldin al-Hilali's remark about women to the assembled faithful: 'If you take out uncovered meat and place it outside on the street, or in the garden or in the park, or in the backyard without a cover, and the cats come and eat it ... whose fault is it, the cats' or the uncovered meat?'

Contempt for women, however, is hardly confined to Islamic fundamentalists. In a small but telling incident in 'enlightened' Europe, men's urinals in the shape of female lips were removed from public toilets in Austria. As it transpired, men had been pissing happily into red-lipped female mouths for three years without any concern. It was only when a political party held a convention nearby that public outcry saw them removed. (Whereupon they were scrubbed up and sold on eBay to enthusiastic buyers.)

So what has it all been about: Isolated events in a free modern society, not amounting to more than the sum of their parts? Or cultural happenings which resonate more deeply, indicative of deeper shifts in society's tectonic plates?

*

These seemingly disparate events have an internally consistent logic. The issue is not about what happens on cruise ships, or the antics of Werribee bogans, Austrian misogynists or Rugby League stars. To look at individual incidents is to concentrate on spot fires without recognising the bushfire that is burning. Nor is the issue cyber-bullying and the abuse of technology, although the problem is certainly intertwined with and intensified by this. All the events are dispatches from the frontline of a much larger, deeper and ongoing cultural clash between the new regime of sexual liberalism and the great movement in the late twentieth century towards women's equality. The whole society, as Helen Garner once put it so well, is seething with issues of sex and power.

To borrow a phrase coined by the Canadian philosopher Charles Taylor, the '60s was the period of the Great Disembedding of Western culture from its religious heritage. Among those elements of the old regime overturned were our longstanding assumptions about human hierarchy: white over black, men over women. One of the transcendent political movements to emerge from that period was the women's movement; another was anti-racism. As Raimond Gaita has suggested, those liberation movements expressed a desire for justice far deeper than mere equality of opportunity: 'Treat me as a person; see me fully as a human being, as fully your equal, without condescension … These are calls to justice conceived as an equality of respect.'

At the same time, though, a sexual revolution was occurring. Alongside patriarchal control of female sexuality, the long-standing oppression of homosexuals was challenged. The contraceptive revolution and widely available abortion saw control over fertility pass, for the first time in human history, from men, church and state to women. A new culture of sexual liberalism was born. It concerned not only how we behaved but also what we viewed. Censorship laws were relaxed; the pornography market exploded; raunch culture emerged.

The women's movement was both a participant in, and the beneficiary of, the sexual revolution. Greater openness about sex, the de-stigmatisation of abortion and contraception, and a less shame-inclined culture enabled women to step down from the garlanded pedestal marked 'asexual madonna' to become, if not Madonna, sexual beings with desires and needs of their own.

Yet the relationship between women's liberation and the new sexual freedom was never an uncomplicated one. The two movements have often been in tension. This was caught in a chance remark of Stokely Carmichael which instantly entered the lexicon. When female activists in the anti-Vietnam War protest movement got fed up with brewing the tea and demanded their own political positions, Carmichael jeered, 'The only good position for women is prone.'

Over time, another reason for the ongoing tension has become clear. Any assumption that now we have 'arrived' at our post-feminist equal-opportunities destination is false. Rather, the sexual revolution is actually much more complete, more successful, more far-reaching than the feminist revolution. And here, the uneven nature of social change matters greatly. It changes everything.

Jostling alongside welcome signs of women's newfound status, and a more relaxed, tolerant, open and liberal society on sexual matters, many of the contours of the new sexual liberalism remain shaped by male dominance. Every so often a truly ugly incident flashes into the public realm, bearing the harsh and indelible signature of misogyny.

All this makes redundant one of the great oversimplifications of modern times, that the new sexual liberalism is either good or evil. Related to this is the false depiction of debate on this issue as a Manichean struggle between the forces of darkness and of light, between Primordialists and Progressives, where the libertarians (the Good Guys) slug it out with killjoy Christian moralists (the Bad Guys).

A useful example is the film *The People Versus Larry Flynt*, which cast Flynt as the 'Loveable Scamp of Free Speech' fighting stupid Christian zealots. This conveniently skips over details of what actually appears in *Hustler* – the misogyny, racism and endorsement of rape myths, the treatment of child sexual abuse. One of its cartoons, for instance, shows a little blind girl trotting down the road with her dog. A man is lying in wait around the corner, with a piece of meat on a string, his pants dangled around his ankles, his engorged penis ready. Hilarious.

In reality, the progressive camp is divided. One group are what the sociologist Arlie Hochschild aptly called 'sunshine modernists', the she'll-be-right libertarian crew whose uncritical embrace of the 'modern' manages to read blithe and breezy narratives of female empowerment into just about anything. When challenged, this gives way to the furious reaction of old generals still fighting the last war, who lay charges of moral panic – the cultural Left's version of the Right's political correctness – as an alternative to thought.

From the political shadows, however, another group is emerging: the critical modernists. These are people for whom the issues with the '60s involve more of a lovers' quarrel than either outright repudiation or wholehearted embrace. Notwithstanding the revival of religious fundamentalism, we live in an increasingly secular society, where new conflicts are emerging. The critical modernists articulate a third position, still from the 'progressive' side of politics, raising questions about the abuse and exploitation of women, and the values of the sexual culture our young people are inheriting. Two of the most recent contributions from the Australia Institute, for example, concern how young people are socialised and, in some instances, sexualised.

'No two reports in our institute's history,' Clive Hamilton told me, 'have caused such reaction, most of it favourable, as the two on sex. There were outpourings of messages and emails of support.' The most recent one, on the sexualisation of children, triggered a national debate. For the first time, Hamilton had to hire a media-monitoring service to keep up with all the commentary (363 media discussions were recorded in the first week).

Interestingly, too, the institute's membership jumped. According to Hamilton, the overwhelming response was, 'Thank goodness someone sensible was saying something.' Someone sensible? 'Not Fred Nile.' The concern came from those who were generally comfortable with the new culture of sexual liberalism, but were not libertarians – at least, not when it involved issues involving children. Support (and relief) also came from members of the women's movement who felt that their concerns over the objectification of women were being swept away by a 'tsunami of pornography and pseudo-pornography and muddled ideas about what sexual liberation for women really means', as a commentator in the online magazine *Slate* put it.

These debates are reopening partly because what is so widely and freely available to people – including teenagers – has radically changed since the last serious debate over censorship. What's out there, just a mouse click away, sure ain't *Lady Chatterley's Lover*.

*

'Three holes and two hands.' That is Robert Jensen, a leftist professor of media at the University of Texas, on pornography's depiction of women.

> Men spend $10 billion on pornography a year. 11,000 new pornographic films are made every year. And in those films, women are not people. In pornography, women are three holes and two hands. Women in pornography have no hopes

and no dreams and no value apart from the friction those holes and hands can produce on a man's penis.

To Jensen's pithy summation, we may add, 'pussy is bullshit'. That last insight comes from the pornographer John Stagliano, interviewed by Martin Amis in an essay called 'A Rough Trade', which appeared in the *Guardian* in 2001. Amis asked Stagliano about the 'truly incredible emphasis on anal sex'. Stagliano shrugged. With vaginal sex, 'you have some chick chirruping away ... With anal, on the other hand, the actress is obliged to produce a different order of response: more guttural, more animal ... Her personality comes out.' Stagliano then explained his shift into the new, harder genre, gonzo porn, with 'Rocco', his favourite 'assbusting' stud:

> Together we evolved toward rougher stuff. He started to spit on girls. A strong male-dominant thing, with women being pushed to their limit. It looks like violence but it's not. I mean, pleasure and pain are the same thing, right? Rocco is driven by the market. What makes it in today's marketplace is reality.

'Reality' in today's marketplace, according to Robert Jensen, is about eroticising dominance and cruelty. 'When the legal restrictions on pornography slowly receded through the 1970s and '80s,' Jensen explains, there was a question of where one went next:

> Anal sex was seen as something most women don't want; it had an edge to it. When anal sex became routine in pornography, the gonzo genre started pushing the boundaries into things like double-penetrations and gag-inducing oral sex – again, acts that men believe women generally will not want. The more pornography becomes normalized and mainstreamed, the more pornography has to search for that edge. And that edge most commonly is cruelty.

As one of the porn directors, Jerome Tanner, explained in a pornography directors' roundtable discussion featured in *Adult Video News*, 'People just want it harder, harder, and harder, because like Ron said, What are you gonna do next?' Another director, Mitchell Spinelli, said:

> People want more. They want to know how many dicks you can shove up an ass ... It's like *Fear Factor* meets *Jackass*. Make it more hard, make it more nasty, make it more relentless. The guys make the difference. You need a good guy, who's been around and can give a good scene, fuckin' 'em hard.

*

Unsurprisingly, how this shapes behaviour, teen behaviour in particular, is a vexed question. No-one suggests the simple Pavlovian thesis: male views pornography and rushes out to drag the nearest woman off the street and rape her. We know that many men who use pornography don't rape, and that some men who don't use pornography do. Fantasy – however grisly – can be an area of 'play-acting', in which aspects of aggression and desire not acted on in everyday life can be expressed. That said, while cautioning against certainty on the question, when Michael Flood and Clive Hamilton reviewed the recent research literature, in *Regulating Youth Access to Pornography* (2003), they found:

> existence of significant associations between use of certain types of pornography and sexual aggression ... regular consumption of pornography and particularly violent and extreme pornography is a risk factor for boys' and young men's perpetration of sexual assault. In addition, it may foster greater tolerance of this behaviour by others.

Nor is the question simply restricted to sexual assault. What is the effect on male attitudes to women when the depictions of them in this powerful medium are so clearly based on misogyny, sexual contempt, degradation and the depiction of a woman as a thing to be used? What is the effect when socialisation into sexual feelings includes regularly masturbating to orgasm over such material? What version of the sexual script unfolds in some men's heads: what is their expectation of what women are willing and ready to do?

The statistics on rape and sexual assault don't bear out any oversimplified thesis, although one Australian Bureau of Statistics estimate suggested that as many as 80 per cent of assaults go unreported. Changes in willingness to report crimes, in police taking responses seriously and so on, can also muddy the waters on how clearly we can 'read' statistical data. The perpetrators of sexual assault are overwhelmingly male, and the victims female. In 2003, the highest number of sexual-assault victims were aged under twenty-five.

Although we are three decades on from the equal-opportunities revolution, sexual attitudes to women remain troubling. Rob Moodie, CEO of the Victorian Health Promotion Foundation (VicHealth), pointed out that Sheikh al-Hilali's comments are far from isolated ones: 'To believe that we live in a tolerant society where the rights of all are respected and protected is to ignore the prevalence of attitudes that support sexual and physical violence against women.' The foundation's recent report, *Two Steps Forward, One Step Back*, found that one in four Victorians believed that women make up rape allegations, and 15 per cent thought that women will say 'no' to sex when they mean 'yes'. What's more, 'A staggering 40 per cent of Victorians actually agree with the myth that men rape because they can't control their sexual urges.'

Clearly, we still have a long, long way to go.

One of the most important elements in the debate over pornography is the possible effects of favourable depictions of rape, the endorsement of the idea that 'no' really means 'yes'. Rae Langton, a philosopher at the Massachusetts Institute of Technology, has developed a nuanced argument in a series of articles about the influence of porn on what she calls 'sexual language games'. Those language games carry powerful presumptions about what women are like. They may be very difficult to contest in a highly charged sexual situation. Power is involved in determining whether our utterances are taken seriously. And porn, Langton argues, casts women in a certain light, enabling assumptions about women's nature – that they all like rape, or forced or rough sex, or that 'no' means 'yes' – to be seamlessly embedded in interactions.

The Australia Institute report on youth and pornography

found that far more teenage boys than girls access porn, a difference of 73 per cent to 11 per cent, and they access it more regularly. Does that fact, alongside the possibility of an overdetermined sexual script ushered in by the mainstreaming of porn, shed light on the Brimble and Werribee cases?

From the female point of view, the initial stages would have begun innocently enough. Perhaps they were flattered, even hopeful that the encounter might lead to a very different form of male attention. Both seemed lonely. Dianne Brimble was a single mother, stoically raising her kids. The cruise was her brief holiday from that unglamorous reality, a moment to kick up her heels. And, regarding the Werribee incident, everyone knows the longings of a teenage girl.

After dancing with the men, before going to their cabin, Brimble was heard to ask, 'Where shall we go next?' The young girl in the Werribee DVD thought she was meeting not twelve but two boys, in the safety of a shopping centre. Whatever was in *their* heads, whether it was even a *sexual* script unfolding, we know that what happened in both cases had elements of a porn script. In the DVD, explicit references are drawn from porn. There are discussions of giving the girl a Brazilian wax and pimping her; she performs oral sex in front of the gang. In the cabin next door to where Dianne Brimble's body was found, a witness, Joanne Muller, heard a protest: 'It was definitely a female voice singing out saying, "I'm not like that and I don't do that sort of thing."'

In the world of porn, *all women* are like that. They take their punishment, and they like it. They smile for the camera.

*

The publisher of Jenna Jameson, the 'world's highest grossing adult-film performer', tells us, 'I believe that there is a pornoisation of the culture.' Jameson's memoir, *How to Make Love like a Porn Star*, was breathlessly and enthusiastically reviewed in publications such as the *New York Times*, the *Los Angeles Times* and the *Philadelphia Inquirer*. To put it mildly, the industry has *not* quietly hung up its dildo, so to speak, after the Glorious Sexual Revolution removed the need for sad little men in their raincoats to sneak into seedy cinemas to catch an 'adult' film. The opposite has occurred. As Martin Amis observed in 2001:

Porno is far bigger than rock music and far bigger than Hollywood. Americans spend more on strip clubs than they spend on theatre, opera, ballet, jazz and classical concerts combined. In 1975 the total retail value of all the hardcore porno in America was estimated at $5–10 million. Last year Americans spent $8 billion on mediated sex.

Porn has gone mainstream. And feminism has not colonised porn; porn has colonised feminism. We all now know its themes and imagery. As William Safire recently noted, the word 'porn' has entered the lexicon, and been unsexed in the process; food porn, for example, has become instantly recognisable shorthand. More interestingly, the values and sexual practices, even the intimate bodily details of the porn star, like the Brazilian wax, have entered popular culture, as commonplace as a manicure at the local beauty salon.

I cannot claim any great nostalgia for the grimmer remnants of the dour sartorial ethos of second-wave feminism: hairy armpits, boilersuits and faces scrubbed bare of make-up. One got the point, though, that it was time to break with the preceding culture, where a collective female memory bank included Chinese foot-binding and whalebone corsets winched up so tight that women fainted. Later, it was just about sacrificing comfort and sometimes self-respect in 'dressing to please'. The fresh hope was for a world where making oneself over into the shape of another's desire, at any cost, would give way to self-acceptance. How quaint that all seems now.

In the bad old days, it was clitoridectomies. In the good new days, it is vaginoplasty. Added to the facelifts and breast implants is a new female bodily terrain to be 'corrected'. Ariel Levy notes that vaginoplasties and 'vaginal rejuvenation' are 'cosmetic operations to alter the labia and vulva so they look more like the genitals one sees in *Playboy* or porn'. These are not, she emphasises, surgeries to increase *female* sexual pleasure. They are designed solely to render a vagina more 'attractive' – and more in line with the quietly universalising standards established by pornography: the surgical version of the Brazilian wax, with its faint resonances of child pornography. Indeed, the US Society for Gynecologic Surgeons warns of the scarring, nerve damage and numbness which may follow vaginoplasty.

How ironic that a movement based around the elimination of such practices as genital mutilation and clitoridectomies has ended up by having female empowerment invoked to support labial pintucks and mutilating surgery on vaginas. It all sells, though, rather better than the boilersuit.

Another aspect of the women's movement encouraged the female sex not to be defined in terms of their value to men, but to be unapologetic about wanting areas of achievement outside the relational world, where you did not 'play dumb'. Yet, for *Playboy* and the emblematically titled *For Him Magazine*, some of the best female athletes in the world were arranged in sexual poses, legs open, garments yanked up or down to expose breasts or pubis, or on all fours in the 'presenting' position, as it is called in the animal kingdom, haunches raised and ready. Then again, Levy says dryly, maybe the athletes thought they were trading up.

*

When is a child's teddy not a bear? When it is a hot-thong teddy – an imitation of the adult version. Such items, alongside 'bralettes' for five-year-olds, are now for sale in children's clothing sections of Australian stores.

To what extent is raunch culture experiencing a kind of downwards age-bracket creep? That was the question raised by the Australia Institute's report *Corporate Paedophilia: The Sexualisation Of Australian Children*. In the appendix, photos from retailers such as David Jones were presented. Some were more blatant than others, but the images of made-up children with glossed mouths, provocative poses and see-through T-shirts displaying bras for non-existent breasts were all aimed at the children's clothing market.

The report's authors, Emma Rush and Andrea La Nauze, pointed to harms children may suffer as a consequence of being sexualised, such as an excessive early concern over bodily shape (hospitalisations for anorexia are increasing for younger age groups), acceptance of children being treated like sexual objects, and distraction from activities better suited to those age groups.

'The messages children receive about desirable behaviour and values incorporate ethical effects that go well beyond simply how to dress,' they pointed out.

Invoking their 'renowned' 'family values', the general manager of marketing for David Jones, Damian Eales, rejected all such criticisms. Likewise Simone Bartley, chief executive of advertising agency Saatchi & Saatchi, who said flatly, 'We have never, ever eroticised children in any way for any client in any communication.'

A second prong of the critique in the Australia Institute's paper – less covered by the press but no less important – was directed at 'tween' magazine culture, the glossy magazines, such as *Barbie Magazine*, *Total Girl* and *Disney Girl*, intended for children under twelve. Apart from the predictable embrace of celebrity culture, in several magazines more than half the content, and in *Barbie Magazine* over three-quarters of it, was concerned with sexual themes. Close to one-third of *Barbie Magazine* was devoted to crushes and boys; only one-fifth of it was 'developmentally appropriate' for the target age group.

Even more disturbing were the 'role models' presented for the tween girls to emulate:

> It is astonishing that Paris Hilton should be considered an appropriate role model for girls who are not yet in their teens; although she is heir to a substantial fortune, Hilton has no particular talent, and is famous largely due to a pirated video showing her engaged in fellatio.

I doubt I am alone among the nation's parents, outside the Hillsong congregation, in agreeing with the report's authors that Ms Hilton's claim to fame is not quite what we have in mind as a role model.

Reading blogs on this topic was interesting. Mothers, mostly, agreed with the report. I call them the 'mothers who mind'. These mothers felt they were continually holding back the floodwaters of a raunch culture threatening childhood. Their relief that someone had finally been called to account was palpable.

The Australia Institute's concern is not an isolated one. In Britain, retailers were forced to remove sexually suggestive children's products from their shelves, including padded bras with a 'Little Miss Naughty' logo. Community outrage also saw a 'sexy' pole-dancing kit removed from the toys and games section of a website run by Britain's biggest retailer, Tesco, which includes items for children aged four to six. The 'Peekaboo' pole-dancing kit came with its very own 'sexy garter' and DVD 'demonstrating suggestive dance moves'. It promised to 'Unleash the sex kitten inside … simply extend the Peekaboo pole inside the tube, slip on the sexy tunes and away you go! … Soon you'll be flaunting it to the world and earning a fortune in Peekaboo Dance Dollars.' For the pre-pubescent child, flaunting *what*, precisely? 'It's the latest exercise craze,' said a Tesco representative piously, with just a hint of injury. 'This item is for people who want to improve their fitness and have fun at the same time.'

Except that the *people* in question were children. What's next? A pacifier in the shape of a dildo?

*

In *Female Chauvinist Pigs*, Ariel Levy tells of a public contretemps between a woman, perhaps one of those mothers who mind, and Robin Nevins, an extraordinarily successful and powerful player in American television giant HBO. She questioned how Nevins, as a mother, was happy to broadcast her program *G-String Divas*, on strippers and their sexual practices. Nevins spun around and snapped, 'You're talking '50s talk! Get with the program!'

For too long, we have been bullied on this question. For too long, frank and reasoned discussion of these matters – raunch culture, the Roman circus sadism of reality TV, the porno-isation of the world, and the rest – has been taboo. For too long, we have been pinned between twin simplicities. In the light of recent events, the libertarian arguments look as tired and morally jaded as a washed-up porn star. The Christian lobby's emphasis on abstinence and virginity seems about as useful as a nineteenth-century douche in the era of AIDS. As Levy says, 'It's time to stop nodding and smiling uncomfortably as we ignore the crazy feelings in our heads and admit the emperor has no clothes.' It's time for other arguments, including those from feminism, to come in from the cold.

Love Me Tender?

How responsive is the new regime of sexual liberalism to the claims of women as equal citizens? How far is it ruthlessly and remorselessly incorporating women's 'liberation' into an even harsher regime of male-dominated sexual relations? These are extraordinarily important questions. Hannah Arendt once remarked that every generation passes something new to the next. To have the daughters of the '60s generation and beyond not prone but down on their knees is hardly an advance on Carmichael. Surely we can do better.

The Monthly

* * *

White Guilt, Victimhood and the Quest for a Radical Centre

Noel Pearson

The audacious idea of a Barack Obama presidency emerged when the first-term black senator from Illinois was invited by John Kerry to deliver the keynote address to the 2004 Democratic Convention. From a gatecrasher without a pass at the previous convention in Los Angeles four years earlier, Obama's exceptional charisma, navigated by a (politically) precise moral compass, led to the fortuitous invitation from Team Kerry.

From his star turn in Boston, Obama stirred the American imagination with the prospect of the first black presidency, and in a flash his 1995 biography *Dreams from My Father* was reprinted and in the bookstores. His application for his 2008 candidature is set out in last year's bestseller *The Audacity of Hope*, where he boldly sets out his 'thoughts on reclaiming the American dream'. It is an impressive statement of beliefs, characterised by intelligent analysis, a candour that may not be completely calculated, and a carefully calibrated self-deprecation. It is counter-weighed by an understandable, but nevertheless disturbing, absence of doubt about whether the contradictions of America can be resolved. Obama attributes the audacity of hope to the salt-of-the-earth characters he parades through his book, but there is no doubt – it is really the audacity of his own ambitions that he has in mind.

My concern with Barack Obama is to ask whether he represents 'the radical centre' of the great dialectical tension in black leadership philosophy in the United States, between the omnipresent legacies of Booker Taliaferro Washington (1856–1915), who fought discrimination behind the scenes, and William Edward Burghardt Dubois (1868–1963), who argued that discrimination should be pursued more aggressively. The history of the Washington–Dubois dialectic remains the prism through which policies for the alleviation of oppression might best be understood. Black Americans have been mostly subscribers to the Duboisian tradition, the tradition in which Dr Martin Luther King Jr stood and Rosa Parks sat: it is the predominant model of black advocacy for uplift. Booker T. Washington's disciples, on the other hand, have been mostly silent, living ordered and industrious lives, valuing education and enterprise, bringing up strong families who desire to take their share of a country much built on the enslavement of their ancestors.

If Obama does transcend these paradigms, his capacity to defy the gravitational pull of the Dubois orthodoxy probably stems from his unique biography: an African-American, but not part of the long history that began with slavery. The stigma associated with the Washingtonian legacy – the allegedly Uncle Tomish belief that American opportunity will reward discipline and responsibility – does not shackle Obama.

Destroying the civil rights promise
Shelby Steele, according to the shallow taxonomy of American political culture, is a black conservative. In his book *White Guilt* (2006), Steele tells how disconcerting it was for someone with his background – son of civil rights campaigners, young Afro-haired wannabe campus radical of the 1960s, fellow traveller with high hopes for Lyndon Johnson's Great Society – to be tagged with this label. That he came to question the post-civil rights trajectory of black America, and to advance a compelling interpretation of the strange twist in the aftermath of the civil rights victories – how retching defeat came from the bowels of victory – earned him the most dreaded black classification: Uncle Tom.

But even as Harry Belafonte denounced Colin Powell and Condoleezza Rice as 'White House niggers' in 2002, a critique was growing in black America that challenged the progressive consensus around race which has prevailed since 1964–65. Shelby Steele is one of the intellectuals leading this critique. He raises troubling issues for those who see themselves as heirs to the radical tradition. By the mid-1960s, he argues, institutions across America suffered a moral authority deficit. When he and a gang of black students burst into the office of his college president with a list of demands he expected to face resistance, even disciplinary action, but didn't. Steele realised the college president 'knew that we had a point, [and] that our behaviour was in some way connected to centuries of indisputable injustice. The result was that our outrage at racism simply had far greater moral authority than his outrage over our breach of decorum.' This was one of Steele's first encounters with *white guilt* – the notion that past injustices perpetrated on a group of people absolve subsequent generations of that group of standard responsibilities.

Whites – and, he asserts, American institutions – must acknowledge historical racism to atone for it, but in acknowledging it they lose moral authority over matters of social justice and become morally – and, one could argue, politically – vulnerable. To overcome this vulnerability, white Americans have embraced a social morality, designed to rebuild moral authority by simultaneously acknowledging past racial injustices while separating themselves from those injustices. Steele calls this dissociation.

Where white guilt forces white Americans to acknowledge historical injustices, social morality may absolve them of it, restoring authority and democratic bona fides. With authority restored, power relations may continue as before. Critically, Steele argues, 'social morality is not a dissident point of view urged ... by reformers; it is the establishment morality in America. It defines propriety ... so that even those who harbour racist views must conform to a code of decency that defines those views as shameful.'

But Steele does not limit his analysis to white America. He expands his argument to assess the effects of white guilt on the freedoms – tangible or otherwise – of black Americans and draws a connection between increasingly militant messages of black power and burgeoning manifestations of white guilt. As new black leaders redefined racism as systemic and sociological, racism was larger than individual acts, and defined social and political events and decisions. Even a hint of racism proved the rule, and the only way to address it was a systemic solution. So, Steele notes, the current generation of black American students, despite never having suffered the oppression or subjugation of their forefathers, enjoy affirmative action with a clear sense of entitlement. Black entitlement and white obligation have become interlocked.

Pushing the argument one step further, Steele unpacks the effects of the interplay. Black consciousness, he argues, led many black Americans to talk themselves out of the personal freedom won by civil rights activism, for the sole (and unworthy) purpose of triggering white obligation. In a reactionary drift, race came to be seen as more important than individuality. In this way, identity played a destructive role in the advancement of black Americans.

When his peers raised their consciousness and embraced the neo-Marxian theories of institutionalised racism, Steele argues they began to think of responsibility as something that made blacks complicit in their own repression. Paradoxically, this historically justified insight started influencing black American ideology at the same time as discrimination and oppression were rapidly and formally being removed from the society.

The realisation that white America had a diminished moral authority to tell black Americans to be responsible led many – black and white – to conclude that white America was *obliged* to demonstrate its reformation by taking on the burden of responsibility for black Americans. White America thus assumed considerable responsibility for improving the socio-economic status of blacks. Underpinning this was the unspoken assumption that it was morally wrong (or unnecessary) for blacks to bear full responsibility for 'their own advancement'.

The devastating effect of this redistribution of responsibility for black advancement to (white) institutions, however, is perpetually to project blacks as weak and incapable of achieving advancement on their own merit. No group in human history, Steele asserts, has been lifted into excellence or competitiveness by another. No group has even benefited from the assistance of others without taking responsibility for itself. And herein lies the nub of his thesis: that social justice is not a condition of, but a mechanism for, an equitable world. It cannot be delivered in the same way as basic services. It cannot be absent one day and present the next. Social justice requires work and collaboration; if it is not accompanied by *individual* efforts to 'get ahead', it is unlikely to generate a better life.

In America, then white guilt now underpins a sense of white obligation to lift blacks up, with disastrous effects. In a 1999 *Harper's* essay, Steele nailed his argument:

> Right after the '60s civil-rights victories came what I believe to be the greatest miscalculation in black American history. Others had oppressed us, but this was to be the first 'fall' to come by our own hand. We allowed ourselves to see a greater power in America's liability for our oppression than we saw in ourselves. Thus, we were faithless with ourselves just when we had given ourselves reason to have such faith. We couldn't have made a worse mistake. We have not been the same since.

The Australian paradox after 1967: black rights become white responsibilities

There are compelling parallels between what happened with black Americans from the time of civil rights and voting rights in 1964–65, and with black Australians from the time of the 1967 referendum, when 90.2 per cent of Australians voted to amend the constitution to count Aboriginal people in the census and to empower the Commonwealth Parliament to make laws in respect of Aboriginal and Torres Strait Islander people.

The American rights guarantees were substantive: they provided freedoms and protections denied to black Americans since the abolition of slavery. So, from the time of their passage, blacks in America could invoke federal law in order to combat discrimination in respect of a wide range of civil rights. The Australian changes did not immediately provide any substantive rights; the Commonwealth Parliament was merely empowered to make laws – a power previously the exclusive province of the states. Protection from racial discrimination was not available in Australia until the Commonwealth Parliament passed the *Racial Discrimination Act* in 1975.

Nonetheless, the symbolic significance of the 1967 referendum, which was the culmination of a concerted ten-year public campaign and redressed the complete exclusion of Australia's Indigenous peoples from the federal compact of 1901, was to mark the beginning of a new era in Indigenous history and policy. It was a hopeful and positive event, and is still mostly seen as such.

Substantive rights and protections for Indigenous Australians were enacted in the years before and after the referendum. But legislation providing affirmative action and access to educational and other institutions was never introduced in Australia. Affirmative action programs have only ever occurred as voluntary policy decisions by public or private institutions.

It is not these rights and recognition events that I (or Shelby Steele) question. They were seminal achievements; it is their aftermath that requires reconsideration.

In the aftermath of the civil rights victories, the politics of 'victimhood' came to dominate black advocacy and public policy thinking. Victimhood relied on a phenomenon within the dominant white societies that had two faces: *white guilt* and *moral vanity*. The rise of victim politics meant that even as there was increased recognition of black rights, there was also a calamitous erosion of black responsibility.

I have often reflected on the downside of the events surrounding citizenship, at least for the remote communities of northern Australia with which I am familiar – particularly Cape York Peninsula. In light of the problems with which we are grappling today, I see three factors as decisive contributors to the descent into hell three decades later. These factors appeared to be positive developments designed to address inequities, but their unintended consequences – particularly for Aboriginal men – were negative:

- The equal wages decision of 1966, which mandated equal pay for Aboriginal stock-workers, contributed to the large-scale exodus from the pastoral industry of northern Australia (and elsewhere). The removal of Aboriginal people to the fringes of country towns and into missions and settlements meant that young men had lots of idle time.

- The Commonwealth Government's solution for Aboriginal people displaced from the pastoral industry was to provide access to social security payments, and the relevant government department undertook a drive through the 1970s to sign people up to income support. This provided young men with work-free income.
- Citizenship brought to Aboriginal people the right to drink.

Young men with idle time, free income and the right to drink created an alcohol abuse vortex which would cause increasing chaos as it widened to include women and older people who had not previously been drinkers. I saw this pattern spread in the three communities with which I am intimate, from my childhood in the late 1960s to the present.

The story of the past four decades is, of course, more complex than this. There were other factors driving the decline in the pastoral industry. The dismantling of the systems of social and administrative control by governments and missions led to growing social chaos. Even where strong and functional cultural norms were maintained by Aboriginal people themselves, their maintenance was broken down by values imported from the wider society, and by the shutting down of Aboriginal authority through the intrusion of the legal system. Legal Aid services to Aboriginal offenders probably did more to undermine the authority of elders and other local justice mechanisms (in Queensland, the Aboriginal courts presided over by local Justices of the Peace) than any other intervention. A workable system of social order based on moral and cultural authority was forced to comply with legal authority – and ultimately had to defer to the law. The moral and cultural authority which had provided structure to life in the settlements withered away.

The decline of religion and of the influence of the churches is also part of this story, including the historically problematic role of the churches in the administrative management of Aboriginal communities. In the case of my home town, I served on the Hope Vale Aboriginal Community Council when the last vestiges of the Lutheran Church's administrative involvement in the affairs of our people were removed in the late 1980s. We cut these last ties with a relishing sense of historic reckoning. The awful truth is that we threw the baby out with the bathwater: the role of the church in the secular and spiritual life of our community was conflated; both the church and our people should have found a way to move beyond the paternalism of the past without destroying the moral and cultural order which had been such a strong quality of our community. But the transfer of moral responsibility that Shelby Steele identified in the United States also played out here. We now repent a social and moral wreckage.

But these are details. The larger context was the growth of the culture and politics of victimhood, which came to be the accepted basis of the relationship between Aboriginal people and the rest of the country.

*

Prior to reading Shelby Steele's thesis on white guilt – and how the success of civil rights transmogrified into the failure of victim politics – I had been thinking about the various positions Indigenous and non-Indigenous Australians take in relation to questions of history and race. There is a dichotomy in popular discussion of racism. It is assumed that people and ideas come from one of two possible sides: those who are racists and those who are not, those who are subject to racism and those who are racists, those who believe that racism is a major social ill and those who do not, and so on. In Australia, the divide is generally seen as being one between those who believe Australia has a problem with racism, and those who believe that Australia is not a racist country.

Since the 1960s, Australians from the left and right have altered their views on racism for the better. While, historically, racism was widely acceptable across Australian society (the 'White Australia' policy was championed by the Australian Labor Party), political opinion and social values shifted fundamentally towards an understanding that overt racism, at least, was unacceptable.

Today, while leading conservatives and liberals (notably former prime minister Malcolm Fraser) are avowed opponents of racism, the polarity between those who consider racism a serious problem and those who do not is generally seen as a left–right split. As progressive people predominately come from left of the cultural and political divide, the ALP (and the progressive minor parties) are generally regarded as opponents of racism, while the Liberal and National parties are considered racist – or at least indifferent to racism. Individuals from both sides often contradict this generalisation.

This dichotomous view of racism is simplistic and misleading. My analysis looks at six positions which Indigenous and non-Indigenous Australians take in relation to race and history concerning the country's original peoples. For non-Indigenous Australians, the arc goes from denial to moral vanity, to acknowledgment and responsibility. For Aboriginal people, this arc ranges from separatism to victimhood, and to pride and principled defence.

There is a strong tradition of *denial* in Australia. The eminent ethnographer W.E.H. Stanner named this tradition in the country's historiography up to the late 1960s the 'Great Australian Silence'. There is a very large constituency which denies that the treatment of Indigenous people in Australia's colonial history (and up to the present) was as bad as historians have demonstrated.

There are two important things to understand about this constituency. First, most of them are defensive about their own identity and heritage. The accusation that they are racist and their colonial heritage is a catalogue of shame and immoral villainy – and they should therefore feel guilt for racism and history – makes them defensive. If race and history are raised in such a sharply accusatory and unbalanced way, people who might otherwise be prepared to acknowledge and take responsibility for the truth end up joining the hard-core ideologues.

The second major constituency in contemporary Australia is *morally vain* about race and history. Its members largely come from the liberal left and are morally certain about right and wrong and ready to ascribe blame. For them, issues of race and history are a means of gaining the upper hand over their political and cultural opponents. The primary concern of the morally vain is not the plight or needs of those who suffer racism and oppression, but rather their view of themselves, their understanding of the world and their belief in their superiority over their opponents. Two things about this constituency need to be understood. This constituency contributes most to, and actively supports, the outlook that casts Indigenous people as victims. Its members have no understanding of how destructive, demoralising and demeaning this mentality is. Their most telling catchphrase in rebuke of their opponents, whenever there may be a suggestion made about the personal responsibility of Indigenous people (or indeed the disadvantaged at large), is 'don't blame the victims'. They excuse and provide a justification for those on whose behalf they advocate, in order to avoid responsibility.

Moral vanity is perhaps an unfair characterisation. Many within this group have decent motivations. They empathise with the plight of Indigenous people who face racism and other real injuries; they acknowledge what has happened through history and recognise that the present is not unconnected with the past. But at some point empathy and acknowledgment turn into moral superiority, and the relative failures of one's cultural and political opponents become the basis of accusations of insensitivity or racism. At this point, racism serves the cultural and political purposes of the progressive accuser rather than the humanity of those subjected to it.

Rather than denial or moral vanity, the optimum position for non-Indigenous people to take is that of *acknowledgment* – of the past and its legacy in the present, recognising that racism is not a contrivance, that Indigenous people endure great hurt and confront barriers as a result of racism. They need to take *responsibility* for the fact of racism, and work to answer and counter it.

On the Indigenous side, the extreme position is that of *separatism*. In the United States, black nationalists such as Marcus Garvey actively pursued separatist agendas. The separatist rhetoric and strategy of Malcolm X was real. But this is a minority view. Generally, African-American issues are thought of as 'race relations' with a goal of ending public programs and practices which recognise African-Americans as a distinct group. The African-American struggle is for socio-economic advancement and equality.

The Indigenous Australian struggle is for socio-economic advancement and equality, but it is also about the recognition of status and rights as a people. Indigenous Australian political issues are 'peoplehood issues'. It is regrettable that this word is so little used in English-language debate. Berkeley professor

John Lie has defined it as 'an inclusionary and involuntary group identity ... It is not merely a population – an aggregate, an external attribution, an analytical category – but, rather, a people – a group, an internal conviction, a self-reflexive identity.'

Indigenous Australians have more of a claim to peoplehood than African-Americans do. However, separatist posturing has largely been a tactical device in Australia, not entirely without (tactical) effect. Separatism has not been the subject of a real and serious strategy, despite the profound sense of alienation experienced by many Indigenous people.

The largest constituency on the Indigenous side subscribes to *victimhood*. Again, this is a strong term, which covers a broad spectrum of outlooks. People will object to my interpretation of the dimensions of victimhood because what many of our people regard as radical, separatist and resistance politics I say is victim politics. Further, what many of our people regard as pride and necessary defensiveness against racism is, I believe, victim politics. Argument arises here because of the dynamic way in which culture and politics evolve over time: what may once have been a truly radical act, such as the Tent Embassy in 1972, degenerates into a sad symbol of defeatist, victim politics, as is plainly seen with the squalid demountables at the Tent Embassy site in 2007.

Argument arises because it is one thing to analyse properly whether some mentality or action proceeds from victimhood, and another to analyse its political or social effectiveness. I am *not* saying the politics of victimhood have not (and do not still) yield returns. They have and do, but at an enormous cost that is sometimes hard to recognise. As Shelby Steele has explained, *white guilt* is a resource blacks in America and Australia have learned to mine.

I want to talk about two problems with victimhood. The first is that we pay a high price for casting ourselves as victims. Victimhood becomes not just a tactic, but an identity. The long-grassers and under-the-bridge dwellers are the most visible, end-stage subscribers to this tragic and self-harming tactic. It damages our people wherever they are – from the young student who believes that academic achievement at school is 'acting white' and defeats him or herself with such a pernicious outlook, to those who tolerate domestic violence because it is 'understandable' given the history of the people concerned.

We indigenes of Australia are confused in our cultural understanding of victimisation and victimhood. Yes, individuals and groups in our society are *victimised* in a variety of ways. But it is a terrible thing to encourage victims to adopt a mentality of victimhood, to see themselves as victims. To adopt this outlook is fatal because it concedes defeat.

The second problem with victimhood is that the access and opportunities it produces are of mixed quality. The 'soft bigotry of low expectations' tends to determine the quality of the opportunities given to people deemed to be victims. In America the hot-button issue is affirmative action. If you take Steele's view, affirmative action is a policy constructed for victims, which does not help them rise out of their victimhood.

Tom Wolfe's perspicacious account of the radical chic posturings of morally vain whites and the mau-mauing of the flak-catchers by the angry 'radicals' in America applied here too, right through the 1970s and '80s. An undergraduate command of some key ideas in international and human rights law led to the new language of 'sovereignty'. I was once told a hilarious story by the late Charlie Perkins of an Indigenous gathering in a Returned Serviceman's League hall in a country town where the entire morning was spent debating whether a portrait of Her Majesty Queen Elizabeth II should remain gazing down at the proceedings as the owners of the establishment intended it to. Those seeking to make a point about the wrongful usurpation of Indigenous sovereignty by the Crown succeeded in their motion, and the rest of the day was spent looking for another venue because the gathering was immediately ejected from the premises.

During my law studies in Sydney in the late 1980s, I expressed interest in working for an Indigenous organisation to a white trade unionist who was well acquainted with some key figures of the 1970s Indigenous leadership. I was taken by this kindly man to the offices of two of the pioneers of the post-Tent Embassy leadership, now 'running things' like Leo and Giovanni Casparo in the Coen Brothers' film masterpiece *Miller's Crossing*. Nothing came of the introductions, but I vividly remember sitting in the office of one of these characters. He was dressed in a black skivvy and smart sports jacket, smoking a cigarette through an elegant cigarette-holder. It could have been a scene out of a 'blaxploitation' film starring Jim Kelly circa 1975.

All of this was victim politics, no matter what the radical pretence. It was scratching bark, not digging out the roots. A prideful and principled defence against racism is what we need as a people. Many ordinary Indigenous people possess this dignity and strength. We must make it our dominant outlook.

The radical centre
People from either side of the cultural and political divide usually believe the distance between their own correct policies and their opponents' wrong policies is substantial. This polarisation leads to problems – a failure to distinguish between a potentially correct policy (for instance, policing relatively minor misdemeanours to restore order to crime-ridden, disadvantaged neighbourhoods) and an obviously incorrect one (police harassment and violence). Typically, the left opposes zero-tolerance policing, although it would be truly progressive to restore social order to disadvantaged neighbourhoods, and such policing is probably critical to achieving this.

This polarisation leads to a failure of the left to appreciate the correctness of policies promoted by the right (and vice versa) because the fine difference between the correct and the incorrect policy is too subtle for (and I use the following phrase advisedly) usual public discourse, which only sees stark tensions that suggest bald contradictions rather than close, more intense tensions that suggest paradox and potential synthesis.

Policy debate about neighbourhood crime centres on questions of freedom and social order. (Obviously) too much social order undermines freedom. (Less obviously) too much freedom with low social order in fact undermines freedom. People who live in optimally free and ordered communities often fail to appreciate the fact that it is the high degree of social order which underpins the freedom they enjoy. Libertarians are either blind to (or careless of) the advantages they take from the strong social order provided by invisible social norms: this is why classical libertarians come from privileged classes.

(Lower-class libertarianism is, of course, the very definition of social dysfunction.)

Where black people are involved, racial discrimination and disadvantage also come into play. Where the problem is high rates of blacks offending, measures aimed at strengthening social order (such as zero-tolerance policing) actually deliver advantage and freedom in the long run. The argument against such measures is that they will result in even greater rates of imprisonment of black people. And indeed, in the short and intermediate term they will. There will be a spike. But if we want black neighbourhoods to enjoy freedom, we need to ask the question: 'What is it about advantaged neighbourhoods that guarantees freedom for their denizens?' The answer is: 'They have social order'. If we don't take the hard policy decisions to increase social order where it is weak because we fear that black involvement in the criminal justice system will increase, then we will never solve the egregious (and, in the case of my home state of Queensland, increasing) over-representation of black people in prison.

The 'radical centre' may be defined as the intense resolution of the tensions between opposing principles (in this example, freedom and social order) – a resolution that produces the synthesis of optimum policy. The radical centre is not to be found in simply splitting the difference between the stark and weak tensions from either side of popularly conceived discourse, but rather where the dialectical tension is most intense and the policy positions much closer and more carefully calibrated than most people imagine.

It is intellectually difficult to analyse and identify the correct (radically centrist) policy because commanding ideologies hold sway and limit the capacity of people to abandon wrong policies and search for better ones. Even where the right policies have been identified, they can easily turn sour because of incompetent implementation, because the calibration is lost: if a police force does not understand the aim of restoring social order to crime-ridden communities and that racism and sharp practice must not be tolerated, policy will degenerate into abuse and victimisation. Even when optimal policies are competently implemented, one must be mindful of the dynamic nature of social, political and economic currents. A progressive measure at one time can produce regressive results later.

*

My first official job was on a task force appointed by Queensland premier Wayne Goss in 1991 – led by his *wunderkind* head of the cabinet office, Kevin Rudd – to develop Aboriginal land rights legislation. In opposition since time immemorial, the fledgling Labor government dreaded its commitment to introduce land rights legislation in the most conservative of states.

To my peoples' disappointment, the new law only provided for a slightly different form of title to replace that previously granted by the National Party government. The practical effect was negligible and did not grant any more land than that already under Aboriginal ownership. Provision was made for Aboriginal groups to claim lands on the basis of their traditional affiliation or historical association, or economic and social need. National parks and vacant Crown lands were the only land that could be claimed before a specially established Land Tribunal – but only those parcels of land that the executive government had decided were available.

My first experience of the *realpolitik* of fighting for Aboriginal rights was bitterly hard. The most shameful thing occurred on the day Premier Goss tabled the Bill. He and his advisers had determined that the best way to sell the new law to an unsympathetic Queensland public was to make it clear he was not giving any free handouts to the blackfellas. The grab on the evening news was to the effect that the provision for the payment of royalties for mining would not allow any Aboriginal 'sheiks' to drive around in Rolls-Royce motorcars.

I learned a bitter truth through this experience: that Aboriginal people are lepers in the Australian democratic process. This got me thinking about pragmatism and realism in political leadership. The new breed of Labor apparatchiks running state governments after the disasters of the 1980s were more hard-headed about the imperatives of holding on to power: no more Whitlamesque indulgences, no more socialism. I understood that Aboriginal causes were political hard-sell, but I felt at the time that Premier Goss could have produced more just legislation without cutting his government's throat in the process. I thought about low-level, poll-driven pragmatism versus ideals. Wayne Goss had been part of the Labor lawyer brigade who had spent time working in Aboriginal Legal Aid, yet in two electorally handsome terms his government did nothing to improve the lot of Queensland's most abject people.

*

We are prisoners of our metaphors: by thinking of realism/pragmatism and idealism as opposite ends of a two-dimensional plane, we see leaders inclining to one side or the other. The naive and indignant yaw towards ideals and get nowhere, but their souls remain pure. The cold-eyed and impatient pride themselves on their lack of romance and emotional foolishness. Those who harbour ideals but who need to work within the parameters of real power (as opposed to simply cloaking lazy capitulation under the easy mantle of righteous impotence) end up splitting the difference somewhere between ideals and reality. This is called compromise. And it is all too often of a low denominator.

I prefer a pyramid metaphor of leadership, with one side being realism and the other idealism, and the quality of leadership dependent on how closely the two sides are brought together. The apex of leadership is the point where the two sides meet. The highest ideals in the affairs of humans on Earth are realised when leadership strives to secure them through close attention to reality. Lofty idealism without pragmatism is worthless. What is pragmatism without ideals? At best it is management, but not leadership.

As one rises above the low-denominator compromise, it takes skill, creativity, strategy, careful calculation as well as bold judgment, prudence and risk, intelligent analysis, insight, perseverance as well as preparedness to alter course, belief and humility, great competence and an ability to make good from mistakes to bring ideals closer to reality. One must be hardheaded in order to never let go of ideals.

Idealism and realism in leadership do not constitute a zero-sum game. This is not about securing a false compromise. It need not be a simple trade-off where one splits the difference.

The best leadership occurs at the point of highest tension between ideals and reality. This is the radical centre. If the idealism is weaker than the realism, then optimum leadership cannot be achieved. And vice versa. The radical centre is achieved when both are strong.

Otherwise, you get the problem of skewing. This occurs when one side of (what I will call) a classic dialectical struggle is weak and the other pronounced. Skewing occurs not just because the intellectual analysis is faulty or weak, but because of the issues involved in working out interests in the real world and the great challenges of reality for any policy and leadership seeking a better resolution in the radical centre. No leadership is immune from the forces that impel confrontation with reality and ideals. Leaders are buffeted by reality and must contend with it – they cannot choose it. Leaders' ideals are not just innate qualities: they are often forced by events and by those around them who most ardently press such ideals. Some of the greatest leaders achieve their apex as much by being compelled by external forces as by their own preferences.

*

I will finish by setting out some reflections on my experience of driving an agenda of rights and responsibilities in Indigenous policy. By the end of the last millennium, it was not possible to continue in the Indigenous policy area without facing up to the gaping responsibility deficit. When I decided that we could no longer go on without saying that our people held responsibilities as well as rights, this was not a repudiation of rights. It was just that all of the talk, all the advocacy, all the analysis, all the leadership, and all the policy and politics was about rights. There was no talk about responsibility. Our responsibility agenda of the past seven years has led us to tackle the largest immediate problems facing our people: substance abuse and the reform of welfare. We have cut through with our advocacy and our policy analysis. The responsibility agenda is now ascendant.

The problem is that, with the rise of the responsibility agenda, there has been a corresponding collapse of the rights discourse. While there has been a lot of talk about 'the rights agenda' in Australia over the past decade, there has been no effective leadership with impactful advocacy, policy and strategy. It is not enough to stubbornly keep up the talk. There has to be *impact*. And in order to have impact, there must be new thinking, new strategies, new tactics – to cut through. We therefore have the problem of skewing in Indigenous policy in Australia. The tensions of the responsibilities agenda are ascending, but the tensions of the rights agenda have receded.

My experiences have led me to three conclusions about the prerequisites for syntheses which allow societies to transcend conflicting tensions and take a historical leap forward: the political analysis must be right; it is not possible for the same actor to play several roles in the dialectical process; and apparently contradictory principles must be carried by strong societal forces.

Shelby Steele has described how faulty analysis can derail promising development. The twin phenomena of 'white guilt' and a problematically conceived 'black consciousness' prevented the United States from achieving a historical breakthrough that would have benefited all Americans.

The second conclusion is that it is difficult for the same actor to play several roles in the dialectical process. Only the primary leaders of a whole society can 'triangulate', to use the practical terminology of Clinton's adviser Dick Morris. People with lesser vantage can only advance one side of a dialectical tension. I and my associates in Cape York Peninsula decided to champion the Indigenous responsibility agenda because this was the most underdeveloped area in the then Australian discourse. The side effect of our decision is that we are perceived to represent only the principle of responsibility.

Australian Indigenous rights consist of both socio-economic rights (which may be referred to as 'race relations' and which we share with African-Americans) and rights derived from our 'peoplehood'. A successful Australian synthesis must reconcile these rights with Indigenous responsibility, and the interests of non-Indigenous Australians. But the Indigenous rights agenda is so weak that non-Indigenous Australians seem unaware of the nature of our people's aspirations. This might seem a strange contention almost two decades after the *Mabo* decision on native title, but it is becoming clear that our opponents do not understand our point.

Six words struck me like a bolt of lightning when I read Shelby Steele's book. Reflecting on the decision of boxing authorities to strip Muhammad Ali of his world heavyweight title when he refused to fight in Vietnam, Steel wrote: 'When he said, "I ain't got no quarrel with the Viet Cong," *even his enemies understood his point* [my emphasis]. Where was the moral authority to ask this black man, raised in segregation, to fulfil his responsibility to the draft by fighting in a war against a poor Asian country?'

Recently we hosted a senior federal minister so that we could explain our reform plans and seek support for them. The minister was supportive, amiable and intellectually astute. I have no doubt he desires our people to rise up in the world. However, as he left he commended our work but said: 'I just don't understand the Indigenous rights stuff.' The minister was not expressing conscious enmity or opposition to my people's aspirations. His remark was a symptom of the fact that the Indigenous rights agenda is politically irrelevant. Tension between rights and responsibilities is impossible, and therefore no synthesis can be achieved. There is no sign of effective carriage of the Indigenous rights leadership. There is no sign of a primary societal leadership that is interested in finding the radical centre – where rights and responsibilities are synthesised.

There is a growing insight in the United States about the nature of their problems – importantly by black intellectuals and leaders – and a successful synthesis of the traditions of Booker T. Washington and W.E.B. Dubois is likely to emerge. I eagerly await Shelby Steele's forthcoming book on Barack Obama and Steele's views on whether Obama has 'the right stuff'.

Edited excerpt from 'White Guilt, Victimhood and the Quest for a Radical Centre', in Griffith Review 16: Unintended Consequences

Pearson's Gamble, Stanner's Dream

Robert Manne

In 1934 the Professor of Anthropology at the University of Sydney, A.P. Elkin, published a small pamphlet which called for 'a positive policy which aims at the welfare and development of the aborigines'. To us, Elkin's words seem anodyne. For his contemporaries, they had a galvanising effect. Before Elkin's pamphlet, Aboriginal policy had passed through just two phases. In the first, the Aborigines, an impediment to the steady expansion of the pastoral economy, were subdued. By the end of this phase, as a result of disease, removal from hunting grounds and water sources and the impact of armed force, perhaps half of the 500 or so tribes that existed at the time of the arrival of the British settlers had vanished altogether from the face of the Earth. In the second phase, those Aborigines who had survived the initial onslaught were segregated, either voluntarily on government stations, Christian missions and reserves or involuntarily in detention camps, and protected by an ever-tightening net of special laws that controlled movement, marriage, sexual behaviour, the fate of children, employment, savings and the consumption of alcohol. At the time of Elkin's pamphlet most Australians believed it was only a matter of time before the surviving remnant would die out. Following his call for a positive policy, a seventy-year journey of government-led policy experiments to build a future for the Aborigines began. The mood of these experiments has since lurched erratically between rather pessimistic realism and over-optimistic hope. The most recent experiment was the decision in June to dispatch police, troops and medical workers to protect Aboriginal children on the remote settlements of the Northern Territory. The Howard government has now altogether abandoned the hopes embedded in the language of reconciliation. Realism once more rules. How did we arrive at this point?

It took a decade and a half for the first positive policy to be formulated clearly. It was labelled assimilation. The post-war minister for territories in the Menzies government, Paul Hasluck, was its philosophical driving force. For Hasluck, assimilation was not a set of administrative devices but a destination. The destination was this: 'All Aborigines and part-Aborigines will attain the same manner of living as other Australians, as members of a single community enjoying the same rights and privileges, accepting the same responsibilities, observing the same customs and influenced by the same beliefs, hopes and loyalties as other Australians.' The policy was frankly paternalistic, although the word was not used. Hasluck described welfare work among Aborigines as 'sheltering, protecting, guiding, teaching and helping, and eventually, as the perhaps most difficult act ... quietly withdrawing without any proud fuss when the Aboriginal entered the Australian community'. The policy was also gradualist. Hasluck assumed that the destination might not be reached for all Aborigines for three generations or more. He did not believe that assimilation implied racial inter-marriage and biological absorption, as many inter-war Australian native administrators did. He did not believe that it was necessary that all Aborigines would ultimately leave their ancestral homelands, although he thought that as a matter of fact very many would.

But where he was insistent was that Aborigines had no future as a distinct or separate people. The government might not actively work to destroy Aboriginal language and culture, but Hasluck believed that eventually both would have to go. In a letter to a churchman he put the point like this. Australians could not 'have it both ways'. If the aim was to facilitate eventual Aboriginal entry into the wider Australian society 'on equal terms', such an ambition was quite simply 'incompatible with full and active preservation of their languages and culture without any changes'.

Towards the end of his life, after his policy had been discredited, Hasluck stated his case about the inevitable end of the Aborigines as a distinct people, about assimilation as their inevitable fate, with uncharacteristic polemical sarcasm. Were Aborigines, he asked in *Shades of Darkness*:

> ... to be living museum pieces? Or a sort of fringe community whose quaint customs are stared at by tourists? Will the drone of the didgeridoo, the clicking of the boomerangs and the stomping in the red dust in the red centre of Australia still be the sufficient employment for the grandchildren of the people of Uluru? Will the separate development that is being pursued with a beneficent purpose today have the result that after two or three generations persons of Aboriginal descent find that they are shut out from participation in most of what is happening in the continent and are behind glass in a vast museum, or are in a sort of open-range zoo?

Aborigines were, in his vision, destined to be nothing more than an ethnicity. At most, Aborigines would have vague memories of what their people once had been. For Hasluck, the idea of a separate people was separatism; apartness was apartheid. He stared at the total destruction of the way of life of the people the British had encountered in Australia, and did not blink.

*

During the late 1960s and early '70s the policy of assimilation was abandoned. The most general explanation for this was the impact in Australia of the profound revolution in sensibility which took hold in the West at that time: the belated recognition of racism as a dimension of Western civilisation. Perhaps only now had the meaning of the Holocaust been grasped. Europeans and European settler societies realised that their history had for centuries been sullied by the assumption of their superiority and the barbarous actions which had been granted permission as a result. In the US the civil-rights movement grew. Western opinion became increasingly sympathetic to the anti-colonial liberation struggles of the peoples in the European empires. White dominance in South Africa and Rhodesia came to seem intolerable. And in Australia, not only were the cultural assumptions underlying the assimilation policy questioned; more deeply, the fate of the Aborigines, which had interested a small segment of the educated public since the 1930s, now became for the first time a matter of general political significance. The old indifference lifted. It was as if, from this moment, many Australians came only now to see with moral clarity what had been in front of their noses since the arrival of the British: what their presence had meant for the original inhabitants, what they and their forebears had actually done. Nor was recognition of racism all that was required of Australians. It seems plausible to suppose that all nations yearn for a noble myth of origin. As Australia was founded by an act of dispossession, coming to terms with what had been done was to prove unusually hard – far more difficult, for example, than for Americans to come to accept the ignominy of black slavery.

Grasping the true meaning of what had occurred in the settlement of Australia required something far less abstract than what I have written so far implies. It required an intimate understanding of the nature of the people which had been dispossessed. For this understanding Australians relied on the work of the anthropologists. Although many were important – Howitt and Fison; Spencer and Gillen, Walter Roth; Radcliffe-Brown; Elkin; Ronald and Catherine Berndt – in this vital task of national education, no-one was of more significance than W.E.H. Stanner, in my opinion if not the greatest of the anthropologists (I am in no position to judge), then certainly the most interesting writer on Aboriginal society Australia has ever seen.

The older anthropologists had looked on the Aborigines they studied as a Stone Age people on the edge of extinction. Baldwin Spencer, for example, introduced his two-volume 1928 memoir, *Wanderings in Wild Australia*, with these words: 'Australia is the present home and refuge of animals, including man himself, that have elsewhere become extinct and given place to higher forms.' Stanner, by contrast, never tired of trying to convince his readers that the Aborigines were a contemporary people. To think of history as 'a linear sequence', with the primitive Aborigines at the beginning and Europeans at the end, he wrote as early as 1958, and to suggest that 'all we have to do is to instruct them in the manifest virtues of our style of life' and wait for them to '"unlearn" being Aborigines in mind, body and estate', was a malignant and self-centred 'fantasy', whose consequences were to be seen 'in a thousand miserable encampments around the continent'.

The older anthropologists never doubted their superiority to the people they studied. 'The idea of putting any of their beliefs to the test of experiment never entered their heads,' Spencer typically informed his readers during a discussion of magic. This was a tone of which Stanner was incapable. Perhaps the finest essay ever written by an Australian is Stanner's portrait in *White Man Got No Dreaming* of one of his lifelong Aboriginal friends, Durmugam. In it, Stanner sails assuredly between the customary rocks of peril waiting for writers on Aborigines – condescension and sentimentality. It is hard to convey the flavour of the essay, but here are snatches from its final pages:

> He was for me the most characterful Aboriginal I have known ... I am sure he was deeply moved to live by the rules of his tradition as he understood it. He wanted to live a blackfellow's life, having the rights of a man, and following up the Dreaming ... He venerated his culture ... I do not believe he ever formed a deep attachment to any European, myself included. He knew I was making use of him and, as a due for good service, he made use of me, always civilly, never unscrupulously or importunately ... [One] young man's remark, 'If I live I live, if I die I die' had seemed to Durmugam monstrous. To him, *how* a man lived and what he lived *for* were of first importance. But he himself had in part succumbed. He now spent much time playing poker (there were five aces in one of his pack of cards) ... He still went bootless, but wore a hat and well-kept shirt and trousers ... Durmugam came to good terms with Europeanism, but found it saltless all his days and, at the end, bitter too ... it never attracted him emotionally, it did not interest him intellectually, and it aroused only his material desires.

Baldwin Spencer and Frank Gillen's *The Native Tribes of Central Australia* is probably the most influential book ever written by Australians. It provided the source material for Freud's *Totem and*

Taboo and Durkheim's *Elementary Forms of Religious Life*. And yet, when Spencer wrote of Aboriginal ceremony it was as if he was peering through the glass of an aquarium. These passages are taken from his memoir:

> The ancestor is rarely represented as doing anything more interesting than looking around, wriggling his body in an extraordinary way, or perhaps eating something ... The natives were very anxious that we should see everything, which sometimes resulted in our spending a good many uncomfortable hours watching dreary performances of no special interest.

W.E.H. Stanner's most important work concerned Aboriginal religion. For him there is no aquarium glass: 'While at song, the celebrants vie rather than compete ... The men's faces take on a glow of animation and tender intent. At the last exclamatory cry – *Karwadi, yoi* – everyone shouts as with one voice. An observer feels that he is in the presence of true congregation, a full sociality at the peak of intimacy, altruism and union.' Because Stanner does not feel superior to what he is observing or to the people he is among, he is capable of entering the Aboriginal world of meaning in a quite extraordinary way. No-one has explicated more lucidly for outsiders the metaphysic of the Dreamtime, for which he coined the neologism 'everywhen'. No-one has taken us more profoundly to an understanding of the Aboriginal world view:

> Murinbata religion might well be described as the celebration of a dependent life which is conceived as having taken a wrongful turn at the beginning, a turn such that the good life is now inescapably connected with suffering ... The Murinbata, like all the Aborigines, gave the impression of having stopped short of, or gone beyond, a quarrel with the terms of life.

And no-one other than Stanner could capture the Aboriginal sense of life more vividly, and in a single phrase: 'A joyful thing with maggots at the centre.'

Stanner's 1968 Boyer Lectures are probably the most influential radio broadcasts in our history. For one thing, Henry

Reynolds tells us that it was only after hearing them that he decided to study Aboriginal history. Most famously, Stanner identified and analysed what he called the Great Australian Silence on the dispossession. 'Inattention on such a scale cannot possibly be explained by absent-mindedness ... Simple forgetting of other possible views turned under habit and over time into something like a cult of forgetfulness practised on a national scale.' But he also captured the depth of Aboriginal attachment to country more powerfully than had any writer until that time:

> No English words are good enough to give a sense of the links between an Aboriginal group and its homeland ... A different tradition leaves us tongueless and earless towards this other world ... What I describe as 'homelessness', then, means that the Aborigine faced a kind of vertigo of meaning.

In the lectures Stanner provided the most devastating critique of the policy of assimilation that had yet been given by a non-Aborigine: 'We are asking them to become a new people but this means that we are asking them in human terms to un-be what they now are.' And, in addition, he provided the most plausible explanation of why the Hasluck policy of assimilation would eventually be rejected:

> Just as in the nineteenth century a sense of physical and biological principle steadily permeated the public mentality so a sense of what I will broadly call 'anthropological principle' may be permeating our own century's mentality. I mean by that a steady awareness that there are no natural scales of better or worse on which we can range the varieties of men, culture and society.

A.P. Elkin stood, in sensibility, halfway between Spencer and Stanner. He could write movingly of the enchanted Aboriginal world, but also about the Aborigines as a primitive people and the supposedly smaller size of the Aboriginal brain. As mentioned, he was the original source of the positive policy that ended in the idea of assimilation. For both these reasons I found very telling indeed an incident recorded in the biography of Elkin by Tigger Wise. Elkin had invited Paul Hasluck to address the 1959 annual congress of Australian and New Zealand anthropologists. In his speech, Hasluck told the audience: 'Looked at from one point of view the weakness of the old Aboriginal society ... is an advantage. The more it crumbles, the more readily may its fragments be mingled with the rest of the people living in Australia.' Elkin was agitated. Wise tells us that he saw in these remarks 'all his ideas twisted and misapplied'. He took to the rostrum to deliver a rebuke: 'The Aborigines themselves will observe a partial and voluntary segregation – an apartness for an unpredictable period ... This apartness is a sense of belonging ... Our task is to see that the phase of apartness does not become apartheid ...'

Elkin had spent his life studying the Aborigines. He had come to admire deeply their way of life. Faced with light-hearted talk about the end of Aboriginal Australia, even Elkin, the intellectual father of assimilation, blinked. So did the political leaders of Australia in the 1970s – Malcolm Fraser no less than Gough Whitlam – as the policy of assimilation was abandoned in favour of a policy of self-determination and reconciliation.

*

There were very real achievements in the new, post-assimilation era. Land rights were granted by statute throughout Australia. In the Mabo and Wik judgments native title was discovered to exist in common law. In 1975 the *Racial Discrimination Act* was passed. In the new school of history pioneered by Charles Rowley and Henry Reynolds, the Great Australian Silence was shattered. The reports of both the Royal Commission on Aboriginal Deaths in Custody and the Human Rights Commission on Aboriginal child removal shook the nation. In 1991 a formal structure aimed at achieving reconciliation was established.

Yet it must be stressed that the generation educated by W.E.H. Stanner, which had finally opened its eyes to the full moral meaning of the dispossession, now hoped for more than this. What this more consisted of is best revealed in the thought of the most influential intellectual figure of the post-assimilation era, the former head of the Reserve Bank, Nugget Coombs, Stanner's close friend and political collaborator. Coombs believed that through the policy of allowing Aborigines self-determination or, as he often preferred to call it, their autonomy, the traditional way of life of the Aborigines need not die. He advocated government support for hundreds of small, decentralised Aboriginal communities in what he called their homelands. He hoped these communities would be formed, so far as possible, according to the pre-conquest divisions of language, tribe and even clan. He hoped for nothing less than the rebirth of the Aboriginal world.

Coombs was not the kind of Rousseauian, 'noble savage' dreamer that his ideological enemies on the Right invariably suggest. He did not believe that these re-established groups would be unaffected in a multitude of ways by the undeniable fact of the dispossession, and by the existence alongside them of an advanced Western materialist-industrial civilisation. This presented no unsurmountable problem. He argued that far from being hidebound or inflexible, Aboriginal culture was dynamic, flexible and adaptive. Coombs imagined a future for the homeland communities where traditional hunting and gathering would be able to be combined with a monetary economy based on welfare payments and small-scale market activities, like cattle raising, emu or crocodile farming, land management, and the production and sale of arts and crafts. He did not deny that all Aboriginal children needed an education that equipped them for some participation in the contemporary world by providing them with basic modern skills. In one of his essays he wrote that he had yet to meet an Aboriginal parent who did not want his or her children to be literate and numerate. Nor did he ignore altogether the evidence of the social ills affecting the remote Aboriginal communities he knew. Coombs wrote from time to time about male violence against women, the indiscipline of the younger generation and the problem of alcohol. After visiting Yuendumu with Stanner, the pair accepted that there was need for a police presence to deal with 'brawls and other disorder arising out of ... abuse of drink'.

And yet, if Coombs' critics on the Right, like Peter Howson or Helen Hughes, offer a distorted picture of him as nothing but a utopian collectivist fantasist, his defensive friends on the Left, like Tim Rowse, now offer an even more distorted portrait of Coombs as a moderate economic rationalist, eminently capable of passing a contemporary neo-liberal respectability test. In the last two decades of his life Coombs was a critic of Western materialist civilisation, capable, for example, of calling it the 'beer and Coca-Cola' culture, or quoting with approval a description of it as 'life without reverence for the past, love for the present or hope for the future'. Because he was open to such a bleak view about his own society, it is not surprising that he often wrote as if he genuinely believed that the Aboriginal way of life was superior to the one in which he lived: 'That human beings are at home in a hunter-gatherer society is not surprising. They have been adapted to it for more than 500,000 years.' Nor is it surprising that he was fiercely opposed to the imposition on Aboriginal children of a Western world view. On one occasion Coombs described purely Western education for Aborigines as 'cultural genocide'. On another he expressed opposition to the idea of compulsory school attendance. Rather, Coombs advocated a 'two-way education', with not only a Western but also an Aboriginal dimension. This would help, he believed, to 'decolonise' the Aboriginal mind. Coombs also wanted to 'Aboriginalise work'. He was enthusiastic about the possibilities offered by the Fraser government's Community Development Employment Projects (CDEP) scheme, which allowed Aborigines to be paid while continuing their hunting and gathering, and gave them time to devote to their religious ceremonies. He supported the re-institution, wherever possible, of Aboriginal customary law. He regarded attempts to interfere with traditional punishments, like leg spearing or the system of 'pay-back', as 'ethnocentric'.

Coombs believed that in the era of self-determination and land rights an authentic revival of Aboriginal life was indeed occurring. 'There are,' he wrote, 'widespread reports of increasing activity in Aboriginal ceremonial life.' Distinctive forms of education were, he believed, thriving: 'There is a quality of enthusiasm, indeed exuberance, about Yolngu education at present.' As traditional life revived, he thought the problems of young people fell away: 'Almost universally the problems of delinquency appear to decline and disappear.' While alcohol abuse might presently be a problem, he seemed convinced that it was coming under control. Indeed, 'Aboriginal concern and action in this matter,' he wrote on one occasion, compared 'favourably with that in Western society'. In the conclusion to his collection of essays, *Aboriginal Autonomy*, published about the time that John Howard regained the leadership of the Liberal Party, Coombs summarised the meaning of all this in the following way:

> In the years since the apparent 'consensus' in approach by the Whitlam and Fraser governments, the direction of change has inexorably been towards greater independence for Aboriginal Australians. Despite the repudiation of that 'consensus', Aboriginals have made by their own initiatives, intelligence and dedication, remarkable progress in the achievement of a lifestyle more healthy, more creative and more characteristically Aboriginal than has previously been possible since their dispossession.

A miracle was occurring. Traditional Aboriginal life was in the process of revival. At the time, few members of the left-liberal intelligentsia would have disagreed strongly with these words.

*

In the 1960s the British anthropologist David McKnight first began fieldwork on Mornington Island, in the Gulf of Carpentaria. He continued regular visits over a period of thirty years. In 2002 he published a study of social life on Mornington Island, *From Hunting to Drinking*. It is the most remarkable portrait of an Aboriginal community in the age of self-determination I have read. For McKnight, by far the most significant event during the period of his visits was the opening of the canteen in 1976. For the vast majority of Mornington Islanders drinking now became the 'main social activity'. McKnight noticed that those who used to go hunting until dusk now returned by two in the afternoon, so as not to miss the opening of the canteen. 'It felt,' he tells us, 'as if all the people were drunk all of the time or at least most of the people were drunk most of the time.' Dreadful alcohol-related deaths soon began occurring: 'Teddy Bell and his brother were drinking and in the middle of the night Pat Bell woke up and discovered that Teddy was drinking methylated spirits. He tried to stop him and in the resulting struggle Teddy accidentally stabbed himself to death.'

By the '90s, of the 900 or so Indigenous inhabitants, McKnight calculated that there were forty women and eight men who did not drink. Most drank to wild excess. McKnight also calculated that by the '90s, on average 50 per cent of income was spent on alcohol. The effects on health were catastrophic: 'After ten years of drinking people were dying at such a rate that the carpenter built spare coffins.' Wild drunken fights became common. Fights had once been about something – kinship loyalty or women – but now they were about nothing. Although McKnight continued to do so, it was now dangerous to walk about the community at night. Going to a film had been a pleasant experience when McKnight first came to Mornington Island. Because of the likelihood of a violent drunken incident, it ceased to be. The cinema was closed.

Children were badly affected. Babies were often neglected. Girls became vulnerable to sexual abuse. Although the community was awash with money, cases of malnutrition occurred. After ten years of schooling most children were illiterate. Even more, some could barely speak. Marital relations deteriorated badly: 'Women appeared to be treated as objects, as if they were things.' Rape had not been a problem in the past. It became so now, especially for white women or Indigenous women who associated with whites. Among the three tribal groups on Mornington Island – the Lardil, the Yangkaal and the Kaiadilt – suicide was unknown before the arrival of Europeans. Before the 1980s it remained virtually unknown. Yet between 1996 and 2000 there were twenty-two suicides on Mornington Island. In Queensland the rate of suicide for these years was 13.7 per 100,000; on Mornington Island it was 466. Between 1914 and 1978 there was one homicide on Mornington Island. Since the opening of the canteen there had been fifteen. All but one of the killers were male. Most of the victims were wives.

McKnight is an anthropologist. He offers some cultural explanations for this disaster. The Mornington Islanders were not a 'moderate' people. They lived traditionally on 'the edge', with dancing, initiation ceremonies, violent clashes. Drinking is also an exciting activity, with people living for the time at a heightened pitch. The Mornington Islanders have egalitarian traditions. Drink drags everyone down to the same level; no-one is better than anyone else. They have no tradition of regulated consumption; everything available was and is instantly consumed. They were also a single-activity people. Once they were hunter-gatherers; now they are drinkers. Yet he also offers more political explanations. Work under CDEP has become meaningless. What the Mornington Islanders have learnt, he tells us, is that 'a job not worth doing is not worth doing well'. Ironically, in the age of so-called self-determination, almost everything is done by the whites who bowl in to work for the shire. They establish less human connection with the Indigenous Mornington Islanders than did the missionaries. The Mornington Islanders, especially the men, feel powerless and humiliated. Life has been stripped of meaning. A people that once lived vibrantly as hunter-gatherers is now profoundly, existentially, bored.

It is difficult to know how typical Mornington Island is of remote Aboriginal communities, at least of those where for some time alcohol has flowed; how far McKnight's terrifying portrait is coloured by his sceptical and sardonic disposition; and whether life has improved on Mornington Island since attempts began in recent years to restrict alcohol there. But there is one thing at least that seems clear. The contradiction between what McKnight and many others observed on remote Aboriginal communities, and what Nugget Coombs and a generation of left-liberals imagined was happening on such communities and, even more, what they dreamt might eventually happen there – nothing less than the revival of a healthy and authentic Aboriginal life – would sooner or later require some new and radical thinking to be done.

*

It was Noel Pearson who broke the ideological stalemate over Aboriginal policy and the remote communities. Pearson had been a land-rights activist and a man of the Left. At one memorable moment in the early years of the Howard government, during the political skirmishes surrounding native title, he had labelled his conservative opponents 'racist scum'. In 1999 he shifted gear. Pearson now acknowledged that over the past quarter-century or so the communities at Cape York had experienced what he would call 'a descent into hell'. For the Left, insofar as problems of violence, sexual abuse, suicide, alcoholism, drug dependency, petrol sniffing, gambling, illiteracy, truancy and child neglect were acknowledged, the historic process of colonisation and the trauma associated with the dispossession were blamed. Although this explanation might in the most general sense be true, for Pearson it was not only useless – by explaining everything it explained nothing – but also misleading. Pearson had grown up on the Lutheran mission of Hope Vale. He knew that conditions then were far less grim. In the early '70s not one Hope Vale Aborigine was in prison. Thirty years later, there were a dozen who were either in prison or had narrowly escaped that fate. Murder on the Cape York of his childhood was unknown. 'In one of our communities,' he wrote in 2000, 'there were three murders within one month.'

The Left was committed to Aboriginal rights. It focused, for example, almost exclusively on the provision of legal aid to Aborigines charged with criminal offences, and was neglectful of the fate of the women and children who suffered abuse at their hands. The Right was responsive to talk of Aboriginal responsibilities but was hostile to Aboriginal rights like native title, the cause for which Pearson had been struggling in recent years. At one level, Pearson's breaking of the ideological log-jam in 1999 was an attempt to refashion the agenda of Aboriginal politics, by marrying the idea of rights with the idea of responsibilities. Yet this formulation is somewhat misleading. In ideological politics, activists are invariably more hostile to the camp from which they have defected than they are to the camp of the former enemy, even when they keep their distance from it. Although Pearson was theoretically opposed to the Right, he was far more emotionally engaged in his conflict with the Left. For their unwillingness to confront the reality of the remote Aboriginal communities, he held the soft-headed Left to blame. Even though he remained committed to native title and Indigenous rights, he postponed the resolution of his differences with the hard-hearted Right for a later day.

What then was to be done? In Pearson's analysis, there were three inter-connected causes of the post-1960s catastrophe of the communities: alcohol, the poison of passive welfare, and disconnection from the real economy.

Pearson believed that the Left saw alcohol as a symptom of deeper problems. For him, it was vital to interpret the emergence of the alcohol epidemic not as a symptom but as a cause. In part, this was because the grog culture on a small community developed a momentum of its own, becoming increasingly difficult for individuals to resist. And in part, it was because seeing alcohol as a symptom of something deeper provided splendid justification for the easy option of inaction. Pearson advocated total prohibition on the communities, total abstinence, rehabilitation programs for drinkers and tough criminal sanctions for those who brought the alcohol in. He saw alcohol abuse as a paradoxical consequence of the citizenship rights won in the '60s. And he saw how the traditional hunter-gatherer ethic of kinship and reciprocity could prove disastrous under conditions of modernity when it was grog rather than food that was being shared.

For Pearson the liberation of Aborigines from the poison of welfare dependency and their return to the real economy was as vital as alcohol control. Here his thought developed. In 2000 he offered a social-democratic distinction between the virtue of the redistributive welfare state and the vice of a life of complete welfare dependency. This year, with the help of seconded Treasury officials, his Cape York Institute completed *From Hand Out to Hand Up*, a sophisticated, fully neo-liberal plan for the future of his people. The plan recommends that all welfare payments be made conditional. Those who are convicted of drug or drink offences, who fail to pay their rent, or who fail to care for their children or ensure their regular school attendance will lose control of family welfare payments, which are to be redirected to those who will act responsibly. The system is to be administered by a Family Responsibilities Commission with both Indigenous and non-Indigenous members. Welfare payments, including CDEP, will be reduced to remove what are called perverse incentives against employment. Worthwhile CDEP activities, like teaching aids, will be converted into real jobs. CDEP will not be available to anyone under twenty-one. Various attempts will be made to let children break out of the cycle of inherited social breakdown. The talented will attend boarding schools. Those seeking work training outside the communities will be supported. Although native title will in general be staunchly defended, residents will be encouraged to purchase their present homes or newly built ones, which taxpayers will heavily subsidise. Businesses will be attracted to the communities with 99-year leases. Because it is accepted that there will never be sufficient employment available in the communities, many members will have to 'orbit' in and out, throughout their lives. 'Orbiters,' we are told, 'are people who periodically return to their communities or homelands and thereby retain their cultural heritage, their languages, their hunting skills, their rituals and cultural rights.' In this way, the very idea of community is re-defined. Membership will consist not of those who live in a settlement but of those who feel connected with it in some way.

Pearson's plan is not merely an audacious (and very expensive) neo-liberal blueprint for the revival of Aboriginal community and the adaptation of Aboriginal identity to conditions of modernity. It is based on the paradoxical belief that the sticks and carrots of a transformative, interventionist policy of social engineering can create the character of the responsible, acquisitive individual on which the philosophy of neo-liberalism is premised. This is Pearson's gamble. It is very far indeed from Stanner's dream – many will think too far. Yet for the hope of the survival of autonomous and viable Aboriginal communities, it seems to me the most coherent policy which has yet been offered. If it too fails, it might turn out to have been the last throw of the dice.

*

As Noel Pearson was handing his report to the enthusiastic Minister for Aboriginal Affairs, Mal Brough, the prime minister, after reading another report into the sexual abuse of Aboriginal children on the remote communities of the Northern Territory, decided to declare a state of national emergency and to send in the troops, police, administrators and doctors. Like the majority of Australians, I was relieved that a decision for action had finally been taken. I am absolutely convinced that the crisis in the communities is real. The analogy drawn by some between this intervention and the children-overboard affair struck me as absurd. I opposed Howard over the question of the detention or military repulsion of asylum seekers because of the almost unbelievable cruelty it showed towards vulnerable children. On this occasion the aim was to protect children from abuse. Nonetheless, like many of those who support passionately the idea of reconciliation, I was dismayed but not surprised at the arrogant disregard for Aboriginal people and their leaders revealed by the failure even to pretend to consultation over issues as sensitive as land rights and the permit system for communities.

There is a Napoleonic streak in the present prime minister. As with the *Tampa* and the blank-cheque commitment to the US in the War on Terror, he has a capacity for advancing basic policy trajectories through apparently instinctive and improvisatory acts. Although much of the policy over the Northern Territory settlements showed signs of being made on the run, behind it the Howard government's new remote-communities strategy was advanced. Those who wish to grasp the general direction of the government's policy should read Helen Hughes's new book, *Lands of Shame*. Hughes is a senior fellow of the Centre for Independent Studies, the most important ideological engine room for Australian neo-liberalism and the Howard government. Hughes supports the elimination of passive welfare and the introduction of private home ownership. In the short run, she advocates the liquidation of most of the settlements but continued support for a small number where decent education and medical services can be delivered, through a population-concentration policy. In the long run, she shows sympathy to the views of the Canadian conservative John Ibbotson, who recently advised young indigenous Canadians living on their settlements to pack their bags and permanently leave. Although Hughes thinks she is sympathetic to traditional Aboriginal values, it turns out that she is hostile to customary law and regards what Stanner called the Aboriginal 'low culture' as little more than contemptible superstition. The policy Hughes outlines – cogently and persuasively, it must be said – is generally unsympathetic to land rights and self-determination, frankly paternalistic, opposed to those who presently exercise power in the Aboriginal communities and openly assimilationist in its ultimate ambition. *Lands of Shame* undoubtedly reflects the general thrust of the thinking of the Howard government and conservative Australia.

The considerable overlap between this and the neo-liberal dimension of the thought of Noel Pearson is clear. Yet the differences between Pearson and Howard are no less important. Pearson supports land rights and native title. Howard is hoping for their erosion. Pearson supports genuine, not phoney, Aboriginal self-determination. Howard supports assimilation, in fact if not in name. Pearson detests Windschuttle's denialist history of the dispossession. Howard is its most influential supporter. Pearson regards the rights of indigenous peoples as politically fundamental. In an essay in the *Griffith Review*, he tells us that when he discussed first-peoples' rights with a senior and sympathetic member of the Coalition government, he was told, 'I just don't understand the Indigenous-rights stuff.' Pearson's life has been dedicated to the struggle for the survival and health of the remote Aboriginal communities. There is no reason to suppose that Howard would be concerned if they all eventually collapsed.

In the final essay of *White Man Got No Dreaming*, W.E.H. Stanner, a supreme realist, warned against the temptation of pessimism. I take the warning seriously. My present hope is that in the next few months, if Labor is elected, Noel Pearson will be able finally to act upon his fundamental differences with Australian conservatives and join cause with Aboriginal leaders like Pat and Mick Dodson, Lowitja O'Donoghue and Patricia Turner and, as importantly, with a new generation of leaders, in their common struggle for the future of the remote Aboriginal communities.

The Monthly

Cowboys and Indians

David Marr

Mohamed Haneef was waiting to board Singapore Airlines flight 246 when two police entered the departure lounge of Brisbane International Airport. 'You are under arrest,' said Detective Sergeant Adam Simms, 'for providing support to a terrorist organisation.' The efforts of the last ten frantic hours to get home to Bangalore had come to nothing. Haneef was led to a room in the airport, cautioned, questioned for fifty minutes by Simms and Federal Agent 2435 Neil Thompson and then driven to the Wharf Street headquarters of the Australian Federal Police. They arrived after midnight.

Haneef was not panicking. He insisted he did not need a lawyer and would stick to that resolve for three days, believing he could straighten this difficulty out: 'I would rather answer it myself.' He told Simms and Thompson he had been trying to ring British police that afternoon to clear up the matter of an old SIM card he had given his cousin Sabeel Ahmed a year ago. Sabeel had been arrested, apparently for misusing the card. Haneef insisted this had nothing to do with him. He told police he believed he was being framed. At about 3 a.m. they brought the exhausted Indian doctor a bed and he slept.

'There is a lot of confusion at the beginning of any complex investigation,' Commissioner Mick Keelty of the Australian Federal Police would confess once the case against Mohamed Haneef had turned into an epic catastrophe. 'Errors in the investigation came to us from the UK ... we're all under time pressures.' The commissioner's men had stopped Haneef at the airport gate in the belief – mistaken – that his old SIM card had turned up at the scene of a terrorist attack in Glasgow forty-eight hours before. The perpetrator of the attack was Sabeel Ahmed's inept brother, Kafeel. After failing to set off two car bombs in London on 29 June, Kafeel had driven north next day in a Jeep Cherokee loaded with gas canisters and drums of fuel which he rammed into a terminal at Glasgow airport. Nothing happened. Having botched the job again, Kafeel leapt from the jeep and set himself alight. An off-duty policeman doused the flames and subdued Kafeel with CS spray. Kafeel was rushed to hospital with hideous burns. The half-dozen arrests that followed swiftly made news around the world for many of the still-unnamed suspects were doctors. One was Kafeel's brother, Sabeel.

Haneef slept for a few hours before police woke him. Simms and Thompson explained they were off to ask a magistrate for authority to detain him. Again he refused a lawyer. This was to be the first time police used machinery designed to fight terrorism by allowing suspects to be held without charge during lengthy police investigations. Theoretically, Haneef could be held for ever but only questioned for a total of twenty-four hours. First up, the magistrate gave them just eight hours. Simms, a Queensland cop seconded to the Joint Counter Terrorism team in Brisbane, turned on the tape at 11.01 a.m. He asked most of the questions. Swift police work meant he wasn't starting cold. The interrogators already had phone and financial records from Australia and Britain. While the prisoner was having breakfast, his Southport flat had been raided, turning up notebooks and diaries. Police had yet to strip Haneef's computer, but they already had evidence of many links – social and financial – between Haneef and his accused cousins. Yet they did not unmask a terrorist that day.

Haneef emerged from the 1616 questions and answers as a nerdy guy with fractured English who has done little in the past decade but study. He denied ever touching a rifle, ever having any training in firearms, explosives or logistics, or ever being part of a terrorist organisation. He denied raising money for political causes and denied knowing anyone who regarded jihad as implying violence. He denied any foreknowledge of the Glasgow attack and the London car bombs. Asked how he felt when he heard of the terrorist attempts in London, Haneef replied: 'Every drop of blood is human, and I feel for every human being.'

Whatever else he may have done along the way, Haneef had performed to perfection the classic role of the good Indian son. He told the police: 'I am the sole carer for my family.' He was eighteen when his father, a teacher in the town of Mudigere, died in 1997. With a little money and a small scholarship, the son entered medical school in Bangalore. His mother, brother and sister moved to town with him and lived very simply in an ugly lower-middle-class Muslim quarter of concrete flats. Old neighbours still speak highly of a wholesome and studious boy. His aim after graduation was to become a physician, an ambition that took him to England in March 2004. Money was tight. His interrogators had found the old diary in which Haneef meticulously noted the sums borrowed to stay afloat in his first eighteen months in Liverpool: £180 from one Indian doctor, £290 from another.

His base was a boarding house run by an Indian charity that looks after trainee doctors and dentists newly arrived in Britain. Though mainly Muslim, Mufeed was not a religious organisation, Haneef explained. But his interrogators were particularly curious about Mufeed's annual summer camp in the Lakes District: was there religious instruction; did you do any self-defence; any white-water rafting; any survival skills? To each, the answer was no. Later police would later claim Haneef lived at the Bentley Road boarding house with his cousins Kafeel and Sabeel. He said the opposite.

Kafeel, a second cousin on his mother's side, was his only family contact in Britain. Haneef described him as a 'short, pretty fat' man of 'reserved personality' with a beard. They had not known each other well in India, but Kafeel rang from Belfast to welcome him when he first arrived. Kafeel was studying aeronautical engineering there but was about to move to Cambridge – the town not the university – to begin a PhD in fluid dynamics at Anglia Ruskin University. It was to his cousin in Cambridge that Haneef went for a few days in May after suffering a short, embarrassing setback to his career: he had failed part two of the qualifying exams set by the General Medical Council. 'I was a bit low. So I thought I'd just go and visit him. Because there was no-one else my family ...' He stayed three or four days looking around Cambridge, eating and praying with his cousin who gave him £300 to tide him over until he could take the exams again. Kafeel didn't want the money back. 'He said: "Just give it to any of the poor people in India."'

He passed at his second attempt in November and spent a day celebrating with Kafeel. It was Ramadan. For the next few months he continued doing unpaid hospital work as a 'clinical observer' mainly at Halton hospital on the edge of Liverpool. Ahead lay a significant hurdle: part one of the Royal College of Physicians exams. These he passed in May 2005. It was a life-changing success. What followed was so Indian, but at every turn, this is a very Indian story.

Haneef returned to Bangalore to bask in his achievement. With the prospects of a fine career as a physician and a good job lined up at the Royal Liverpool Hospital, he found a wife. She was an IT graduate from a family way up the ladder from Haneef's. They lived in a beautiful house in a beautiful suburb of the city. They were modern Muslims. They read and travelled. Haneef's engagement to Firdous Arshiya was announced in July. This alliance did not come cheap: from his brother-in-law-to-be, Haneef borrowed £3000 to settle his English debts and to pay for the wedding. Here was a source of rich misunderstanding for police who would later be trawling through Haneef's financial records: his brother-in-law is Dr Siddique Ahmed and his second cousin is Dr Sabeel Ahmed. Both figure in records as 'S. Ahmed.' It could be so confusing.

Haneef returned alone to Britain to begin work and Sabeel followed a few weeks later. They knew each other well. For many years his younger cousin had been following in his footsteps. They were at Bangalore medical college together a year or so apart, and now Sabeel was in England preparing to take his General Medical Council exams in Preston. One day that summer, brother Kafeel picked Haneef up in a rented car and they drove to Preston together to deliver luggage to Sabeel while listening to a CD of the Koran. After this trip, Kafeel disappeared to India and, it seems, began to drift into extreme Islamic circles.

Once he began earning a decent wage at the hospital, Haneef sent money home to his family. This was done in a way that puzzled Australian investigators but makes perfect sense to Indians: in October 2005, he paid £960 into Kafeel's English bank account on the understanding that his cousin in India would pay the same sum to his family in Bangalore. Haneef told the police: 'He made arrangements to pay ... in India to my family.'

The wedding was in Bangalore in November that year. Both his cousins were guests. 'Was it a traditional Islamic wedding?' asked Detective Sergeant Simms, while admitting in the next breath: 'I don't know what that means.'

Haneef reassured him it was, indeed, traditional: 'A lot of people are gathering.'

'A lot of colour?'

'Yes.'

'And what part did Sabeel play?'

'He just stood there.'

The newlyweds returned to Liverpool and moved into a flat in Pembroke Place near Liverpool hospital. About this time, Haneef bought a mobile phone with a one-year plan from Orange. Relations between the newlyweds and Sabeel were close. Sabeel visited them and ate with them. They spoke on the phone. Theirs was his postal address. They were family. Sabeel was the driver on trips round Britain: to London for a day to see the sights, to a bird sanctuary in Wales and up to the Mufeed summer camp in the Peak District.

'What's that?' asked Simms.

'It's a district in UK.'

'Peak?'

'Yes. Peak District is a spot there.'

'Sorry, just not aware of that.'

The expedition that fascinated Haneef's interrogators was the family trip to the Lakes District and Scotland in the spring of 2006. Haneef rented the car. Sabeel drove. With them were Haneef's wife, her parents and her brother. In Edinburgh they photographed themselves in front of the castle. In Glasgow, they prayed at the mosque, and slept the night in a motorway hotel. Haneef's computer was filling with family snaps.

But for his ambition to be a physician, this young doctor may well have stayed in Britain. But he wanted to continue his studies in a good teaching hospital. Such jobs were hard to find.

'The competition is very fierce there.' So he answered an ad in the *British Medical Journal* for a post at Southport Hospital on the Queensland Gold Coast, was interviewed on the phone, accepted and prepared for the journey to Australia. The expense of the move was compounded by needing a large sum to pay for his sister's wedding: 'I being the only earner and looking after her, for the whole of my time.' From his bank he borrowed £2000.

Just before they left, Haneef and his wife took a pile of gear to Sabeel's flat by taxi: a duvet, sheets, crockery, a food processor, a framed picture of Mecca, a winter overcoat and a number of medical and religious texts. Some of this stash was for Sabeel and some to be ferried out to India as friends and family moved back and forth. Haneef also gave his cousin his SIM card. Keeping in contact with their families was obligatory and expensive. In these years they both used Yahoo chat rooms, Skype and mobile phones. Haneef said of Sabeel: 'He is talk a lot on the phone, always on the phone.' The card had a few weeks and a couple of hundred minutes' credit left to run. But as Haneef explained to his interrogators, the big plus for Sabeel were the discounts offered when the card was renewed for a second year. 'They used to … give more minutes at a less cost.' The arrangement was that Sabeel would take over payment and transfer the card to his own name. Step two never happened.

Haneef and his wife arrived in Australia in mid-September 2006 with few plans. The taxidriver suggested a motel somewhere near the hospital and after two or three nights at the Motor-Inn, the young couple found a flat nearby in Pohlman Street, Southport. Haneef began work as a senior House Officer and enrolled with the Australian College of Physicians to continue his studies. He paid his debts; lived frugally; sent as much money home each month as he could; worshipped at the Gold Coast mosque; and took his wife on brief trips to Sydney and Surfers Paradise. A photograph of Haneef on that excursion was later leaked by the police to suggest he may have had plans to blow up one of the apartment blocks.

By November, Firdous Arshiya was pregnant and in March this year she returned to Bangalore. 'We didn't have enough support here,' explained Haneef. 'We thought it would be better for her to be there with the parents.' Her blood pressure was high so their daughter Haniya was delivered by emergency caesarean on 26 June. A few days later, the child contracted jaundice and was brought back to hospital. Haneef was uncharacteristically hazy about the exact date. He said everyone was ringing everyone through this crisis and by Sunday, 1 July he felt he should fly home for a visit. But he did nothing until he turned up for work on Monday. That was the previous day, the day in question.

With breaks for meals and prayers, Haneef's interrogation continued until 5.30 p.m. The tone was mostly polite. The prisoner was willing. His answers were detailed. He refused only to give his views on the political situation in Iraq and Afghanistan. 'I don't like to comment.' Simms and Thompson didn't press the point. They did their chores: quizzing their prisoner about every name in his notebook and everyone he met through Kafeel and Sabeel. They tracked through his studies, his work and his financial transactions. The SIM card was a principal focus. So was the narrative of the previous day from the moment Haneef received a message that Sabeel was in custody because of some 'misuse' of the card. Over the next jumbled hours, Haneef was given a week's leave; called his father-in-law for a ticket home; was told Sabeel's mother on the phone from Bangalore that he must ring a London police officer about the card; tried and failed four times to get through; then travelled to the airport where he was arrested.

Before the tape was turned off and the prisoner taken down the road to the Brisbane Watchhouse, Haneef told his interrogators: 'I haven't done any of the crimes. Just want to let you know. And I don't want to spoil my name and my profession. That's the main thing. And I've been a professionalist until now and I haven't been involved in any kind of extra activities, what sort of activities which you were discussing earlier. And I just want to live in life as a professionalist in the medical profession. That's what I want.'

*

News of Haneef's detention had broken even while he was being interrogated. The political leadership sang its usual double song: the presumption of innocence and presumption of terrorism. That evening Commissioner Keelty told the ABC his officers believed the Indian doctor was 'connected' to a terrorist group. It's a word that can mean anything, of course, but in light of what police had learnt from their prisoner that day, 'connected' was a bold claim. Even more graphic accusations were being made by police staking out the Gold Coast Hospital. According to later reports, officers were telling the hospital staff their colleague may have been part of a terrorist sleeper cell.

A tabloid portrait of Haneef emerged rapidly: an Islamic radical from his student years; a ruthless terrorist working under the perfect cover of a man dedicated to healing; a prime suspect in an al Qaeda plot; an absconder from his job fleeing the country to escape detection; and a collaborator in the Glasgow operation with his cousin, the dying Kafeel Ahmed. But from the start, Haneef had vigorous supporters. He was vouched for by family, colleagues and neighbours. Queensland's premier, Peter Beattie, declared him a 'model citizen with impeccable references.' As the press began to suggest Haneef's detention was overkill, Keelty stepped in to say there was 'a lot more' to the case than mobile phone records. A few days later the commissioner declared: 'The links to the UK are becoming more concrete.' By this time the press had learnt – and only the police could have leaked the information – that Haneef's international financial transactions were being investigated.

The magistrate's order to detain him, renewed on the evening of his first interrogation, was due to expire late on Thursday, 5 July. That afternoon the hard-bitten Brisbane criminal lawyer Peter Russo had a call: 'Do you mind coming down to the watch-house? There's someone who needs a lawyer.' The facts are a bit murky at this point, but it seems one of the old cops had finally persuaded Haneef it was time to get help. Russo was not surprised to be rung. 'I've been called to the watchhouse on numerous occasions over the years, sometimes just to pacify people who are refusing to give their fingerprints. The guys at the watchhouse know me, and I'm easy to find I guess.' But this wasn't a drunk or a petty crim needing a hand. It was the nation's most famous terrorist prisoner.

Haneef had spent two days and two nights waiting in a double cell with a small five-metre by seven-metre yard attached. He had access to magazines but no daily papers. He had made only one phone call, to the Indian consulate on the morning of his interrogation to warn his family he would not be arriving home.

He had been refused permission to speak to his wife. He had not been questioned again. Russo spent less than an hour with his client, whose instructions were simple: 'I want to go home.' The hearing began at 7 p.m. Russo was not allowed to hear the police evidence and the magistrate's decision was made in his absence. All the lawyer could do was put on record the fact that his client had been co-operating. Police were given until the evening of Monday the 9th to hold their prisoner.

Extraordinary resources were being thrown at the case. 'There is something in the order of 170 AFP officers involved,' Keelty told ABC radio's *AM*. 'And there would be up to an additional fifty state police officers from Queensland and Western Australia.' Keelty and the Attorney-General, Philip Ruddock, urged the public to be patient while an overwhelming mass of evidence was assessed. Keelty spoke of 18,000 files stripped from the doctor's laptop. Ruddock was sombre about the prospects of an early resolution of the investigation: 'I am told it is the equivalent of reading 31,000 pages of paper to look at the amount of material that actually has to be analysed that has been retrieved through the exercising of search warrants.'

Haneef waited. At Monday's hearing Russo was joined by Brisbane barrister Stephen Keim SC. A week after his arrest, Haneef had still not been told why he was being held. His lawyers were also in the dark. When their lawyers handed magistrate Jim Gordon a dossier of secret information, Keim protested: 'That's not natural justice. I've got a right to make submissions. I've got a right to know generally what your case is.' He was shown nothing, but the magistrate cut the police request for five days down to forty-eight hours. Canberra's lawyers mulled over Keim's demands. He was eventually handed a small dossier. 'They gave me thirteen pages of material that two days earlier was so secret and so highly protected, I could not get one letter of it.'

At about 3.45 p.m. on Friday 13th, Haneef was driven in a police van 200 metres from the watchhouse to Queensland Police headquarters in Roma Street for his final interrogation. Why the police chose to go at this point isn't clear. The press was restive; lawyers were thundering on opinion pages; the magistrate was growing sceptical; and the manoeuvring of Haneef's legal team had seen the first cracks in the wall of secrecy behind which the prisoner was being held. The dividends of further delay were uncertain: squads of police working on the investigation were turning up nothing of much use. Indeed the case was going backwards.

When Scotland Yard corrected its big mistake is not clear, perhaps as early as 5 July when a chief inspector of the Yard's counter-terrorism command arrived in Brisbane. Certainly by the time Haneef's final interrogation began, the Australian Federal Police knew the old SIM card had had nothing at all to do with terrorism. It was not a bomb component, had played no part in the London and Glasgow attacks and was not found – as the public would continue to believe for a week or more – in the wreckage of Kafeel's Jeep Cherokee. It was with Sabeel in Liverpool.

By this time police should also have been briefed that Sabeel was no terrorist. Suicide bombers traditionally send a message before their deaths. It appears that Kafeel, heading north after failing to set off those car bombs in London, sent his brother a text message with a password that would open an email. According to the *Guardian*:

> Those who have seen the email regard it as Ahmed claiming responsibility for the attempted attacks on London and the one he was about to stage in Glasgow. According to a source, Ahmed says his actions were carried out in the name of Allah. Ahmed writes that his relative would be shocked to read what he is about to tell him about his involvement in terrorism, praises God, and says he wants martyrdom.

Shocked. If this account is correct, Sabeel was clearly not in on Kafeel's plot nor aware of his brother's terrorist ambitions. The *Guardian* also claimed Sabeel was in no position to stop the Glasgow attempt. According to the paper, he did not open the email until an hour and a half after his brother had driven the Jeep into the airport terminal. Sabeel was in custody – but still not charged – for failing to alert police to Kafeel's confession hours after the crime had been committed. So what had this to do with a cousin on the far side of the world?

*

'Geography was not one of my better subjects at school,' Adam Simms admitted in the sixth hour of the interrogation. 'Bangalore, where's that in relation to Pakistan?' Detectives on three continents had been gathering whatever evidence they could find about the Gold Coast doctor for ten days, but Detective Simms hadn't opened an atlas. The name Mysore meant nothing to him. He didn't know where Liverpool was from London. The ways of Skype were a mystery: 'I'm a bit of a dinosaur when it comes to this sort of thing.' His grasp of the ordinary steps in a doctor's career was nil. He had no clue what Muslims do in Ramadan. 'OK,' he said when Haneef explained. 'Excuse my ignorance, yeah.'

Simms emerges as a decent man from the transcripts of these interrogations. He dealt with Haneef politely, hour after hour. But his ignorance of Islam is bewildering. He was, after all, the officer to whom the AFP had delegated the urgent task of discovering whether Australia was holding a man in league with fanatical Islamists who had tried to slaughter large numbers of people in London and Glasgow. Simms knew the term jihad. He was aware of a division between Shia and Sunni. But Islam comes for Simms in only three strengths: moderate, strict and extreme. He showed no expertise in the nuances of fanaticism. Hours were spent that last night asking the prisoner if this or that colleague, friend or cousin was moderate, strict or extreme.

Leafing through Haneef's photographs of family holidays in Britain, Simms asked if religion had been discussed on these travels. 'Not normally,' Haneef replied. 'Just about the faith and the prayers and things we used to say, praying time.'

'What sort of discussions were they?' Simms persisted.

'Just the normal things.'

'You'll have to tell me because I don't know what you mean by that.'

This was strategy. Simms was stumped every time by Haneef's replies: these people said their prayers, they listened to the Koran in the car, they went to the mosque, they were just normal. He never seemed to know what to ask next.

Questioning began at 4.15 p.m. and continued with breaks roughly every hour until just before dawn on 14 July. Simms took the running but Federal Agent Thompson asked the occasional question after receiving prompts on his laptop. Ramzi Jabbour, manager of domestic counter-terrorism for the AFP, was supervising the interrogation from a nearby room. Sitting with the prisoner was Russo, his knockabout solicitor, with a nasty cough turning into flu.

Though Simms would remind Haneef all through the night that the crucial issue was the SIM card, these hours of interrogation have the feel of a fishing expedition: a team of police hoping to find some more tangible link to terrorism in Haneef's past. So they crisscrossed the narrative of his time in Britain, his travels, his colleagues, his career and the sums of money – mostly small – that flowed in and out of his bank accounts. But always the questioning returned to the SIM card and his cousins Sabeel and Kafeel.

What emerged was a much clearer picture of the intimacy between Haneef and Sabeel. Under questioning, the prisoner revealed a couple of meetings between the cousins not admitted in the first interrogation. None connected him to terrorism. Just before midnight, Simms revealed that in June this year, Kafeel paid a month's fees on the SIM card. 'We believe Kafeel was using the phone also. Does that surprise you?' asked Simms. It did. 'Dr Sabeel wanted it for his use. He said he just wanted to make normal calls to India and friends.' That line of questioning went no further.

At 3 a.m., having thrown everything they had at Haneef, the interrogators turned to the suspicious circumstances of his rushed attempts to leave Australia on the night of 2 July. These were crowded hours and police had to judge his account against a timeline of events in Britain and Bangalore:

Tuesday June 26.
His daughter is born.
Friday June 29.
London bombs discovered.
Saturday June 30.
Haneef's daughter readmitted to hospital with jaundice.
Kafeel rams the Glasgow terminal.
Sabeel taken into custody.
Sunday July 1.
Reports of the terrorist outrages and arrests are flashed round

the world but the names of Kafeel and Sabeel would not be released for another three or four days.

Monday July 2.

Haneef says he was too busy at work that morning to do more about getting away to Bangalore than make a brief phone call to ask the hospital about family leave. Then at about 2.30 p.m., his colleague and friend Dr Mohammed Asif Ali brought him a message: 'You need to call India.' Haneef's brother had rung to say Sabeel was in custody; there had been some 'misuse' of his old SIM card; and Sabeel's mother wanted to talk to Haneef. Ali had only been brought into the loop because the brother had been trying and failing to make contact with Haneef all morning.

Haneef went home to his nearby flat and made a number of rapid calls: to his brother Shoaib in Bangalore, then to arrange a week's leave from the hospital; and then to his father-in-law, Ashfaq Ahmed, to ask for a ticket home. Whether he asked for a one-way ticket isn't clear. Haneef's rather confused explanation was that at this point he had only about $100 in his bank account – as usual all his spare cash had been sent home to support his family – and he would buy the ticket back himself after his next pay.

Simms asked Haneef: 'Was the decision to go and take leave made because you found out about this telephone issue?' He replied: 'No. Not about that at all.' Later he would concede in the interrogation: 'This was the second reason probably why I would have gone.'

Sabeel's mother now rang and gave Haneef the number of a London police officer who wanted to speak to him about the SIM card. According to Haneef, she didn't explain why there was an issue with the card. Haneef claimed he was still some hours away from learning there was a connection between Sabeel's troubles and the terrorist attempts. Haneef rang the officer's number three times between 3.08 and 3.29 p.m. but couldn't get through.

Late in the afternoon, he returned to the hospital and put in his leave form. He looked for Ali and found him in the emergency department. The two doctors had known each other since their days together in Liverpool and were neighbours in Southport. Haneef gave him spare keys to his flat and to his new Honda

Jazz. When he told his colleague he'd been trying without success to call a policeman in London, Ali lent him an international calling card to try again. This attempt at 4.32 p.m. didn't work either.

Back at the flat, Haneef had one more favour to ask of his friend: to come and collect for safekeeping his laptop and his wife's jewellery. Giving the computer to Ali was later cited by police as an attempt to conceal evidence. And Simms was sceptical about the jewellery. Haneef explained it was 'some bangles and some necklaces and things.' Why not take them home to his wife? 'She had enough with her,' replied Haneef. 'I mean, obviously we were going to come back.'

When his e-ticket came through in the early evening, he spoke again to his father-in-law, telling him for the first time about Sabeel and his own name being somehow mixed up in his cousin's troubles. Haneef says Ashfaq reassured him that if he had done nothing wrong there was nothing to worry about. 'You're going to come here and we'll have support here for you.' Haneef settled down to wait for the airport transfer van due at 8 p.m.

The flat was tidy. Journalists who saw the place a day or so later reported a couple of unwashed dishes in the sink but no signs of a rushed departure. As he waited, Haneef exchanged messages in Urdu with his brother Shoaib on a Yahoo chat line. It was at this point, says Haneef, that he learnt for the first time how serious the situation was: 'He told me about the thing what was going in the UK. Then he explained to me that Sabeel might have been arrested for this reason. There was the same a terrorist attack.' Together they watched the latest report on the attacks on BBC.com which still did not name Sabeel or Kafeel. How Shoaib knew of the link is not clear, but the transcript indicates the source of the information was their cousins' mother. But whatever the source, the news was clearly travelling from Bangalore to the Gold Coast. Not the other way around. Yet the AFP believed this exchange between the brothers 'may be evidence of Haneef's awareness of the conspiracy to plan and prepare the acts of terrorism in London and Glasgow.'

Haneef didn't wipe these exchanges. The police would take them from the computer and have them translated. The result was gibberish. Haneef had the original Urdu in front of him, but

Federal Agent Thompson brushed aside his protests: 'We can go back through it then I'll ask your version.' That never happened. Urdu is spoken by a couple of hundred million people, but Australia's front-line counter terrorism force couldn't find a decent translator. They were undeterred.

The interrogation ended without fanfare at 4.42 a.m. The police called a break and never came back. Instead they conferred with Jabbour and the team briefed the office of the Commonwealth Director of Public Prosecutions. The police knew they didn't have a case against Haneef, but they had high hopes. Their optimism was infectious. A decision was taken to charge Haneef. The DPP Damian Bugg QC later tried to spread the blame a little:

> This decision was made following advice provided to the AFP by one of my officers that on the basis of the information available at that stage and what was said to be likely to be available and other potential sources of information, the police could have reasonable grounds for believing that Dr Haneef had committed that offence.

My guess is that something else lay behind the decision to charge: after the song and dance of using the nation's new anti-terrorism machinery to hold Haneef for eleven days, it would look like a failure *not* to charge him. A couple of years would pass before his trial came to court. Anything could come up in that time – and if it didn't, the courts could take responsibility for letting the terror suspect go. But it was a strategy that required what evidence there was to remain secret for a long time: secret and heavily defended.

At about 5 a.m., the flu-raddled Russo was told his client would be charged with intentionally providing a SIM card 'to a terrorist organisation consisting of a group of persons including Sabeel Ahmed and Kafeel Ahmed, being reckless as to whether the organisation was a terrorist organisation.'

*

Noël Godin, the great Belgian *entarteur* or pie-thrower, observes that a great deal about a person's character is revealed in the first seconds after they've been hit by a pie. The immediate response of John Howard, Ruddock and Keelty to the leaking of the transcript of Mohamed Haneef's first interrogation was blind rage. 'Whoever has been responsible,' snarled the Prime Minister, 'is not trying to make sure that justice is done.' The Attorney-General put on a grave, grey face and declared it 'inappropriate, highly unethical' that these questions and answers had seen the light of day. Keelty was almost distraught on morning radio: 'It's undermined the prosecution.' He was right.

Four days had passed since Haneef was charged. He had been bailed by a magistrate and then held behind bars by fiat of the immigration minister, Kevin Andrews. Police leaks had further blackened his character. On 17 July, Stephen Keim sent a copy of the transcript by taxi to Hedley Thomas, a journalist in the Brisbane office of the *Australian*. Next day, it was everywhere. For the first time, we read Haneef's protestations of innocence and learnt of his many attempts to reach the British police and his reasons for trying to leave the country in a rush on a one-way ticket. The subtle analysis of the commentators would add further details to the case emerging against the police. But even at first reading it was clear they really had no evidence Haneef had done anything.

Ruddock and Keelty threatened Keim with disciplinary action and contempt of court. Those threats collapsed. Two days later, the ABC's Raphael Epstein broke the news on *AM* that the famous SIM card was no nearer the scene of the crimes than Sabeel's house in Liverpool. The headlines told the story: Terrorism Case Imploding; Inept Game of Cowboys and Indians; SIM dim link Haneef phone card doubt; Terror Case Outrage; A Case of Plain Old Verballing; Haneef Case Turns to Farce. A week later after a brief review by the DPP, the charges were dropped. That weekend, Haneef sold himself to *Sixty Minutes* and flew home to Bangalore. Would Australia have let him leave the country if the British police were remotely interested in prosecuting or even questioning him? Never.

In the parallel world of politics, Haneef's persecution continues. Keelty has announced his officers will continue working on the investigation 'until such time as we exhaust all avenues of inquiry about a number of people, including Dr Haneef.' Kevin

Cowboys and Indians

Andrews continues to mutter darkly about Haneef's sins, releases garbled and misleading material to damn him and expresses his regret that the AFP will not allow him to reveal more. John Howard is signalling it's time to close a few loopholes so the next Mohamed Haneef doesn't get away:

> All of this is a reminder that terrorism is a global threat. You can't pick and choose where you fight terrorism. You can't say I'll fight it over there but I won't fight it here. It's also fair to say that the anti-terrorism laws that this Government has enacted are all, to their very last clause needed … If we need to strengthen them, we will.

The Turning Tide

Judith Brett

'There is a tide in the affairs of men / Which, taken at the flood, leads on to fortune.' But tides also recede. The big question for observers early in this election year is, has the tide finally turned?

Still running John Howard's way are the economy and the resources boom, as well as the momentum of incumbency. But there are also powerful currents pulling the other way, deeper than the surface froth of political debate and the play of issues. There are three turning points with the potential to shift the basis on which Howard has built his political success: from age to youth; from fear to hope; from private to public.

From age to youth. This is the most obvious. When he turned sixty-five, Howard promised to stay in the job for as long as the Liberal Party and the voters wanted him. And he reiterated the promise when Costello challenged last year. There is a deep disingenuousness in this promise. Taken at face value – and this is how Howard wants it taken – it disavows personal ambition and puts him at the service of the party and the nation. But it also says, if you want me to leave, you will have to throw me out. Hence Keating's rather improbable image of Howard as a coconut glued to his chair, and his reminder of the brutality of his own disposal of Hawke. 'You know, prime ministers have got Araldite on their pants, most of them. They want to stick to their seat. And you either put the sword through them or let the people do it.'

Howard, of course, will argue for the benefits of experience and a wise head. But whatever he says or promises, he cannot escape the fact that he is getting old. And all of a sudden, with Rudd rather than Beazley as his opposite number, he looks it. Howard turns sixty-eight in July this year. When the next election comes round, in 2010, he will be seventy-one. What is he to say to the electorate about his intentions? Elect me and I promise to say on till I'm seventy-one, and then I may even run again, like my hero Robert Menzies, who stayed on till he was seventy-two! Or: elect me, and at some unspecified date before the next election, I will retire and pass the leadership on to my loyal and patient deputy, he of the down-turned mouth, who lacks the common touch and already looks worn out from all those hard years in Treasury.

Old leaders often believe that after them, the deluge: it seems to be a hazard of the psychology of ageing. So, on the whole, they stay on too long. It would have been much better for Menzies' subsequent reputation had he lost the credit squeeze election in 1961 (which he won on Communist preferences); for Margaret Thatcher not to have waited till she was pushed; for Mao Zedong not to have launched the Cultural Revolution. At stake here is not just the age of leaders and their waning physical and intellectual energy, but their inevitable disconnection from the social and cultural worlds of people born twenty, thirty, forty and even fifty years after them – and from their futures. Sometimes, ageing leaders are reckless with their country's future because they won't be around to bear the consequences. So Howard seems remarkably unworried about the consequences of global warming, responding to it more as a political challenge to be managed than a real-world danger.

From fear to hope. Critics of Howard argue that much of his political success is due to the way he has used fear: fear of asylum seekers, terrorists, rising interest rates, loss of jobs and so on. The most sustained argument for this is found in Carmen Lawrence's book *Fear and Politics*, and it is a standby of the so-called Howard-haters. I don't completely agree with this position: it is overblown, and relies on a sloppy conflation of Howard's characteristics with those of the Australian people. Because it interprets Howard's political success in essentially negative terms, it fails to engage with the full range of reasons why voters have supported the Coalition. The Coalition has always been the preferred party of the cautious, and caution is not the same as fear. However, I think a slightly different and more complex claim takes us to the heart of Howard's prime ministership.

Howard's leadership style is shaped around combat and control. He thrives in a crisis, is quick to point out threats in the environment and to create division between friends and enemies. He believes that one should stick to one's guns, never give ground, stay till the job is done, and so on. Howard has embraced the war in Iraq with such enthusiasm because war suits his leadership style, and he focuses on enemies real and imagined, because he needs them. Real terrorists are a boon, but his obsessive battle with a largely imaginary left-wing educational establishment shows that there is more going on here than a hard-nosed confrontation with a nasty reality. It is a timeworn cliché, but if he didn't have enemies, he would need to invent them. Howard needs the war in Iraq and the War on Terror at the top of the political agenda because this is his psychological home ground.

His foolish attack on the American Democratic candidate Barack Obama, in an interview with Laurie Oakes in February on the *Sunday* program, shows this clearly. He said, 'If I were running al Qaeda in Iraq, I would put a circle around March 2007 and pray as many times as possible for a victory, not only for Obama, but also for the Democrats.' Obama's position on Iraq is shared by many American politicians and by most of the American public. So why was it Obama he singled out? I think Obama is such a threat to him not because of his different position on Iraq, but because he works with a very different psychological palette. 'We can build a more hopeful America,' Obama told the crowds at his campaign launch. 'And that is why, in the shadow of the Old State Capitol where Lincoln once called on a house divided to stand together, where common hopes and common dreams still live, I stand before you.' Howard knows that if the political mood in the US and Australia shifts from fear to hope, he is done for.

Harold Stewart and James McAuley's Ern Malley put into the mouth of Lenin a truth political leaders mostly ignore: 'The emotions are not skilled workers.' Sometimes, no matter what the penalties in their AWAs, people simply down tools and go looking for a different boss who will allow them to feel things differently.

As my late friend and colleague Graham Little showed in his work on political leadership, all leadership styles are unstable. Each has a particular emotional and psychological shape, but each also casts the shadow of the emotional possibilities it excludes. Strong leaders, like John Howard, are emotionally organised for survival in a difficult world. They thrive on competition and stress the virtues of independence, individual responsibility, hard work and tough decisions. Competitors are often treated as enemies, even if they are only the mild-mannered members of the parliamentary Opposition. When real enemies appear, such leaders rally their team behind them for the fight. Graham Little contrasted strong leaders with group leaders, who pay attention to the many ways human beings need and depend on each other and believe in the creative possibilities of collective action. Group leaders specialise in the politics of sympathy and compassion; strong leaders dismiss them as weak and not to be trusted with the tough tasks of national leadership. They, in turn, see strong leaders as uncaring and many of the dangers that they guard us against as delusional.

Little also had a category of inspiring leaders, leaders who are able to break through the habitual stand-off between strength and compassion and suggest that perhaps we can find political solutions that encompass both. This is a less coherent leadership style than the other two, a sort of midpoint, but it captures the way some leaders can break through with the promise and hope of solutions.

Each of Little's leadership styles has characteristic strengths, and characteristic ways of failing. The danger for strong leaders is that they become too rigid, demand too much repression of individual initiative in the name of loyalty or security, invent enemies and stifle the new ideas needed to respond effectively to a changed world. They may offer a safe pair of hands, but the hands are often only holding solutions to yesterday's problems.

The characteristic shortcomings of strong leadership are displayed on our television screens every time Howard has to discuss the challenge of climate change. Human-induced climate change is a new and urgent problem, and it transcends all the battlelines and solutions of the old politics. Facing up to it, Howard squares his shoulders, sets his chin and stares resolutely into the camera. Everyone knows he has been denying the reality of climate change for the past decade at least, and everyone knows that the politics of this situation are changing fast. But he can only do what he can do – so he gives ground slowly and reluctantly. Having been forced to accept the scientific consensus that carbon emissions are causing the earth's climate to change, he refuses to admit any link between either of these and the drought, even though a connection is highly probable. He searches for enemies to attack: global panic merchants, loony greenies. And he tries to turn the problem into a conventional conflict of economic interests. In this scenario, he presents himself as the guardian of a national economy pitted against other national economies. And he turns the challenge from one of the long-term sustainability of life on the planet to short-term issues of economic prosperity, and the threatened jobs of coalminers. You can almost hear the cogs whirring as he calculates the margins in the Labor electorates with coalmines.

It is abundantly clear that Howard simply does not *get* climate change, and certainly that he has no solutions. He may well be able to win the next election by targeting voters with jobs in the old energy sector, but this is not a solution to climate change.

From public to private. Obama called for more than hope in his launch speech. He called for generational change, and 'an awakened electorate'. 'It hasn't been an absence of sound plans that has stopped us,' he said, 'but the failure of leadership, the smallness of our politics. People have looked away in disgust and disillusion. We're here to take politics back.'

Hugh Mackay reports that among the people he's interviewed over the years, there is a widespread nostalgia for the Whitlam era – and this from people who disliked Whitlam, as well as from the fans. The nostalgia, he argues, is for the political intensity of the times, the sense of engagement and that politics mattered. It's much like the nostalgia sometimes expressed for World War II, that it brought people together, lifted them out of their small lives into an enlarged sense of collective purpose. In an elegant little book called *Shifting Involvements*, the political economist Albert Hirschman has argued that there is an oscillation in modern Western political history between periods of engagement with collective and public purposes, and periods of retreat into the concerns of private life and the pursuit of individual material wellbeing. This oscillation, he says, can only partly be explained by outside events and crises; there is also a psychological dynamic at play in such turnabouts, which can be very rapid. Hirschman was writing in the wake of 1968, when a new political engagement appeared, as if from nowhere, and swept large numbers of people into public action. And then this spirit ran its course. Disappointed with the inevitable failures of activism, people went back to the more manageable but smaller concerns of their private lives, leaving politics to the professionals.

There is a match between a strong leader and a disengaged polity. The strong leader's message is, leave it to me, I'm in charge. He may, as Howard has done with the anti-terrorist legislation, demand to be given more power, but he does not ask for more involvement. His peacetime purpose is to provide the safe shield behind which people can get on with their lives. Obama offers a different relationship, inviting people back into public life and the exciting possibilities of public action. Obama's critics point out that he is short on policy specifics. And people may well not heed the invitation – or not quite yet.

But they may. The looming environmental crisis is one which confronts us with our interdependence, not just on the environment but on each other, and so it is likely to propel increasing numbers of people into public action to seek collective solutions to a collective problem. It is becoming blindingly obvious that the West cannot go on as it has done, consuming resources as if there is no tomorrow, year after year, decade after decade, into an open-ended future which is simply more of the same. Popular culture, with its fascination with disasters, knows this. Global business leaders know this. Politics is paralysed.

Many people, I am sure, feel as I do, that they are living in two clangingly discordant timeframes. In one, life goes on as usual, turning on lights and taps, driving cars, complaining about the weather, organising holidays, bringing up children, calculating superannuation ...

In the other, we know that the scientists are right, are haunted by images of polar bears swimming between melting ice floes, and feel powerless to do anything. The enthusiasm with which water is being saved shows that people know things have to change. But most of the solutions are far beyond anything people can do as individuals, and if you think too much about the future, you just get depressed. Howard says he prefers to be optimistic about the future. So would we all.

What Howard doesn't seem to get is that on climate change, our preferences are irrelevant. If the climate is changing, it is changing, no matter what he would prefer or how he describes it. And this is not a problem that can be turned into a conflict between us and them. He can fire insults at the messengers as much as he likes, but if the message is right, there will be simply be more messengers.

Much of Howard's political success has come from the intensity of his focus on the minutiae of day-to-day politics. He knows the margins in all the electorates and the names of his backbenchers' children; he dominates the media; he calculates the days till the next election; he devises handouts for disgruntled groups and keeps money in the coffers for government advertising campaigns; he studies his opponents to find their weaknesses and public opinion polls to craft his arguments. And he has won again and again. But none of this tells us anything about whether the long-term public interest is being served by his victories. Keeping his eye so firmly on the present, Howard seems unable to focus on the long-term future of the nation, let alone the planet.

Howard knows his strengths, and in the coming year, he will play to them. He will warn us of the threats of terrorism and Labor's mismanagement of the economy, try to wedge Labor on climate change among blue-collar workers, blame the Labor states as much as possible for health crises and the skills shortage. He will stress the inexperience of youth against the wisdom of age; he will pour scorn on the illusory and insubstantial promises of hope; he will promise that with him as prime minister, our individual prosperity will continue for ever and ever, and that global warming can be dealt with by the pragmatic politics of incrementalism, in which no-one will be a loser. He will fight to keep the election on his chosen ground. It will be a remarkable feat if he can pull it off.

The Turning Tide

The turning points from age to youth, from fear to hope and from private withdrawal to public engagement have their own separate dynamics. But they also overlap with and reinforce each other. If they start to run together, they will sweep Howard from office. And he knows it.

The Monthly

* * *

Extravagant Stillness

Luke Davies

'If you don't have time to read this ad, it was written for you,' announces an advertisement for a philosophy course that appears in newspapers from time to time. The implication clearly being: slow down your life; get in touch with something more essential. Always a tall order, of course. Yet, in a similar vein, it can be said of Philip Gröning's *Into Great Silence*, an exercise in pure contemplation, a glacial and austere documentary about life in a Carthusian monastery high in the French Alps: If you don't have time to see this film, it was made for you. It may not lead you to slow down your life but, for two hours and forty minutes, it will almost certainly lower your heart rate and divest your mind of a little clutter.

No visitors are allowed to the twenty or so Carthusian monasteries scattered across the world, where monks take a vow of silence. In 1960, two journalists were given access to shoot inside the Grande Chartreuse monastery – the mother house of the order and the subject of *Into Great Silence* – on the condition that no actual monks were filmed. In 1984, Gröning, a young German film-maker, asked to shoot a documentary about life inside the walls. The head prior refused permission, but implied that perhaps at some future date the order would be ready for him. Fifteen years later, Gröning received an invitation to come and film.

The shooting conditions laid down were very specific. There

was to be no artificial lighting: only what the camera could capture. No voice-over commentary. No other crew: just Gröning and his equipment. And no additional music on the soundtrack: only live sound recorded on location. (Interestingly, this last requirement is more than made up for by the monks' exquisite deep-voiced chanting of the liturgy, which spreads through the film like a rich treacle.)

Gröning spent about five months living at the monastery between 2002 and 2004. Apart from the two or three hours a day during which he filmed, he lived like the other monks, in his own bare wooden cell, participating in the domestic routines of cooking, cleaning and gardening, as well as those of prayer, chanting and contemplation. Of the 120 hours of footage he shot, he has crafted a film about meditation that becomes, somewhat surprisingly, a meditation in itself.

In his great work *Arctic Dreams: Imagination and Desire in a Northern Landscape*, Barry Lopez describes walking in the Brooks Range, in Alaska, among the tundra birds who build their nests on the ground and whose 'vulnerability is extreme'. 'I took to bowing on these evening walks,' he writes. 'I would bow slightly with my hands in my pockets, towards the birds and the evidence of life in their nests – because of their fecundity, unexpected in this remote region, and because of the serene arctic light that came down over the land like breath, like breathing.' In a profound sense, *Into Great Silence* seems to be a film about breath, about breathing. Certainly it is a film that breathes. Certainly it captures something of the sense of reverence of which Lopez so eloquently writes. I don't just mean the gentle reverence of these monks for their God. It is in the film-maker's reverence for the objects and events on which his camera continually lingers: the fecundity of the forgotten corner or the hidden moment, suspended in stillness. Dust motes float in the air in a shaft of sunlight. Snow gathers on the eaves. A hunchbacked monk pushes the ancient food trolley down a long corridor, the rattling wheels bumping over the flagstones. The monastery, a vast Gormenghast-like complex, sits nestled in the snow as the stars wheel silently overhead in a stop-motion sequence. A tin plate rocks gently in a stone sink, moved by some unseen wisp of breeze.

The first hint that this might be a kind of anti-film comes early, as Gröning extends the opening scene – a monk kneeling in the half-light, head bowed, features indistinct, knuckles clenched in prayer – far beyond mere set-up. (The scene lasts more than four minutes.) The monk prays ... and prays. Stands and kneels, stands and kneels; keeps right on praying. The floorboards creak. Logs crackle in the wood stove. We are plunged into the 'great silence' at the film's heart. The effect, until we settle into the film's rhythms, is a sort of cinematic weightlessness. We wait for the story to begin, for the pace to pick up. And we will wait in vain.

For those who like their entertainment snappy, expect some discomfort. What is unusual in this film about silence and contemplation is that the passage of time is undivided by filters or markers. We sit inside it, as in physical space, more than we are swept along by it. What Gröning wants to explore is something that has been marginalised by the market pressures of the industry: the capacity for cinema, at some primal level, to entrance, to open us to an ecstatic engagement with the film-as-lyric. His film reactivates some of the old magic of this newest of art forms: that moment when utter peace and letting go descend upon us, collectively, in the dark of the multiplex.

And yet, for all the stasis and immersion and non-linearity, there is a narrative of sorts in *Into Great Silence*, and a haunting forward movement. What plays out is the induction and integration into this severe life of the two novitiates we meet at the beginning of the film: in particular, the young black man, named in his new life Dom Marie-Pierre. Prostrate on the floor, the men are provisionally accepted into the order. They rise and move around the room, and embrace the other monks, one by one. Here, the tiniest hints of personality emerge from within the silence and reserve. One of the older monks steals a furtive peek at the newcomers as he waits, head bowed, for his awkward embrace. It is such a recognisable glance, so deeply human. It could be the curiosity of the small child for the new student who arrives mid-term, that yearning for an interruption to the flow of relentless sameness.

Elsewhere, other moments of personality emerge; flashes of interaction, at least, in which we see these ascetic, pared-back men as tender, even playful. An old monk fits out Dom Marie-Pierre in his new surplice and cowl. It's just one man fitting out and dressing another – in silence, of course, and almost neutrally, like a tailor – but the moment is spring-loaded because there is so little direct human contact in the film. Later still, a wizened old monk, frail and paper-thin, with sagging emaciated flesh, sits patiently while a younger monk delicately applies ointment to his bare arms and shoulders. A tableau of silent reticence, it is perhaps the film's most tender moment.

The whole of *Into Great Silence* works in this way. The smallest elements become energised, and the narrative of everyday things begins to take on a kind of supercharged intensity. Thus, when some of the monks, on their customary Sunday walk outside the monastery grounds, slide down a steep snowdrift using their shoes as rudimentary skis and tumble in a heap of delighted giggling at the bottom of the run, it seems a hilariously transgressive moment. As for the *other* 159 minutes: what becomes intriguing about these men is their deep level of acceptance, if for nothing else than the unchanging rhythms of the days. They eat, they pray, they chant, as if to do otherwise, or to do anything more, would be to crowd their lives with inessentials.

Into Great Silence brings to mind a recent documentary with a similar title, *Touching the Void*, Kevin Macdonald's extraordinary film – a spiritual thriller in the truest sense – about the dreadful ordeal of two mountaineers who suffer a climbing accident high in the Peruvian Andes. While *Touching the Void* is the more gripping of the two films, both share the same heightened sense of a fiercely devout determination. They make wonderful companion pieces. I'm reminded too of *Rivers and Tides*, Thomas Riedelsheimer's documentary about Andy Goldsworthy, one of the world's great living artists, who works almost exclusively outdoors, often in the snow and ice, and whose work, devotional as much as it is obsessional, is almost entirely consumed with notions of presence, reverence, attention. Goldsworthy has made the entire natural world his monastery.

There is also in *Into Great Silence* a sense of intensity and expansiveness co-existing, of an intimate immensity and a deeply felt obsession contained within a great vastness. Kurosawa's late-career film *Dersu Uzala* captured this sense of vastness out in the

Siberian wastes: the expanse in that film was spatial, and raised the hairs on the neck. For the monks of the Grande Chartreuse, the expanse that they live with and within is temporal, but no less intimidating for that. They are, like Dersu, in some sense travellers in the Outlands.

It is easy to admire the Andy Goldsworthy model of the artist as monk/devotee, the world-acolyte assisting Nature in the performing of its rites. What is harder to conceive of is the stark sacrifice that the monks of the Grande Chartreuse make, and the ritualistic formality of their devotion. In *Into Great Silence*, Philip Gröning affords us the vicarious pleasure of a temporary submersion in an extreme existence.

If nothing else, this is a film that encourages us to ponder deeply how we might practise greater awareness in life: how to be mindful, how to pay attention. Here and there in our world are pockets of calm, and *Into Great Silence* is one such pocket. If you don't have time to see it, it was made for you.

The Monthly

Scale by Scale

Susan Hampton

Lucy Ellen Swinfield and her two daughters were the sopranos who held the Church of Christ together in the upper registers. During hymns I looked at Grandma Lucy's profile, the notes soaring in the air near her mouth, her stern face concentrated on the Lord, singing, usually for help – for her earlier self, a young widow with four children – and for herself now, with a paralysis in the legs, holding herself up on the back of a pew.

She was so stern and good and righteous. When I was twenty and watching the fish mobile move over my son's cot, I thought there must be a natural balancing that makes its way through families: I was neither stern nor good, and righteousness only made me feel uncomfortable. My response was to turn the holiness into laughter, or to run away. Until I was sixteen, when we left that area, I often climbed up the tank stand and onto the roof. From this vantage point I studied the ways to leave.

There were four main roads out of town. My parents talked about these roads all the time. The Old Graman Road. The Glen Innes Road. The Tingha Road. Bannockburn Road was the way we went to Lucy's old farm. No-one lived there now. In that small wooden house she taught her daughters piano, and when her husband died at forty-three of a brain tumour, her sons became resentful dairy farmers. These were boys who did not even like cows. They wanted to live in town and finish school.

These boys, my father and his brother, could sing too – people say. I never heard my father sing. Uncle Allen sang in church, along with his cousin Angus and other Mackie men. My father was the only defector from their small church. Resolutely he stayed away. At Sunday lunch, unless Grandma was there, he preached a small sermon. 'And God said unto them come forth, but Moses slipped on a banana skin and came fifth.' And while he sent his children to church with his brother, at home he satirised everything about religion.

My mother had taught Sunday school at the Methodist church around the corner from the Church of Christ, but stopped teaching when she married him. Kind of an unspoken rule. She was nineteen. Years later we talked about it.

'It wouldn't have been worth it – it didn't matter that much.'

'But Mum, did you believe in God?'

'I have an open mind. I wouldn't say God, exactly.'

'But you liked teaching Sunday school?'

'Who wouldn't like the loaves and the fishes?'

She also liked children, and would've had more than six, if the doctor and her husband had not made it obvious they wanted her tubes tied. Also, for the first five kids, when she went to hospital, relatives offered to take in the existing kids for the fortnight they allowed women then to give birth and recuperate. With the sixth child, no-one offered, right up to the pains beginning, and she had to ask. The town had decided she had enough.

'I would've had seven.' she said. 'Or more.'

*

If religion was meaningless to Dad, what was important to him? It became clear that his daughters were expected to come first at school. This held true for athletics and for academic work. You had to be able to out-run and out-articulate anyone. This was a thing that gave you standing in the community. Then too, it was important to face reality, not to kid yourself, or be naive. Truth was more important than God.

Then why did he allow or encourage his brother to take us to Sunday school and church? Was that not hypocritical? (We didn't think of this at the time.) Actually, I realised as an adult it was his only private time with Mum, that bit of Sunday morning. It was due to their sex life that I was filled with religion.

*

A few years back I stood next to Uncle Allen in my old town in their church when his wife of fifty years died, to sing with him. A sweet tenor voice in a rebuilt church, ugly like so many churches built in that era. Blond brick things with aluminium window frames. The town where I live now, Canberra, is full of these ugly churches. The first church, in my old town, had decent stained glass and a decent pitch on the roof, but had been built in a dry creek bed which shifted in the drought, and the whole building cracked. They did not take anything symbolic from this, but simply rebuilt it a bit further away from where they thought the creek might have been. The second version was built during the '50s and here I spent the first half of the funeral service trying not to notice the architecture and the thin stained glass, where pink doves intersected crosses over backgrounds of magenta and khaki. My uncle sang falteringly but prayed with firm tone on the Our Father.

Though at the time I was an atheist, or thought I was, I prayed with him.

*

If I never heard my father sing, I heard about it from other people. At twenty when he stopped going to church, he stopped singing. I've heard of this happening in other families, where a person suddenly gave up music for some reason, and never sang or played the instrument again. All their singing was church-related. Until I went to school, I didn't know any songs but hymns. Since these were mostly Wesley hymns, rather than the pop song hymns you hear today, they outclassed the things taught at school; 'Incy Wincy Spider' for example seemed tame compared to the poetry which then existed in church, and which children like me responded to without ever needing to believe in God as such.

When my aunts sang to me, or while they were sewing, they sang 'When Mothers of Salem, their children brought to Jesus, the stern disciples drove them back and bade them depart.' My aunts never commented on my father's rather cruel behaviour.

They simply sang this song constantly to any of the children who came to visit. 'But Jesus saw them ere they fled and sweetly smiled and kindly said, 'Suffer the children to come unto me.'"

As the oldest child I may have needed the song more, since I often stayed with them for months. It was one of the places I ran away to. These were old adopted aunts, also good and righteous, but not stern. It was often noted by the women in the family that I copped what was called the brunt of Dad's behaviour. I wondered about this word brunt, and how to bear the blind reaches of his anger. Part of it was, not that I realised it then, we were being educated, and he had wished for that knowledge. He seemed filled with resentment. Sometimes it was a witty resentment. I joined the chess club in high school and he asked me to teach him to play – then he set about beating all of us. But we fought back and had some significant wins.

Aside from 'brunt', I learnt many new words from the *Collected Shakespeare* Dad unaccountably gave me the year I was studying *A Midsummer Night's Dream*. It was his only present to me. Printed in Poland, it cost quite a lot of money, fifteen shillings. At the time I was receiving two shillings a week in pocket money.

Because I had such a bad memory, I had been cast as one of the rude mechanicals, a man called Quince, who held up a tilley lamp and said, 'This lanthorn doth the hornéd moon present.' I went around saying this for some weeks. We must have done a much-stripped-down version of the play, since we did it in one English lesson.

Quince – perhaps it was his name, or perhaps because he was part of the inner play – seemed to relate to the feeling I had sometimes hearing the singers or reading certain hymns. While it's true many of the hymns were dreary and mournful-sounding, some had a line here or there that electrified me, and had dance rhythms: 'As pants the hart for cooling streams / when heated in the chase.'

Reading the play forty years later, I find the rude mechanicals rehearsing on a green plot in a wood, where a hawthorn-brake is their dressing room. They argue about whether or how soon to kill the hero, who must die gallantly. Once it is agreed he must die for love, they're worried this will upset the ladies. Bottom says he has a device to make all well, a prologue must be written to explain that their hero is an actor called Bottom who does not really die. Similarly, they agree the man who plays the lion, not to frighten the ladies, must show half his face through the lion's neck, and must *speak through the neck*, and must first name himself as Snug the joiner.

Quince then says there are 'two hard things'. One is how to present the moon, and the other, presenting the wall that separates the lovers of 'this lamentable comedy'. For the moon he suggests someone come in 'with a bush of thorns and a lanthorn, and say he comes to disfigure, or to present, the person of Moonshine'. I wondered here at the use of 'disfigure'.

*

As a child, looking through the index of the hymnal out of a terrible boredom with the sermon, the words that mystified me were the ones that followed the first lines of the hymns. After 'Jesus, the children are calling,' it said Rickmansworth; after 'Joy to the World!', Antioch; 'Judge eternal, throned in splendour' was Rhuddian, 'Judge me God of my Salvation' was Blaenhafren, a word I specially liked, and used to recite to myself to try and sleep when my parents were arguing in the next room. *Blaenhafren.* 'King of my life, I crown thee now' was Duncannon. 'Lead Kindly Light' was Lux Benigna, though of course 'Lux' to me meant soap; only much later reading CD booklets for sung masses did I find 'lux aeterna' meant 'eternal light'. 'Out of the Depths' was Gelineau.

I see now these are the names of the tunes. I don't know why I didn't realise it at the time. These mysterious words put me straight into the liminal zone, a place where I understood nothing but was free to play around with possible meanings. There in these words was a world not already fixed, a place of floating signifiers before any of us were concerned about the relation of the signifier to the signified. Here happily I floated, and where everyone else read 'Lord, keep us steadfast in thy word,' I read Erhalt Uns, Herr. Since many of these words were in German, I sent away for a correspondence course in German. Some of the words were inches long. And I was never sure how to say them.

Another thing that mystified me was the idea of the soul.

*

Today on ABC radio the violinist Pinchas Zuckerman was describing the opening of Berg's Violin Concerto, *To the Memory of an Angel*. Zuckerman plays segments to explain technical matters to do with twelve tone and also inversion, then he says, maybe Berg wouldn't have composed it if a friend had not asked him to write something for their newly dead 18-year-old friend. Despite the complex technique behind the composition, Zuckerman says, there are no extra notes, only what is needed. 'And why? Because it's coming from the soul of Alban Berg.'

He describes how Berg takes a Bach chorale and uses it in this requiem – but then it seems to be about more than Manon Gropius, the girl who died; it seems personal, as if he's feeling his own death. Zuckerman describes how the opening finishes on a high G, thus using four octaves, 'the whole range of the instrument – of life.' The presenter says, 'Yes, Berg finishes writing this, then gets stung by wasps, then they turn to boils and get infected, then he dies.'

'Yes,' Zuckerman says, 'almost as if he knew.'

*

The famous short lyric 'An die Musik', set by Schubert, addresses the spirit of music, which seems to hover over all creation: 'Du holde Kunst, in wie viel grauen Stunden, wo mich des Lebens wilder Kreis umstrickt': 'You holy craft, in many an hour of sadness, when life's hard toil my spirit hath oppressed' – it is music which revives the heart and bears the soul to realms of rest. While the heart needs reviving, the soul is what needs rest. Here, music is what stands in for the Holy Spirit, or attunes us to it.

There is no way to convey in words what Schubert's melody does with this lyric, but it's a song that can be listened to over and over, keeping its interest because of the tension between the many notes of the bass and the simplicity of the treble which works like a lullaby. To hear a soprano go from the B below middle C within a few phrases to the E above top C, and then return, creates a soaring effect so that the self, in the original *umstrickt* or 'ensnared', is by implication released. In the English translation, the self is described as 'oppressed', for the later rhyme with 'rest', but the figurative use of the German 'ensnared' is much stronger. Similarly, the line 'Hast thou my heart revived with love and gladness' in the German reads 'hast du mein Herz, zu warmer Lieb ent zunden' where 'revived' is 'warmed', and instead of 'gladness' we have 'zunden', meaning 'ignited'. My heart is warmed and ignited. Working your way back from a translation to other deeper layers of meaning may be a type of soul-work. Taking nothing at face value.

*

In the Christmas school holidays we packed the Falcon wagon and drove the eight hours to Newcastle where my mother's side of the family lived, the other side of life, where people drank and smoked and hit their wives and went fishing. This grandmother, Nana, had been a Catholic, but again, the man wasn't interested in God and she stopped going to mass. It was only in my fifties that I found out she had even been raised a Catholic: she never mentioned it. By this time I'd become interested in the mass because of sung masses, and because I was teaching a course in narrative at a university.

In Nana's back bedroom, where I have lived various parts of my adult life, I found wrapped up in the bottom of the wardrobe a very small book containing prayers and sacraments. The opening pages had been torn out, and it began with a Table of Moveable Feasts. I thought the phrase had been invented by Hemingway. I wonder what 'the Ordinary of the Mass' means. I didn't think Nana would ever look at this book again, but I also didn't think she'd give it to me if I asked for it. I don't know why I thought this. So I stole the little book.

The people on this side of the family didn't sing – at least, I have never heard any of them sing, including my mother. Possibly they think they are tone deaf. Maybe they don't want to sing. When I first met a family who sang together – anything – silly songs, Gilbert and Sullivan, 'Green grow the Rushes O', 'The Internationale', 'On Ilkley Moor Baht Hat', I admit I burst into tears. What joy so many people have missed out on. I have a friend who sings lullabies to me in adult life and it never fails to move me. I have tried to imagine growing up in a family who sing together – what would that be like? And in fact when I met a Yugloslav man once, who sang with his friends while they played cards at night, I married him. It wasn't the right thing to do really, but it shows among other things how affected I was by the feeling created when people sing together.

*

A friend has sent me his translation of 'An die Musik', noting that the one I used is antiquely Victorian. Also, it is pretty far from the original, he says: 'holde' doesn't mean 'holy' but 'charming' or 'lovely'; 'wilde Kreis' means 'wild circle'. In the opening line, 'in many an hour of sadness', his translation reads 'in how many grey hours'. The original: 'in wie viel grauen Stunden'. I feel the stirrings of my old wish to understand German.

*

Back in the country town where I lived and back at school and back in the fresh tablelands air I continued to run away and my schemes became more sophisticated and even desperate. Across the river on the common outside a long caravan I once begged a man from Bullen's Circus to abduct me. Not that I knew the word abduct, but that was my intent. I said my parents were dead, I showed him a handstand and a double cartwheel but he was unconvinced.

That Sunday in church we sang:

Holy Holy Holy
Lord God Almighty,
casting down his golden crown
around the glassy sea

I suddenly saw the rising sea out Nana's front door and thought – yes – the sea glitters and the sun across it is the spikes of his crown. But without saying 'glitter' the word 'glassy' makes me realise it – further, a metaphor (not that I knew that word) was like God, in that the meaning was sideways, and was implied rather than directly spoken. Then I thought of the way all the meanings of the word 'crown' are at the side or back of your mouth as you sing those words. I couldn't have said I believed in God, but I believed in the dense and articulate power of the image.

It was a little hymn to light, and why not? It gave you an image, and you did the thinking from that. All this went through my mind that day in an instant. And maybe that's the only way God will ever visit me. A quick and thorough visit, it primed me for a life of reading and writing. More, because the poetry came in by music, I was open-eared when as an adult I heard the Fauré Requiem, or Kiri Te Kanawa singing Mozart's 'Laudate Dominum' from the *Solemn Vespers of the Confessor*. Then the Latin and all its prior and peeped-at meanings fed back into the word-hoard.

That day, it also occurred to me to ask, Why call a powerful image or a moving piece of music 'godly'? Can't it just be empirically what it is? High art, not godly? Of course it can, and secularism is based on that thought.

*

Years later when something in me wanted the sung mass, I started to think 'god' and 'godly' were simply shorthand. For no good reason other than the effect of the shape of the mass, and the poetry and music – and a cultural tradition built up and perfected over 2000 years – I started using 'god' as a term. A deracinated term, perhaps, but still, useful shorthand for things, which were often wordless, and their power was in their wordlessness.

It was a paradox then that at times poetry could bring you to this point where wordlessness and timelessness took over and rested you.

*

No-one really helped me look for poetry in the Bible and say if they had shown me the Book of Job, I would only have been horrified or frightened. Would I have understood God was making a bet with Satan over who could win and keep the soul of Job? When despite all his losses Job continues to believe in God, would I have heard the poetry in Job's wife saying 'Curse God and die, Job'? or in his reply:

> Naked came I out
> of my mother's womb and naked
> shall I return thither: the Lord

gave, and the Lord hath taken away;
blessed be the name of the Lord.

And these lines are repeated whenever the people around him fall into doubt. It is his chant of survival. I've thought a lot on these lines, and particularly of the time I first read them when I was perhaps forty-five and really ready to receive them. I was in Armidale visiting friends and there was a concert that night at the cathedral. It was a requiem I knew well from my CD, and so I hoped the singers would be good.

When the solo tenor first came in, I heard him falter, just before each held high note, and physically reach for it in the air – it was excruciating to watch – he had a fine voice but was not confident of his high notes – and each time with effort and quaveringly sometimes, he sent his note out into the vaulting spaces of the cathedral. I couldn't watch any more, so I picked up a book that was on the back of the pew and opened it at random. As the tenor reached for his next difficult note, I read 'Naked came I out of my mother's womb' and engrossed I read on. Job had lost all his oxen. He had lost his camels. I forget whether God or Satan was causing his catastrophes, but the aim was to see who could keep Job believing in him. A big wind comes up, and Job's ten children, feasting together in the eldest brother's house, all die. But the Devil doesn't win his bet with God, and can't tempt Job away from his faith even though his wife and friends and advisers all say he has no further reason to believe God cares for him in any way. And I relaxed then, because it seemed this tenor had the same quality of faith as he got his throat ready to throw out the high notes. It was an experience I would never have with a CD. I was trembling and sweating when the concert finished. I wanted to go and thank the tenor for singing when he did not quite have the voice for it. Except that he did eventually reach each note. And the locals at the concert knew and loved him, and wanted him to sing – this must have helped. If ever I felt in the air a benign atmosphere it was in that church in Armidale. My friend asked why I was crying. I opened the Bible and pointed at the Book of Job. She took my arm and laughed, 'You must've read this before, no?' 'No.'

*

Scale by Scale

Back in Sydney, Joan Sutherland was being interviewed on the radio about her early life with Bonynge and how he convinced her she could sing both mezzo and soprano – and helped her increase her upper register while singing in the shower – then on stage whispered to her: 'Just pretend you're in the shower.' Sutherland spoke about her years of lung gymnastics, how long she could go between taking breaths, and how her effort was in making all this seem effortless – as if the sound just flowed from her. I heard her singing the duet from *Norma* with Marilyn Horne and that was sublime but not heart-wrenching in the way of the Armidale tenor. I wonder if God is sublime then maybe Jesus is the heart-wrenching part.

I still don't know whether I could say I believe in God. But I want to be alert to, for want of another shorthand, godliness. And in fact I think it's the remnant pagan in me who responds to the Catholic Mass – for originally where did it come from? The Rites of Eleusis spring to mind as one source. Whatever it is I receive by going to Mass I imagine multiplied by the ancients, by having the ceremony outside, if nothing else. By the time Bach and Mozart and Pergolesi and Fauré have enriched the traditional shape of the ceremony with their sung masses, the sublime has re-entered culture. It's hard to find this sublimity in secular work and that may be one reason I'm drawn – still kicking perhaps – to the sacred.

When I heard for possibly the twentieth time the Benedictus from the Bach mass in B minor I realised it was the tenderness of the intervals, especially in the repetitions of *in nomine Domini*, that were so affecting. But it couldn't really be explained. Quantum physics and string theory may have related to the musical structures and even the timing; a singer could advance towards it scale by scale; but its mystery was intact.

Publication Details

'The Heart of Desire' by **John Armstrong** appeared in *Meanjin*, Vol. 66. No. 1, 2007.

'The Turning Tide' by **Judith Brett** appeared in *The Monthly*, March 2007.

'Fire Down Below' by **Dan Chiasson** appeared in the *New Yorker*, 11 June 2007.

'Lost in the Woods' by **Inga Clendinnen** appeared in *The Monthly*, April 2007.

'Portrait of the Monster as a Young Artist' by **J.M. Coetzee** appeared in the *New York Review of Books*, Vol. 54, No. 2, 15 February 2007.

'Extravagant Stillness' by **Luke Davies** appeared in *The Monthly*, April 2007.

'What is a Tree?' by **Tim Flannery** appeared in *New York Review of Books*, Vol. 54, No. 2, 15 February 2007.

A shorter version of 'The Innocence Manoeuvre' by **Anna Funder** appeared in the *Guardian*, 5 May 2007.

'From Frogmore, Victoria' by **Helen Garner** appeared in *The Monthly*, May 2007.

Publication Details

'Like Love in a Marriage' by **Anna Goldsworthy** appeared in *The Monthly*, September 2007.

'Bons Mots No Match for Nazi Bullets' by **Clive James** appeared in *The Australian's Review of Books*, March 2007.

'Blow-ins on the Cold Desert Wind' by **Kim Mahood** appeared in *Griffith Review 15: Divided Nation*.

'Love Me Tender?' by **Anne Manne** appeared in *The Monthly*, December 2006.

'Pearson's Gamble, Stanner's Dream' by **Robert Manne** appeared in *The Monthly*, August 2007.

'Being There' by **Mark McKenna** appeared in *The Monthly*, March 2007.

The excerpt of 'Alive in *Ant and Bee*' by **Gillian Mears** is from *Harpers Gold, HEAT 13* new series: (Giramondo, 2007).

The edited excerpt of 'White Guilt, Victimhood and the Quest for a Radical Centre' by **Noel Pearson** is from *Griffith Review 16: Unintended Consequences*. The full essay was shortlisted for the Victorian Premier's Alfred Deakin Award for an Essay Advancing Public Debate and the Queensland Premier's Harry Williams Award for a Literary or Media Work Advancing Public Debate.

'Born in the GDR' by **Gert Reifarth** appeared in *Meanjin*, Vol. 66. No. 2, 2007.

A shorter version of 'Many Me' by **Kate Rossmanith** appeared in *The Monthly*, February 2007.

'Hard Cases and Hearts of Darkness' by **Nicolas Rothwell** appeared in *The Australian's Review of Books*, April 2007.

An earlier version of 'The Ups, the Downs: My Life as a Biographer' by **Hazel Rowley** appeared in *Australian Book Review*, July–August 2007.

Publication Details

'Faith in Politics' by **Kevin Rudd** appeared in *The Monthly*, October 2006.

'It's Too Easy To Say "God Is Dead"' by **Guy Rundle** appeared in the *Australian Financial Review*, 27 April 2007.

'In Fealty to a Professor' by **Anne Sedgley** appeared in *Meanjin*, Vol. 66. No. 1, 2007.

'In Shiraz' by **Don Walker** is excerpted from a longer account of a trip to Iran.

Notes on Contributors

John Armstrong's books include *Conditions of Love: the Philosophy of Intimacy* and *Love, Life, Goethe: How To Be Happy in an Imperfect World*.

Judith Brett is Professor of Politics at La Trobe University. She is the author of *Robert Menzies' Forgotten People*, *Australian Liberals and the Moral Middle Class*, *Quarterly Essay 19: Relaxed and Comfortable* and, with Anthony Moran, *Ordinary People's Politics*.

Dan Chiasson's first book of poems, *The Afterlife of Objects* appeared in 2002. He is also the author of *One Kind of Everything: Poem and Person in Contemporary America*.

Inga Clendinnen is the author of several books, most recently *Agamemnon's Kiss*.

J.M. Coetzee was awarded the Nobel Prize for Literature in 2003. His most recent novel is *Diary of a Bad Year*.

Luke Davies has written four collections of poetry and two novels. In 2006 he jointly won an AFI award for the adaptation of his first novel, *Candy*.

Tim Flannery was 2007 Australian of the Year and is the author of *The Weather Makers*.

Anna Funder is the author of *Stasiland*.

Notes on Contributors

Helen Garner is the author of many books, including *Joe Cinque's Consolation* and *The Feel of Steel*.

Anna Goldsworthy is a concert pianist and a member of the Seraphim Trio. Her solo-piano CD, *Come With Us*, is forthcoming.

Susan Hampton is a poet, whose work includes *The Kindly Ones*. She edited *The Penguin Book of Australian Women Poets*.

Clive James is the author, most recently, of *North Face of Soho: Unreliable Memoirs Volume IV* and *Cultural Amnesia*.

Kim Mahood is an artist and author. Her *Craft for a Dry Lake* won the 2001 NSW Premier's Prize for Non-fiction.

Anne Manne is the author of *Motherhood: How Should We Care for Our Children?*, published in 2005.

Robert Manne is Professor of Politics at La Trobe University. His books include *Left Right Left: Political Essays 1977–2005*, *The Petrov Affair* and two *Quarterly Essay*s, *In Denial* and *Sending Them Home*.

David Marr is the author of *Patrick White: a Life*, *The High Price of Heaven*, *Quarterly Essay 26: His Master's Voice* and co-author with Marian Wilkinson of *Dark Victory*.

Mark McKenna is the author of *Looking for Blackfellas' Point: An Australian History of Place*, *This Country: A Reconciled Republic?* and a forthcoming biography of Manning Clark.

Gillian Mears is the author of *The Grass Sister*, *The Mint Lawn* and many short stories.

Noel Pearson is the director of the Cape York Institute for Leadership and Policy.

Gert Reifarth has taught in the School of Languages and Linguistics at the University of Melbourne. He is the author of a radio play about Heinrich Heine.

Notes on Contributors

Kate Rossmanith is a lecturer in the School of Letters, Art and Media at the University of Sydney.

Nicolas Rothwell is the author of *Another Country*, *Wings of the Kite-Hawk* and the novel *Heaven and Earth*. He is the northern correspondent for the *Australian*.

Hazel Rowley is the author of *Christina Stead: A Biography*, *Richard Wright: The Life and Times* and *Tête-à-Tête: Simone de Beauvoir and Jean-Paul Sartre*.

Kevin Rudd is the leader of the Australian Labor Party.

Guy Rundle is the writer of political satires performed by Max Gillies and the author of *Quarterly Essay 3: The Opportunist*.

Anne Sedgley is Manager of Heritage Information at Heritage Victoria.

Don Walker is a songwriter and performer. *All is Forgiven* by Tex, Don & Charlie was released in 2005, and his solo CD *Cutting Back* in 2006. His book of recollections will be published in 2008.

The Best of 2007 from Black Inc.

The Best Australian Stories 2007
Edited by ROBERT DREWE

In this seductively diverse collection, Robert Drewe has assembled the country's best short fiction of the past year. Here are sparkling stories from Kate Grenville, David Malouf, Shane Maloney and Marion Halligan, alongside exciting new work from a younger generation, including Alice Pung, Will Elliot, Cate Kennedy and Nam Le. Drawn from all over the country and spanning a remarkable range of styles, *Best Australian Stories 2007* showcases Australia's most vibrant contemporary writing. As Robert Drewe says, 'Don't let anyone tell you the Australian short story is dead. It's thriving.'

OUT NOW ✷ $27.95

The Best Australian Poems 2007
Edited by PETER ROSE

Following on from the success of previous years' Best Poems anthology, new editor Peter Rose is taking only the best of our established poets, as well as discovering hidden gems by emerging writers. *The Best Australian Poems 2007* is the ultimate showcase of Australian poetry.
Contributors include: Judith Beveridge, John Kinsella, MTC Cronin, Bruce Dawe, Dorothy Porter, Peter Goldsworthy, Jennifer Harrison, Barry Hill, Clive James, David Malouf, John Tranter, Les Murray, Peter Porter, Craig Sherborne, Chris Wallace-Crabbe, and many more.

OUT NOW ✷ $24.95

www.blackincbooks.com